FROM HABIRU TO HEBREWS
AND OTHER ESSAYS

FROM HABIRU TO HEBREWS
AND OTHER ESSAYS

ROBERT WOLFE

MILL CITY PRESS

MINNEAPOLIS

MILLCITY
PRESS

Mill City Press, Inc.

212 3rd Avenue North, Suite 290

Minneapolis, MN 55401

612.455.2294

www.millcitypublishing.com

ISBN-13: 978-1-936780-58-7

LCCN: 2011930958

Cover Design and Typeset by Madge Duffy

Printed in the United States of America

TABLE OF CONTENTS

PREFACE

Assembled in this volume are ten essays which I have written over the course of the past fifteen years which, taken together, provide a comprehensive picture of my understanding of Jewish history and the Jewish people. It is an understanding based on many years of study both of Jewish history and world history. And at the same time, it is an understanding based on a strictly secular world view, one which takes for granted the obvious fact that there is no king or queen in the sky, no realm of the supernatural on earth and no heaven or hell anywhere save the ones which human beings themselves create.

For reasons which I explain in the first essay, "From Habiru To Hebrews", it has been my fate to combine in thought and deed a profound faith in the value and worth of the Jewish people with a refusal to be swayed by any form of religious ideology, whether pro-Jewish or anti-Jewish. To put it another way, to me it seems most unjust that a non-existent invisible entity should get the credit when it is the Jewish people that has done the work.

But what work? That is the question which these essays seek to answer. My main goal is to bring out the true nature of the Jewish role in world history. In particular, the Jewish role in the origins of Christianity and Islam is explored in three essays: "Jewish Influence", "Calendar Wars" and "Zion". Another two essays, "Jewish Ideas" and "The Judeo-Masonic Tradition", examine the Jewish contribution to the development of modern progressive thought. My basic thesis which I substantiate in these essays is that Jewish influence on world history was not just the result of the efforts of a few outstanding thinkers but rather of the activity of the Jewish people as a whole.

An additional essay, "The Seleucid Era", deals with a little known facet of world history, namely the persistence of the Seleucid calendar system in Middle Eastern and Jewish culture long after the Seleucid empire had been overthrown. This essay can be seen as a sample of the kind of integration of Jewish history and world history which I advocate in general terms in the essay, "Jewish History and World History". Finally, two essays, "The Future of Jewish Secularism" and "Why I Am A Zionist", set forth my understanding of the significance of Zionism in modern Jewish life.

I suppose some might call me a Jewish nationalist, but in my own eyes I am first and foremost a historian. I was trained as a historian, have a PhD from Harvard University (1965) to prove it, and taught history on a professional level for thirty years. If you want to understand anything, you must understand its history, where it came from and how it got the way it is. Jewish history may be unique in certain ways, but when all is said and done, it is the history of a people, the same as any other. To put it another way, a strictly secular understanding of Jewish history and integration of Jewish history into world history are two sides on the same coin.

The key to demythologizing Jewish history may be found in the first article, "From Habiru To Hebrews". There I show that the myth of Hebrew origins contained in the Torah is based on a real event, the conquest of Canaan by bands of runaway slaves and other fugitives known at the time as Habiru. Most of the unique features of later Jewish history can be traced to this one fact. States founded by runaway slaves are rare in human history, and there is no other example of such a state that survived, first in fact and then in memory, for over 3000 years. It is impossible to understand the meaning of Zionism and the modern state of Israel without reference to this history.

It is no coincidence that the founding of Israel took place in the context of the victory of the progressive forces in the world over the most murderous and also the most anti-Semitic empire that has ever existed. The triumph of the Zionist ideal and the triumph of the progressive forces were linked together because not only the Zionist ideal but also many progressive ideals were ultimately rooted in the history, customs and beliefs of the ancient Jewish nation established by runaway slaves. It is because of the unique origins of the Jewish people that Jewish history cannot be understood apart from world history or world history apart from Jewish history. The purpose of the essays contained in this book is to demonstrate the truth of this assertion in a scholarly and objective way.

However there is one point on which I feel compelled to deviate from standard scholarly practice. I have always felt that there was something medieval about footnotes. No one reads them except for other scholars, and yet they contain information which is important for evaluating the objectivity of the text. It is therefore my practice to embody the information normally contained in footnotes within the text itself. If I think a particular citation is important, I give the precise source, down to the page number, from which it was taken. All historians build on the work of those who have gone before them, and I want very much for the reader to know on whose work I am relying, or not relying, as the case may be.

There is one more point I need to mention. Although each essay is different, there are certain themes which appear in many of them. For this reason, some material appears in more than one essay. I don't like to repeat myself, but the alternative would have been to completely rewrite the essays, which I thought inappropriate. And since much of what I have to say will be unfamiliar to many readers, perhaps a little repetition is not such a bad thing. In any case I thought it best to let the essays stand just as I wrote them, at different times and for different audiences, but al;ways with the same goal in mind, to make the truth of Jewish history accessible to a wide audience.

FROM HABIRU TO HEBREWS

I come from a secular Jewish background, the son of Jewish parents
who belonged to the Communist Party during the 1930s. They left the
Party in 1939, around the time of the Nazi-Soviet Pact, and also left
each other, getting divorced when I was about two years old. I was
raised in the home of my mother in Washington Heights, a neighborhood in Manhattan which at that time was about half Jewish. Most of
my boyhood friends were Jewish, and so too were most of my mother's
friends, who tended to the same "progressive" point of view as she
did. My father too remained a "progressive", meaning someone who
agreed wiith many of the positions of the Communist Party without
necessarily belonging to it. So from an early age I received a heavy dose
of Jewish secular culture along with a sense of identification with the
progressive current in American life.

By the time that I graduated from college in 1958, that current
had been very much submerged by the anti-Communism of the
1950s. I decided to go to graduate school and was fortunate enough
to be admitted to the history program at Harvard University with a
Woodrow Wilson scholarship. I formed the resolve to specialize in the
study of revolutions and wrote my PhD thesis on the subject of the
popular organizations in the Paris Commune of 1871. In 1965 I got a
job teaching history at the Washington Square College of New York
University, but unfortunately for me, I was even more interested in
making revolutions than I was in teaching about them. My involvement with the radical student movement at NYU led eventually to
my participation in the spring of 1970 in the student takeover of the
Courant Institute at NYU, a building which housed a huge computer
belonging to the Atomic Energy Commission. To make a long story
short, I ended up fired from my job at NYU and sentenced to three
months in prison for helping to hold the computer for ransom.

After I got out of prison in 1971, I remained active in what we called "the Movement" for about five years, but I gradually came to feel alienated from it due to its slow descent into anti-Semitism. For the first time in my life, I began to take an interest in Jewish history. My initial motive in doing so was to prove both to myself and to my friends in the Movement that Jewish tradition contained a progressive component and was not the bastion of reactionary thinking which so many on the left now claimed it to be. But the more I learned about Jewish history, the more convinced I became that Jewish tradition not only contained a progressive component but was itself the source of many of the progressive ideas disseminated in an anti-Semitic form by Christianity, Islam and Marxism, the three dominant ideologies of the modern world. Starting in the late 1970s, I began work on a book intended to validate this insight, while at the same time earning a living teaching history as a lowly adjunct at a number of small colleges in the New York area.

THE HABIRU

It was at this point in time that I discovered the Habiru. Even though I was a professional historian, I had never heard of them until I began to study Jewish history. A hot topic in the small world of "Biblical scholarship", their existence had remained almost completely unknown to everyone else. For 100 years, archaeologists had been unearthing clay tablets in the Middle East which made reference to a group of people variously described as "Habiru" or "Apiru" in the scholarly literature. Hundreds of such references were found, all dating from the 2nd millenium BCE. None of these clay tablets discussed the Habiru at length but rather made reference to them in passing in some larger context. Sometimes the Habiru were described as mercenaries, other times as day laborers, yet other times as bandits. The Biblical scholars were in general agreement that the reality behind these different descriptions was that of bands of armed men, most of them fugitives, who camped on the outskirts of the more settled areas and made a living as best they could. References to such Habiru bands were found in many different parts of the Middle East, making it clear that they did not constitute a tribe or nation but rather a social class, one that was generally viewed by the scribes who mentioned them with a mixture of fear and contempt.

What really got my attention in the scholarly literature about the Habiru was the evidence that many of them were fugitive slaves. For example, William Albright states on page 86 of *Yahweh and the Gods of Canaan*:

> We read in the tablets of Ugarit that escaped slaves had been accustomed to find asylum with the 'Apiru, preferably on the other side of the border between the Hittite empire proper and the vassal state of Ugarit. This practice was explicitly forbidden and runaway slaves had to be extradited.

And on page 273 of Volume 1 of James Pritchard's anthology, *The Ancient Near East*, appears a passage from a letter dating from the 14th century BCE which makes reference to "slaves who had become 'Apiru". So not only did "Habiru" (or "Apiru") sound something like "Hebrew", but the two groups seem to have shared a similar social status as well. Jewish tradition portrays the original Hebrews as runaway slaves, and the authors of the Torah took this tradition seriously enough to write, in Chapter 23, Verse 16 of the *Book of Deuteronomy*:

> You shall not turn over to his master a slave who seeks refuge with you from his master. He shall live with you in any place he may choose among the settlements in your midst, wherever he pleases; you must not ill treat him.

Would the authors of the Torah have promulgated such an injunction unless they were themselves in actual fact descended, at least in part, from fugitive slaves? I doubt it, and therefore the fact that many of the Habiru were also fugitive slaves made a connection between the two groups appear highly probable in my eyes.

However it soon became apparent to me that most Biblical scholars did not share my assumption. Virtually without exception, Biblical scholars both past and present approach the question of Hebrew origins from a religious point of view. Rather than adopt what is reliably known about the Habiru as the starting point of their investigation, their normal tendency is to try to fit the Habiru into a picture of Hebrew origins which is ultimately derived from the story told in the Bible. But approached from this angle, the Habiru simply don't fit. In particular, the Hebrews described in the Bible constitute a tribe or nation, but the Habiru were clearly a social class. While many Biblical scholars are willing to admit that there may be a connection between the words "Hebrew" and "Habiru", only a small minority are willing to entertain the possibility that the Hebrews may have actually been Habiru. James Hoffmeier, on page 124 of *Israel in Egypt*, published in 1996, presents the standard view as follows:

> At an earlier date, identifying the Hebrews with the *habiru* was common, but in recent decades, the association has been discouraged, largely because *habiru* is now understood to be a sociological term, not indicative of any one ethnic group. More recent studies consider the *habiru* to be more specifically groups of refugees who lived out of reach of urban, settled areas, who nevertheless preyed upon such states. This generally accepted meaning need not preclude the term *habiru* from being applied to the Hebrews who were dislocated in Egypt and then again when they returned to Canaan.

Reading between the lines, it is apparent that Hoffmeier felt uncomfortable with the idea of the Hebrews as Habiru not only because the Habiru constituted a social class but also because he felt that this particular social class "preyed upon" the good people of the towns and cities.

The bottom line is that most Biblical scholars simply don't want the Hebrews to be Habiru. Even George Mendenhall, who is thought by many to have affirmed the identity of the Hebrews and the Habiru, did not really say this. In *The Tenth Generation*, published in 1973, he raised the question of why the term "Apiru" came to be applied to the "Israelites", and answered it this way, on page 137:

It came to be applied to Israel because there was a continuity in pre-Israelite tradition and history of refusal by villagers and shepherds to become assimilated to the existing political organizations in whose environs they lived. When the political empire became intolerable and unable to preserve order, they withdrew from *all* obligation and relationship to it in favor of another nonpolitical overlord (whose obligations were of an entirely different and functional order).

In other words, the Hebrews were not real Habiru, but rather "villagers and shepherds" who were slandered as Habiru by others because they refused to accept the rule of the Canaanite city-states. Needless to say, the "nonpolitical overlord" whom Mendenhall thought they obeyed instead was God, an "overlord" in whom Mendenhall too believed.

Founded by German Protestant theologians in the 19th century, modern Biblical scholarship has had a dual character throughout its history. On the one hand Biblical scholars have made great strides in the direction of developing a realistic understanding of when and by whom the Torah was written and what was the historical background behind it. Yet on the other hand the great majority of Biblical scholars have continued to believe that somewhere at the core of the "Biblical" tradition was a divine revelation which formed the original basis not only for Judaism but also for Christianity. One of the few Biblical scholars to have commented on this dichotomy is Niels Peter Lemche, author of *Early Israel*, published in 1985. Lemche pointed out that most Biblical scholars adopt a sceptical attitude towards the historical narrative in the Torah, while at the same time treating its religious ideology as the result of a "divine intervention in history". Lemche rejected this approach, concluding on page 413: "Therefore it is out of the question to regard Israel's hypothetical religious experience as a starting point for a survey of the early history of Israel."

Since he wasn't interested in forcing the Habiru to fit into the Biblical narrative, Lemche had no difficulty in seeing them as the original Hebrews. He put it this way, on page 427:

> Therefore, as a working hypothesis I propose the following sce-
> nario: at least as early as from the first half of the 14th century
> and subsequently the mountainous regions were 'inhabited' by a
> para-social element, the *habiru*, who consisted of runaway former
> non-free peasants or copyholders from the small city-states in the
> plains and valleys of Palestine.

Lemche believed that the Habiru, who originally "were not a sedentary element" but rather "outlaw groups of freebooters", eventually settled down in the hill country of what he called "Palestine" starting perhaps around 1200 BCE. He saw their transformation into a "sedentary element" as due to a number of factors, including the spread of iron tools, the development of slash and burn agriculture and the introduction of terracing of hilly slopes, all of which tended to increase the agricultural productivity of the previously heavily forested hill country.

But just how and why did the Habiru become the founders of the Biblical tradition? Since Lemche thought that the Exodus narrative was more or less entirely mythical, he had to find an origin for the Biblical tradition within Canaan itself. However he was most reluctant to credit "outlaw groups of freebooters" with the creation of such a prestigious tradition. He therefore argued, on page 434, that "the phenomenon which came to be the specifically Israelite religion was fundamentally what might be termed an isolation of one particular aspect of Canaanite culture, namely the ethical." These Canaanite ethical thinkers, Lemche added, must have come from "the upper strata" of Canaanite society. To me it seems obvious that Lemche did not actually like the Habiru any more than the other Biblical scholars did and hence felt compelled to invent an upper class Canaanite ethical tradition, no evidence of whose existence he was able to cite, in order to explain the origins of Biblical religion. Moreover I am not so sure that "ethical" is the most precise term to describe the religion of the Hebrews, which might be more accurately characterized as "egalitarian".

One Biblical scholar who made a point of describing this religion as "egalitarian" is Norman Gottwald, author of *The Tribes of Yahweh*, published in 1979. As he put it on page 643, "The religion of Yahweh appeared from the start exclusively as the religion of socially egalitarian peoples." Gottwald saw the Habiru as part of the social movement that gave rise to what he called "the religion of Yahweh", but not the dominant part. Like Mendenhall, he thought that the nation of Israel originated in a rebellion of Canaanite "villagers" against the rule of the Canaanite city-states, but unlike Mendenhall, he thought that many Habiru also participated in this rebellion. He argued, on page 408, that the line between Habiru and villagers "was probably a rather indistinct one in many cases, becoming less and less distinct as central authority crumbled". As time passed, the Habiru began to settle down, while the villagers started to develop self-defense groups. Finally:

> At some hypothetical point in this expansion and slow convergence of nonfeudally organized peoples, the preconditions for a wider unity developed. In such a setting early Israel took its rise.

This scenario sounds plausible, but while there is ample evidence of Habiru participating in armed attacks against the Canaanite city-states, there is little or no indication that Canaanite villagers did the same.

Moreover, although Gottwald saw Habiru culture as "egalitarian", he did not feel that it was the source of "the religion of Yahweh". Gottwald tended to emphasize the references that described (or could be interpreted as describing) the Habiru as "mercenaries", making it possible for him to argue that despite their rebellious outlook and outsider status they were nonetheless integrated into the Canaanite social system and hence incapable of evolving an alternate social ideology on their own. That ideology, Gottwald believed, could only have come from the "Moses group", which Gottwald depicted, on page 39, as "composed of a mixture of stock breeders (sheep, goats, and cattle), small gardeners, and fishermen, including war captives or migrants from Canaan". Just where he got this information Gottwald did not say, nor did he explain why he chose to omit from this list the Habiru who were known to have been brought to Egypt as prisoners of war and set to work there as slaves on building projects.

Open to criticism as it may be, the work of Mendenhall, Gottwald and Lemche still contained many valid insights into the question of the relationship between the Hebrews and the Habiru. Their books came out in the 1970s and 1980s, at a time when the memory of the 1960s was still fresh in many minds. But in recent decades, as Hoffmeier rightly claimed, linking the Hebrews and the Habiru "has been discouraged". Gottwald for one was clearly influenced by the "Liberation theology" of the 1960s and 1970s, but the political and intellectual climate since the 1980s has been quite different. The notion that the Biblical tradition originated in a revolution of some kind, possibly led by outlaw bands of armed men known as Habiru, has lost what little appeal it ever had for Biblical scholarship. Yet in reality, the evidence of the identity of the Hebrews and Habiru is overwhelming. The reason why I began this article by describing my background is so readers will understand why I am more open to this evidence than many others. But in the final analysis it is the evidence itself which is decisive, and although I am no Biblical scholar, I have enough experience as a historian to recognize a buried truth when I see one.

SHECHEM

Although references to the Habiru have been unearthed all over the Middle East, far and away the most important source of information about them is the large collection of clay tablets unearthed at Tell el-Amarna in Egypt towards the end of the 19th century. Many of these tablets consist of letters written in Accadian cuneiform hieroglyphics during the 14th century BCE and sent to the Pharaoh in Egypt from various Egyptian puppet rulers in Canaan. The letters are filled with complaints about the Habiru, who are said to be leading a rebellion against Egyptian rule in Canaan and plundering the cities of those local rulers who still remained loyal to the Pharaoh. And in one such letter, reproduced on page 200 of *Shechem* by G. Ernest Wright, appears a threat by Abdu-Hiba, the ruler of Jerusalem, to align himself with the Habiru unless he receives more support from the Pharaoh. In particular, Abdu-Hiba threatened: "Now shall we do as Lab'ayu, who gave the land of Shechem to the 'Apiru?"

Labayu is mentioned in many letters: he was the ruler of Shechem and the main rival of Abdu-Hiba for control of the hill country of Canaan. Whether he actually "gave the land of Shechem" to the Habiru is not clear. Perhaps Abdu-Hiba exaggerated, perhaps not. The important point is that his letter shows that the Habiru exercised a considerable degree of control over the region of Shechem in the 14th century BCE. And the reason why this point is important is because Shechem was without a doubt the main political and religious center of the Hebrews throughout their early history.

Numerous indications of the significance of Shechem for the Hebrews may be found in many of the books of Tanach, the Hebrew word (acronym actually) for what is commonly called the Jewish Scriptures or the Old Testament. In the *Book of Genesis*, Shechem is the place where Abraham first sets foot when he arrives in the land of Israel and where he builds a sacred altar. In the *Book of Joshua*, Shechem is the place where Joshua convokes the Hebrews just before his death in order to enter into a solemn covenant to remain faithful to God. In the *Book of Judges*, Shechem is the place where Abimelech, the very first would-be king of the Hebrews, goes in order to declare his candidacy. And in the *First Book of Kings*, Shechem is the place where Rehoboam, the son of Solomon, is forced to go in order to try to get the Hebrew tribes assembled there to accept him as king. When the tribes decide to elect Jeroboam instead, Jeroboam makes Shechem the first capital of the kingdom of Israel. Even if some of these references are wholly or partially legendary, they still show that for the authors of Tanach, Shechem was thought to be a place which had a special meaning for the early Hebrews.

These indications are all the more significant in that almost all of the books of Tanach were composed by the scribes of the kingdom of Judah, centered in Jerusalem, which was a bitter rival of the kingdom of Israel for authority over the Hebrews. The scribes of the kingdom of Judah had no reason to exaggerate the importance of Shechem in early Hebrew history, given the fact that it was so closely associated with the origins of the kingdom of Israel. If they nonetheless included material in Tanach, such as the convocation of the Hebrew tribes at Shechem by Joshua, which could be seen as legitimizing the kingdom of Israel, it must have been because they thought that the importance

of Shechem in Hebrew culture was too well known and well established
to be glossed over or denied. This importance was not only political but
also religious, in that an altar of some kind was in fact set up there and
religious ceremonies conducted in conjunction with the political decisions made there. These indications tend to suggest that Abdu-Hiba
did not exaggerate and Labayu really did make some formal grant of
authority to the Habiru in the region of Shechem which provided the
original basis for the subsequent Hebrew view of Shechem as a holy
meeting place.

Additional evidence of the central position of the Habiru stronghold of Shechem in early Hebrew history is provided by an unlikely
source, the so-called "victory stele" of Merneptah. Sometime around
1207 BCE the Egyptian Pharaoh Merneptah set up a stone monument
commemorating his alleged victories over the Libyans and Canaanites.
The specific areas in Canaan which he claimed to have conquered are
listed in geographical order proceeding from south to north. Near
the end of this list comes a reference to the conquest of "Israel".
Hoffmeier, an expert on Egyptian hieroglyphics, translates the reference as stating, "Israel is wasted, its seed is not." He then goes to
state, on page 29 of *Israel in Egypt*, that based on the position of this
reference in the list of geographical place names, "The tribes of Israel
appear to have been located primarily in the central Hill Country and
Upper Galilee."

The "land of Shechem" too was located in the central hill
country, in the northern part, bordering on the Jezreel Valley and
Galilee. Nadav Na'aman, in an essay entitled "The Contribution of
the Amarna Letters to the Debate on Jerusalem's Political Position
in the Tenth Century BCE", appearing in Volume 3 of his *Collected
Essays*, states on page 5 that at the time of the Amarna letters, "Two
Canaanite kingdoms occupied almost all of the central hill country:
Shechem and Jerusalem." What all this suggests is that by the end of
the 13th century BCE, the Habiru centered in the region of Shechem
had begun to call themselves by the name of "Israel". Just when they
adopted this name is not known, but it is a reasonable hypothesis that
they did so not long before the arrival in Canaan of a small band of
Habiru fugitives fleeing slavery in Egypt and bringing with them a new

ideology of Habiru rule over the entire "land of Israel".

That there were in fact Habiru slaves in Egypt at this time is shown by a number of sources quite apart from the story in the Torah. Hoffmeier refers, on page 113, to a "victory stele" of the Pharaoh Amenhotep 2, dating from the 15th century BCE, which lists the various types of captives brought back to Egypt by the Egyptians after a successful campaign in Canaan and Syria. Included in the list are 3600 "Apiru". Additional Habiru prisoners must have been seized on other occasions, for by the 13th century BCE we have evidence of Habiru slaves working on construction projects for the Egyptians. Abraham Malamat, on page 42 of his article in Haim Ben-Sasson's anthology, *A History of the Jewish People*, cites the following inscription dating from the time of the Pharaoh Ramses 2: "Distribute grain rations to the soldiers and to the 'Apiru who transport stones to the great pylon of Ramses." And Hoffmeier, on page 115, has reference to an article by Ellen Morris describing scenes of forced labor in Egyptian wall paintings. Hoffmeier states: "The text accompanying the wine pressing scene in the tomb of Intef at Thebes, Morris observes, specifically identifies the workers as Apiru (i.e. *habiru*)."

What this evidence suggests is that there must be a kernel of truth in the Torah account of Hebrew slaves fleeing Egypt and taking up residence in Canaan. However, most of the details of the story as it appears in the Torah are clearly legendary. According to the Torah, some 600,000 Hebrew men fled Egypt at the time of the Exodus. If we include women and children, plus the "mixed multitude" which was said to accompany them, we are left with at least one million people subsisting for forty years in a barren desert on food which fell from the sky. A more likely scenario would be a small band of Habiru slaves, numbering perhaps some hundreds, escaping Egypt and making a quick passage across the Sinai to link up with the Habiru already in control of the region around Shechem. Very possibly the Habiru fugitives from Egypt were in fact led by a man named Moses, but in any case they seem to have brought with them a new ideology which played a key role in the subseqent Habiru conquest of Canaan.

A significant detail in this context is the fact, noted by a number of Biblical scholars, that most of the members of the tribe of Levi mentioned in the Torah and the *Book of Judges* had Egyptian sounding names. According to Tanach, the tribe of Levi was the only tribe that was not assigned a specific territory in the land of Canaan. It was the tribe of Moses, and its original function was to officiate at the religious ceremonies of the Hebrews. It seems probable that the tribe of Levi originated as the small band of Habiru slaves who escaped from Egypt and linked up with the Habiru already established in Canaan. Habiru are known to have been held as slaves in Egypt for a period of at least several hundred years, from the 15th to the 13th century BCE, and it would be only natural if many of them had become assimilated to the Egyptian language and culture. Yet assimilated as they may have been, the Egyptians continued to refer to them as Habiru, a usage which perhaps reflected the social gap which separated slaves from the rest of society in Egypt and Canaan alike.

In my opinion the greatest weakness of modern Biblical scholarship is to be found in its failure to deal with the issue of slavery. Most Biblical scholars act as if it were a minor or trivial point that there are numerous indications that many of the Habiru everywhere in the Middle East were fugitive slaves. And by the same token, the Biblical scholars never stop to ask: how likely is it that the authors of the Torah would have described themselves as the descendants of runaway slaves unless it were true? Throughout the world, in most times and places, there has been a stigma attached to people who have been enslaved, a presumption that they would not have become slaves if there were not something wrong with them in the first place. Yet each year, in the Passover ceremony, Jews are told to remember that their ancestors had been slaves in Egypt. And even though only a small percentage of the Habiru who conquered Canaan could have been slaves in Egypt, this tradition still reflects the reality that the Habiru as a group were composed in large part of fugitives from one or another form of bondage.

Putting it all together, the known facts suggest that sometime towards the end of the 13th century BCE, perhaps following the death of Ramses 2 in 1213 BCE, a small group of Habiru slaves fled Egypt and made their way to Canaan, bearing with them three things:

(1) The practice of circumcision. According to the Greek geographer

Herodotus, circumcision was an Egyptian custom. Whatever it may
have meant for the Egyptians, for the Habiru it became a way of distinguishing themselves from the rest of the Canaanites and transforming
their self image from that of a band of outcasts into that of a warrior
elite.

(2) The use of alphabetical writing. So far as is known, alphabetical writing was first developed by Semitic miners working for the
Egyptians in the Sinai desert around the middle of the 2nd millenium
BCE. They wrote on stone using letters partially derived from Egyptian
hieroglyphics. Although it is often asserted that the Hebrews subsequently received their alphabetical writing system from the Canaanites
or Phoenicians, it was the Habiru in Egypt who were most likely to
have contact with the Semitic miners working for the Egyptians in the
Sinai. In view of the importance attached by the Torah to the story of
the writing of the ten commandments on stone in the Sinai, it seems
likely that it was the Habiru fugitives from Egypt who introduced the
knowledge of alphabetical writing into Canaan.

(3) The concept of a ruler god who sided with the slaves rather than
the slavemasters. The concept of a supreme ruler god was well developed
in Egyptian culture, but it was invariably associated with the person of
the Pharaoh, who was said to be the earthly incarnation of this or that
supreme god. Having endured forced labor on behalf of the alleged
"son of Ra", the Pharaoh Ramses 2, the Habiru in Egypt had every
reason to reject this association. Their influence was no doubt reflected
in the Hebrew ban on the worship of graven images, the production of
which was a speciality of the Egyptians. At the same time, the Habiru
in Egypt also had a strong motive to appropriate the Egyptian concept
of a supreme ruler god and utilize it for their own purposes.

The Hebrew language narrative and literature found in Tanach
appears to reflect a synthesis between the revolutionary adaptation
of Egyptian culture associated with the Habiru fugitives from Egypt
and the political culture of the Habiru bands already centered around
Shechem. This political culture is reflected in Tanach first and foremost in the legend of the sons of Israel. It is apparent that this legend
provided a mechanism whereby the Habiru active in the region of
Canaan could identify themselves as members of one big family, which

functioned in practice as a confederation of Habiru bands, and hence achieve a greater degree of unity than had previously been possible.

That this legend originated among the Habiru already established in Canaan rather than among the Habiru fugitives from Egypt is strongly suggested by a number of indications. Merneptah's "victory stele" shows that the Habiru in the region of Shechem were already generally known as "Israel" around the time that the flight from Egypt took place. In Tanach, the "patriarchs" Abraham, Isaac and Israel are depicted as receiving a claim to the land of Canaan that was prior to and independent of the claim associated with Moses and the Exodus. Moreover, it would appear that the real life fugitives from Egypt were treated by the Habiru in Canaan as just another tribe, the tribe of Levi, which was not even given a territory of its own. No doubt the Levites did exercise a certain degree of authority relative to the other "tribes" by virtue of their religious role and beliefs, but it nonetheless appears that they were integrated into an already established political structure rather than establishing a new structure of their own.

However, it must have been just as obvious to the Habiru in Canaan as it is to the Biblical scholars today that the story of the sons of Israel was incompatible with their status as Habiru. The members of scattered bands of fugitives could not possibly have been related to one another to any significant degree, much less be all descended from the twelve sons of one father. In order to become the sons of Israel, they had therefore to cease being Habiru, or at least cease being known as such. There is every indication that they set out to do just this, spurred on by the fact that they had never liked being called Habiru in the first place.

THE HEBREWS

What was the precise meaning of the term, "Habiru", in its original context? And for that matter, was the term actually "Habiru", or rather "Apiru"? These questions need to be answered in order to address the larger question of the relationship between the terms "Habiru" and "Hebrew".

For many decades after the tablets from Tell el-Amarna and elsewhere were first unearthed, no one doubted that they made reference to people called "Habiru". In the English language translation of the Tell el-Amarna tablets published by Samuel Mercer in 1939, the term "Habiru" is used without any hint of the possibility of a different reading. By the way, in an "Excursus" at the end of the book, on page 843, F.H. Hallock stated:

> But we must admit some association between Hebrews and Habiru; linguistic and historical considerations make this inevitable, even though in the light of present-day knowledge we cannot speak with too great certainty concerning that association.

But starting in the 1950s, questions began to be raised about the accuracy of "Habiru" as a reading of the cuneiform text, with "Apiru" increasingly suggested as an alternative reading.

Accadian cuneiform hieroglyphics, which is the writing system in which the Tell el-Amarna tablets were written, consist of wedge shaped indentations in clay. According to the experts, in the particular hieroglyph in question, the initial consonant could be read either as a "b" or as a "p". The Accadian writing system apparently did not make any distinction between the two. However, by the 1950s a few references to Habiru in other writing systems had been discovered, and in these references the initial consonant seemed to be a "p". At the same time, it was also asserted, for reasons which are not entirely clear to me, that the word should be read without an initial "h". Some Biblical scholars were not convinced by these arguments and continued to use the term "Habiru". but the majority gradually switched over to "Apiru", which is generally considered to be the correct term today.

I don't consider myself qualified to pass judgment on whether "Habiru" or "Apiru" is the correct reading, nor does it appear to me that the evidence is conclusive either way. In *Le probleme des Habiru*, published in 1954, Jean Bottero surveyed the relevant data at considerable length, concluding on page 156 that he was not able to resolve the issue. He himself continued to use the term "Habiru" however. On the whole it appears to me that, with a few exceptions, those who deny the identity of the Hebrews and the Habiru prefer the term "Apiru", whereas those who affirm the identity of the two groups tend to prefer

"Habiru". I too affirm the identity of the two groups, and therefore I too use the term "Habiru", which sounds more like "Hebrew". But ultimately it doesn't really matter which term resembles "Hebrew" more closely, because of course "Hebrew" is not the Hebrew word for "Hebrew". The word is "Ivri", which doesn't seem to resemble either one all that closely.

On the other hand, it's not all that different either. In Hebrew, the letter "bet" can denote either a "b" or a "v" sound, depending mainly on its position in the word. "Ivri" is written with a "bet", which is why many translations of this word, such as "Hebrew", use a "b" rather than a "v" sound. As for the possibility that the Accadian word was pronounced with a "p" rather than a "b" sound, Manfred Weippert deals with this issue in *The Settlement of the Israelite Tribes in Palestine*. Weippert doesn't believe that the Hebrews and the Habiru were the same, and he prefers "Apiru" to "Habiru", but like many other Biblical scholars, he sees a linguistic connection between the Accadian and the Hebrew terms. In particular, he lists no less than 14 different examples of a "b" sound shifting into a "p" sound (or vice versa) in various Semitic languages, concluding on page 82: "In other words, the equation *apiru* = Hebrews can certainly be substantiated with linguistic proofs." My own feeling is that the linguistic evidence doesn't really prove the identity of the Accadian and Hebrew terms, but it does leave room for this possibility. The main reason why most Biblical scholars believe the two terms are related is because they were used in very similar ways.

Biblical scholars are generally agreed as to who the Habiru were, but there is a certain range of opinion as to how they were perceived. Bottero thought "refugee" was the most accurate term, while Weippert preferred "outlaw". The one trait that defined the Habiru as a group is that they stood outside the established social order both literally – they camped on the outskirts of the settled areas – and figuratively. But there were evidently degrees of difference from one place to another as to how antagonistic was their relationship to that order. If they served as mercenaries, they might have a relationship to the state that was defined by some kind of formal agreement. Some Biblical scholars believe that they were generally seen as "foreigners", whereas others emphasize their status as "fugitives". There is no obvious reason for preferring one term over another, since all of them undoubtedly have some basis in fact.

However, a clue to how the term "Habiru" was generally understood in the 2nd millenium BCE is provided by the existence of similar terms in other Middle Eastern languages. In particular there is the Sumerian expression, "SA.GAZ". I don't know enough about Sumerian hieroglyphics to understand why it is written this way, but since that is how most Biblical scholars write it, I am following suit. The Sumerians were a people whose ethnic and linguistic background is not well understood and who were settled in the southern part of what is now Iraq by the time that they developed a hieroglyphic writing system around 3000 BCE. The Accadian writing system was derived from the Sumerian and it also took over the Sumerian term "SA.GAZ", which was widely used in Accadian texts, including the Tell el-Amarna tablets, as a synonym for "Habiru". Bottero, on page 82, notes that the two terms were used alternately in texts unearthed at Boghazkoy, the capital of the Hittite empire in what is now Turkey, and the Biblical scholars all agree that the meaning of the two terms was more or less identical.

According to Bottero, on page 149, the root meaning of SA.GAZ in its original Sumerian context "is pejorative and indicates a violent and criminal act of aggression, and most often the perpetrator of that aggression" [my translation]. Hence Bottero thought that "SA.GAZ" should be translated as "brigand" despite the fact that he also thought that "refugee" was the best translation for "Habiru". But this contradiction is more apparent than real, for it would appear that the Habiru were refugees (or fugitives) who became brigands.

This is precisely the conclusion suggested by an article by Nadav Na'aman, "Habiru-like Bands in the Assyrian Empire and Bands in Biblical Historiography", appearing in Volume 1 of his *Collected Essays*. In Assyrian inscriptions dating from the 7th and 8th centuries BCE there are references to a group called "urbi" in the Assyrian language. The meaning of the term has been variously given as "fugitives", "bandits", "irregular troops", "a special type of soldiery" or "elite troops". According to Na'aman, the term "urbi" was derived from a verb, "merubu", which meant "to flee, run away, escape". Na'aman continued as follows, on page 299:

> The term *urbi* refers to groups of fugitives who, in the face of Assyrian military campaigns, destructions or annexations, fled from their homeland and found shelter in peripheral areas. These uprooted people tried to adapt themselves to new circumstances by forming a band under the command of a prominent leader. The bands were independent armed bodies, restricted in number and characterized by their predatory nature and military ability. Often they became dangerous to sedentary and pastoral societies. Thanks to their military ability they served on occasion as mercenaries in the armies of neighboring rulers.

And Na'aman concludes: "All of these characteristics are typical of the bands of Habiru, which are so well known from late third-and second-millenium BCE ancient Near Eastern documents."

The important point which emerges from all this is that for the people who wrote and read the texts in which terms like "SA.GAZ" or "Habiru" or "urbi" appear, all of these terms must have had a negative connotation. Sometimes this connotation became explicit, as in one of the Tell el-Amarna letters, appearing on page 261 of Mercer's translation, where one Canaanite official says of another that he has become just like the SA.GAZ people, "a runaway dog". The Habiru were outlaws by definition since they did not form a part of the established social system and did not consider themselves bound by its laws. Furthermore, the fact that many of them were fugitive slaves added an additional element of criminality to their image, since in all slave holding societies, flight from slavery is considered a serious crime, often punishable by death. To be sure, the Habiru also had the image of constituting a serious military force, but while this might have endeared them to some, for the established social order it was probably just another count in the indictment. Whether the Habiru themselves felt proud of their outlaw status is hard to say, but the weight of the evidence indicates that proud or not, they were eager to get rid of it.

The best way of finding out how the Habiru felt about being called "Habiru" is by examining how the Hebrews felt about being called "Hebrew". All the texts which mention the Habiru were written by others and therefore don't reflect a Habiru point of view, but the Hebrews had ample opportunity to make their views known. And the first thing which every Biblical scholar has noticed about the way the term "Hebrew" is used in Tanach is that it is hardly used at all. In the whole of Tanach, the term "Hebrew" appears only 33 times. In the Torah, the Hebrews are almost always described as the "sons of Israel" ("b'nei Israel" in Hebrew, usually translated as "children of Israel" or "Israelites"). In the later books of Tanach other terms are used, but hardly ever "Hebrew".

Moreover, when the term "Hebrew" does appear, it is used in certain specific ways. Nadav Na'aman has probed this issue in depth in his illuminating essay, "Habiru and Hebrews: The Transfer of a Social Term to the Literary Sphere", appearing in Volume 2 of his *Collected Essays*. Like most Biblical scholars, Na'aman doesn't think that the Hebrews were Habiru, but he has no doubt that the term "Hebrew" was derived from "Habiru". He points out, on page 270, that in Tanach, the term "Hebrew" is typically used to describe "Israelites in exceptional circumstancs". In particular it is used to describe "Israelites migrating to a foreign country" or "Israelites in a position of slavery". He adds that the use of the term "Hebrew" is especially prevalent "in the stories of the book of Exodus, in which it is applied to Israelites who were enslaved and exploited by the Egyptians for hard labor." And he concludes, on page 271: "It seems clear that all biblical references to the 'Hebrews' reflect some traits borrowed from the image of the second millenium Habiru".

A good example of the way the term "Hebrew" is used in Tanach may be found in Chapter 29 of the *First Book of Samuel*. After being forced to flee from the territory of "Israel" because of the wrath of king Saul, the future king David has gathered a band of malcontents around him and found refuge among the Philistines. Now the Philistines are preparing for battle with the forces of king Saul, and David and his band are ready to join them. But the "princes of the Philistines" cry out: "What do these Hebrews here?" Achish, David's protector among the Philistines, is compelled to send David and his men away, because the other Philistine leaders do not trust him and fear he will join forces with king Saul when the battle is imminent. The use of the term "Hebrews" in this context may of course be understood as a reference to the ethnic group of which David and his men were members; but it also makes perfect sense as a synonym for "Habiru", implying a ragged band of mercenaries viewed with disdain by most of the Philistine leaders. It would seem that the authors of Tanach could not help but make occasional use of the term "Hebrew" as a way of adding a note of realism to their story, while at the same time systematically avoiding any explicit identification of the Hebrews as Habiru because it would have conflicted with the legend of the "sons of Israel".

According to Na'aman, what then happened is that the term "Hebrews" was rescued from oblivion by the Jewish writers of the late Second Temple period, who increasingly used it as a way of describing the ancestors of the Jews. It appears to me that by this time the connection between the Habiru and the Hebrews, which was clearly well known at the time the books of Tanach were written, had been largely forgotten, and the term "Hebrew" came to be surrounded with an aura of religious sanctity quite unlike its original connotations. Perhaps through the influence of Josephus, who used the term quite frequently, the word "Hebrew" then entered Christian (and ultimately also Jewish) discourse as a respectable alternative to the invariably pejorative term, "Jew".

However the Hebrew language has still retained a trace of the original meaning of the term. The Hebrew word "Ivri" comes from a Hebrew root, ayin, bet, resh, whose basic meaning is to pass or cross over. The Hebrew word for the "past" is derived from this same root. But there are also a number of words in Hebrew derived from this root whose meaning is precisely equivalent to the English word "transgression", namely to pass or cross over the line between permitted and forbidden. Thus we have "avaryan", meaning "transgressor", and "avera", a violation of the rules. Indeed, several Biblical scholars have even gone so far as to suggest that the term "Habiru", whose root in the Accadian language is not clear, was actually derived from the same "West Semitic" root as "Ivri" and had the same root meaning, namely to pass or cross over, whether as fugitives or as law breakers. Be that as it may, there can be no question that the terms "Hebrew" and "Habiru" are closely related, and the one obvious explanation for this relationship is that the Hebrews were in fact Habiru.

THE JEWS

There remains the Jewish question, which is: what was the legacy of the Habiru for the Jews?

The word "Jew" is a shortened and humiliated form of the word "Judah", which is the standard English language translation of the Hebrew word, "Yehudah". Judah was the name of the Hebrew kingdom centered in Jerusalem that was founded by David sometime around 1000 BCE. The kingdom was called Judah because David came from the tribe of Judah, who was said to be one of the sons of Israel. The Persians called the kingdom "Yahud", the Greeks called it "Ioudaia" and the Romans called it "Judea" until 135 CE, at which time they officially changed the name of the entire country to "Palestine" (in honor of the Philistines), at the end of the so-called "Second Jewish War", during the course of which they murdered some 580,000 Jews according to the body count of the Roman historian Dio Cassius.

Just about everything which is known about the Hebrews, apart from the texts which mention the Habiru, is known because of what the Jews wrote about them in Tanach. According to the account in Tanach, after the death of David's son Solomon, the kingdom of Judah split into two parts, a kingdom of Israel in the north and a much smaller kingdom of Judah in the south. However the kings of Israel allowed themselves to be seduced by pagan beliefs and practices, and therefore the kingdom of Israel was overthrown by the Assyrians and the ten Hebrew tribes who inhabited it were sent away into exile, never to return. Eventually the kingdom of Judah was also overthrown, by the Babylonians, and the Jews sent into exile, but because they had at least tried to resist pagan influence, they were permitted by God, acting through Cyrus, the conqueror of the Babylonians, to return to Jerusalem and rebuild the Temple.

Many Biblical scholars agree on a slightly more sophisticated version of this account according to which the split between Judah and Israel was due to the existence of two distinct religious tendencies among the early Hebrews, the cult of "Elohim" and the cult of "Yahweh". The cult of Elohim, they argue, grew out of the indigenous Canaanite worship of "El", the supreme god of the pagan Canaanites, while the cult of Yahweh was introduced into Canaan by the "Moses group" coming out of Egypt and the Sinai. The Jews, it seems, were more drawn to the worship of Yahweh, while the supporters of the kingdom of Israel preferred Elohim. Although rarely stated explicitly, the clear implication of this version of events is that the worship of Yahweh was somehow more monotheistic than the worship of Elohim. Perhaps this was because it supposedly came out of the desert, and some Biblical scholars even speculate that the word "Yahweh" may have been derived from the belief system of a nomadic people living in or around the southern Sinai.

In any case, it has become an article of faith among Biblical scholars that first some Hebrews and then the Jews worshipped a god called "Yahweh". The word appears in the title of some of their most prestigious books, such as Albright's *Yahweh and the Gods of Canaan*, or Gottwald's *The Tribes of Yahweh*. With the exception of a number of Israeli authors, it is used by virtually every Biblical scholar accorded the status of Biblical scholar by the other Biblical scholars. It has also made its way to a wider public, so that while most educated people remain unaware of the very existence of the Habiru, they think they know that Yahweh was the god of the Jews. Some like him and some don't, but thanks to the Biblical scholars, no one doubts that "Yahweh" is what the Jews called him.

They are wrong. The word "Yahweh" is a 19th century German language rendition of the Hebrew letters yod, hay, vav, hay, normally written in English language versions of Tanach as YHVH, which are used interchangeably with "Elohim" as representing the name of God in Tanach. Out of respect for the German Protestant theologians who founded the whole field of Biblical studies, modern Biblical scholars writing in English have not even bothered to replace the "w" in Yahweh with a "v". The Hebrew letter "vav" is normally represented by a "v" in English, but in German, the "v" sound is represented by a "w", hence "Yahweh" rather than "Yahveh". According to the German Protestants, "Yahveh" was the correct way of pronouncing the letters YHVH, which had previously been pronounced as "Jehovah" by English Protestants. Just how they knew this they did not say, nor could they, because YHVH is not a word and was never pronounced as a word by any Jew prior to the discovery of Yahweh by the Germans.

Had the Biblical scholars both past and present even a modicum of respect for the Jews, as opposed to the Hebrews or "Israelites", they would have paid more attention than they do to the fact that religious Jews are forbidden to pronunce the letters YHVH as a word. Wherever these letters appear in Tanach and elsewhere, religious Jews are supposed to pronounce the word "Adonai", meaning "Lord", in their place. The Biblical scholars know this, but they attach no importance to it, evidently assuming that the Jews don't understand their own religion as well as the Protestants. Rainer Albertz deals with this issue in a typical manner on page 49 of Volume 1 of his book, *A History of Israelite Religion in the Old Testament Period*, published in 1994. According to him, "because of the reluctance to utter the divine name which began in the Hellenistic period, its pronunciation is not completely certain". However, "Yahweh is the most probable pronunciation". Albertz cites no evidence to show that the Jews pronounced YHVH as a word prior to "the Hellenistic period", nor does it even occur to him that it might never have been intended as a word in the first place. Nonetheless there is abundant evidence to show that from the start YHVH was not considered to be a word but rather a place holder for the Hebrew sentence, "ehyeh asher ehyeh", meaning "I will be what I will be".

The sentence appears in Chapter 3 of the Book of Exodus; the relevant passage reads as follows:

> Moses said to God, "When I come to the Israelites and say to them 'The God of your fathers has sent me to you,' and they ask me, 'What is His name?' what shall I say to them?" And God said to Moses, "Ehyeh Asher Ehyeh." He continued, "Thus shall you say to the Israelites, 'Ehyeh sent me to you.'" And God said further

to Moses, "Thus shall you speak to the Israelites: The LORD, the God of your fathers, the God of Abraham, the God of Isaac, and the God of Jacob, has sent me to you: This shall be My name forever, This My appellation for all eternity."

More often than not, the sentence "ehyeh asher ehyeh" is translated as "I am that I am" in English language versions of the Torah, but what the sentence actually says is "I will be what I will be". Either way, the important point is that God tells Moses that his name is "ehyeh asher ehyeh", or "ehyeh" for short, and not "Yahweh". Once you realize this, then the reason for the ban on pronouncing the name of God out loud becomes obvious. It is that you cannot pronounce the sentence "ehyeh asher ehyeh" or the word "ehyeh" without assuming the identity of God.

But why did the Jews adopt the letters YHVH as a place holder for the forbidden name of God? The most likely explanation is that they did so because these are the letters out of which almost all of the forms of the verb "to be" are constructed in Hebrew. In modern Hebrew grammar, the root of the verb "to be" is normally given as hay, yod, hay, or HYH, but there is also a related form, hay, vav, hay, or HVH. However, these grammatical forms only date from the start of the systematic study of Hebrew grammar by Jews in Spain during the Middle Ages. It would have been only natural for the Jews who wrote Tanach to combine the two roots into one in the form of YHVH. In general, roots in Hebrew grammar are not supposed to be pronounced; they merely indicate the letters out of which various related words are formed.

The Biblical scholars know all this yet they persist in the obsessive use of the term "Yahweh" (and also "Yahwism" and "Yahwistic") anyhow. For example, George H. van Kooten in his Introduction to his anthology, *The Revelation of the Name YHWH to Moses*, published in 2006, states on page ix: "The name 'Yahweh', connected with the phrase, *ehyeh asher ehyeh* ('I am that I am': Exod 3:14), is of central importance in Judaism, and 'Yahwism' became tantamount to Jewish monotheism." But how could the name "Yahweh" be of "central importance in Judaism" when there is no evidence that one Jew ever used this name for some 3000 years? Moreover, in this same anthology, van Kooten himself shows in his essay, "Moses/Musaeus/Mochos and his God Yahweh, Iao, and Sabaoth, Seen From a Graeco-Roman Perspective", that the Greeks, who had no more respect for the Jews than the Biblical scholars, did not think that the name of the Jewish God was "Yahweh" but rather "Iao". Van Kooten, on page 130, attributed the Greek ignorance of Yahweh to "the declining willingness of Jews to pronounce and invoke the name of Yahweh". but like Albertz he could cite no indication that the Jews had ever used this name. It was probably precisely because the Greeks had never heard of Yahweh that Albertz and van Kooten asserted that the Jewish reluctance to pronounce this name began "in the Hellenistic period".

To top it all off, Biblical scholarship has also obfuscated the meaning of the other name of God in Jewish tradition, namely "Elohim". The god "El" was indeed the supreme god of the Canaanite pantheon, and the word "El" was used in exactly the same way as the word "God" in English, namely to indicate not only God Himself but any "god". A "god" in Hebrew is an "el", and the standard plural form of "el" is "elim", meaning "gods". However, there is also an archaic plural form of "el", and that form is "elohim". The word "Elohim" does not literally mean "God", but rather "gods". So which should it be: "The Lord our gods is one" or "The Lord our gods are one"? By an amazing coincidence, this question doesn't arise in Hebrew, because in Hebrew the use of the verb "to be" in the present tense is banned. You cannot say "I am thin" but only "I thin". In Hebrew grammar there is a form of the present tense of the verb "to be", namely "hovay", but this form is never used as a verb, only as a noun to mean "the present". Seeing as the "Shema", the affirmation of the unity of "Elohenu", meaning "our gods", is probably the single most frequently repeated sentence in the entire Jewish liturgy, I find it hard to believe that there is not some connection between this fact and a grammatical system that makes it unnecessary to decide whether "our gods" exist (or exists) in the singular or the plural.

So there you have it: the Jewish religion is founded on the worship of a god called "gods" whose real name is said to be "I will be". Were the Biblical scholars not blinded by their need to personify the god of the Jews (perhaps so that he could become a father), they would have noticed that they are dealing with a complex, dialectical mode of thought not unlike the complex, dialectical mode of thought associated with later generations of Jewish revolutionary thinkers and leaders. The one thing that "gods" and "I will be" have in common as names of God is that it is more or less impossible to personify them. It is hard to imagine a plural entity as a singular person or to form an image of an unknown future entity. Yet at the same time, these hard to personify names are attached in Tanach to the figure of a ruler god who constantly observes, warns, punishes and rewards just like a person might do. It seems evident that what we have here are two conflicting tendencies, on the one hand a need for a ruler god, on the other a profound suspicion of authority, both of which are amply represented in the pages of Tanach. To me it also seems evident that both of these tendencies grew out of the culture and mode of thought of the Habiru.

The Habiru who became known as Hebrews appear in the Torah and the other early books of Tanach not as they were but as they wished to be. Who they were was a warrior elite who gained control of the greater part of the land of Israel starting around 1200 BCE. There is no indication in Tanach that the early Hebrews differed from the Canaanites to any appreciable extent either in language or in physical appearance. They differed because they constituted a social class on the margins of Canaanite society, and they adopted the rite of circumcision as a way of formalizing this difference and defining themselves as fearless conquerors rather than hapless victims. But as conquerors they needed a ruler god to provide them with a title deed to the land of Canaan and to validate the way of life they wished to follow there. However, their ruler god differed from other ruler gods in that he was not originally associated with the institution of monarchy. It is only in the time of Saul and David, some 200 years after the start of the Hebrew conquest of Canaan, that God in Tanach shows the slightest interest in the political form of Hebrew rule. It seems that the Habiru did not want a ruler god with monarchical features and that it was for this reason that they extended the ban on the worship of graven images into the conceptual sphere, where it functioned as a ban on the personification of YHVH or Elohim.

Yet in order to rule over Canaan as a united force, the Habiru needed more than a ruler god: they also needed the legend of the sons of Israel, and it was for this reason that they did not portray themselves as they were in the Torah but rather as they wished to be. Instead of depicting their ancestors as fugitives and refugees, they depicted Abraham, Isaac and Israel as peaceful bedouin wandering around the Middle East tending their flocks. This was because the whole concept of the "b'nei Israel" was a bedouin concept, identical to that of the many bedouin tribes who traditionally described themselves as the "sons" ("banu" in Arabic) of some patriarchal ancestor. And having invented an idealized past as bedouin, the Habiru could not be seen as a warrior elite, but had to win all their battles through divine intervention vouchsafed to Hebrews who were entirely lacking in military experience and equipment. By the same token, all the Hebrew tribes had to experience the Exodus from Egypt, even if this made the Sinai rather crowded during their passage, just so the "tribe" of Levi could not lord it over all the other "tribes". The end result was a Torah that is almost entirely mythical yet still conveys in a powerful way its attachment to the cause of the slaves as opposed to that of the slave masters.

How you feel about the Torah depends in large measure upon how you feel about the concept of a ruler god, but how you feel about the Habiru depends in even larger measure upon how you feel about the concept of revolutionary violence. Revolution implies violence, or as Mao Zedong put it back in 1927:

> A revolution is not a dinner party, or writing an essay, or painting a picture, or doing embroidery; it cannot be so refined, so leisurely and gentle, so temperate, kind, courteous, restrained and magnanimous. A revolution is an insurrection, an act of violence by which one class overthrows another.

But was the conquest of the land of Israel by the Habiru a real revolution: did it result not just in the overthrow of the rule of the Canaanite city-states and their Egyptian overlords but also in the creation of a new and more progressive social order? The weight of the evidence is that it did. The social ideal of Tanach is that of the small farmer whose right to the land was to be guaranteed by the law of the Jubilee according to which land lost through debt was to be returned to its rightful owners every 50 years. The accumulation of large land holdings was frowned on, the institution of slavery sharply curtailed, the provision of charity to the poor mandated. The perpetuation of these social values and practices was to be assured in the same way as they were originally established, through the use of armed force. In Jewish tradition, this notion of armed force in the service of social equality came to be associated with one man in particular, the founder of the kingdom of Judah, David.

DAVID

As you might expect, the Biblical scholars who don't like the Habiru don't like David either. One of the most influential Biblical scholars in recent decades is Israel Finkelstein, co-author along with Neil Asher Silberman of *The Bible Unearthed*, published in 2001, and *David and Solomon*, published in 2006. On page 44 of *David and Solomon* the authors expound on the meaning of the term, "Apiru", as follows:

> This term, sometimes transliterated as Habiru, was once thought to be related to the term "Hebrews" but the Egyptian texts make it clear that it does not refer to a specific ethnic group so much as a problematic socioeconomic class. The Apiru were uprooted peasants and herders who sometimes turned bandits, sometimes sold themselves as mercenaries to the highest bidder, and were in both cases a disruptive element in any attempt by either local rulers or the Egyptian administration to maintain the stability of their rule.

What is most amazing about this dismissal of the "Apiru" as disruptive troublemakers unrelated to the Hebrews is that nowhere in either book do the authors even attempt to show that the Hebrews did in fact constitute a "specific ethnic group" separate and apart from the Canaanites. Finkelstein in particular has built his reputation in large part on attempting to debunk much of the historical information in Tanach as legendary, yet when it comes to the obvious myth of the "sons of Israel", he neither accepts nor rejects it, thus enabling him to use it to deny the identity of the Habiru and Hebrews without actually having to pretend that he believes in it.

High on Finkelstein's list of things in Tanach to debunk is the story of David and the rise of the kingdom of Judah. According to Tanach David established a large kingdom ruling over the greater part of the land of Israel, but according to Finkelstein and Silberman David was a petty "chieftain" ruling over a small part of the southern hill country. And in order to denigrate David still further, the authors can think of nothing better than to identify him with the "Apiru". As they put it on page 46 of *David and Solomon*: "Put simply, the description of the rise of David in the first book of Samuel contains many distinctive parallels to the activity of a typical Apiru chieftain and his rebel gang." Over and over the authors characterize David as a "bandit" at the head of a "gang" of "ruffians and freebooters". Yet the passages in Tanach on which the authors rely to substantiate these characterizations could just as well be viewed as descriptions of the formation of a revolutionary army. Silberman and Finkelstein gives these passages a negative spin for the same reason that they see the Habiru as "problematic", because they don't like revolutionaries.

For example, there is the well known passage in Chapter 22 of the *First Book of Samuel* describing how David first formed his little band: "And every one that was in distress, and every one that was in debt, and every one that was discontented, gathered themselves unto him; and he became captain over them; and there were with him about four hundred men." Silberman and Finkelstein have a point, in that it was undoubtedly in just this manner that many Habiru bands were formed. But the issue is not whether David and his followers resembled the Habiru, which they undoubtedly did; the issue is whether both David and the Habiru in Canaan were mere "bandits" or rather revolutionaries intent on imposing a new social order, one of whose key features was the avoidance of the loss of land through debt. It seems clear to me that David was indeed a revolutionary, but one who differed from the Habiru in one essential respect, in that his revolution was founded on the institution of monarchy.

Not only did David get himself named king of Judah, but he founded a dynasty that ruled over the kingdom of Judah in uninterrupted succession for some 400 years. And even after that, the notion that "the" Messiah would be a direct descendant of David remained a significant feature of Jewish Messianic culture right on down to modern times. Just why did the figure of David come to loom so large as the ideal monarch in Jewish tradition? No doubt his personal qualities, as described in Tanach, played a role here, but there is only one obvious answer to the question of why David became such an important figure. It is the answer that is supplied by Tanach, namely that David defeated the Philistines, conquered Jerusalem and extended the authority of the Hebrews further than it had ever been extended before. He did so by forming the Hebrews into a unified military force under his command, whereas previously they had fought mainly as a confederation of independent tribes without any centralized command structure. It is evident that the Hebrews were not enthusiastic about the concept of monarchy, but they accepted David's version of it because it worked and won them the battles they needed to win in order to implement their vision of the ideal social order.

Ancient Jewish culture, the culture that is reflected in the pages of Tanach, was a monarchical version of the revolutionary culture of the Habiru. It substituted the monarchy for the tribes, the priesthood for the Levites and the Temple in Jerusalem for all the local shrines, yet at the same time it remained far more egalitarian and humane than the culture of the kingdoms and empires which surrounded the land of Israel. And it was precisely because of the progressive features of Jewish culture that the Jewish people has been subjected to such savage persecution throughout our history. In particular, it is impossible to understand the genocidal assault on the Jewish people by the Romans and their Greek allies, which resulted in the death of over 2 million Jews during the era of the so-called "Jewish wars" of the 1st and 2nd centuries CE, without reference to the fact that Jewish law frowned on the institution of slavery whereas the Roman empire was built on it. In later years, Christianity, Islam and Marxism, each in their own way, drew on the progressive current in Jewish life for their own inspiration, yet far from recognizing their debt to the Jewish people, they invented one anti-Semitic stereotype after another in order to distance themselves from the Jewish fate.

This dynamic has continued unto the present day in the form of the demonization of the state of Israel by the international left. When I first began to write and lecture on the subject of Jewish history, I thought I would find my most appreciative audience in the progressive community. I was, after all, demonstrating that the entire "Biblical" tradition, which still remained such a formidable competitor with the secular left, was in fact an outgrowth of a social revolution and not the result of some divine plan. But as it turned out, most progressives didn't want to hear about this particular social revolution because it made the Jews look good and hence, by implication, made Israel look good. They much preferred to believe that the Jews of old worshipped a cruel patriarchal god named Yahweh and therefore deserved what they got at the hands of the tolerant, easy going pagans. This point was brought home to me with particular clarity by a book called *When God Was A Woman*, by a woman named Merlin Stone, which was serialized with great fanfare by the progressive radio station WBAI in New York during the 1980s. Drawing largely on studies published in Germany during the 1930s, Stone tried to show that the patriarchal cult of Yahweh was actually introduced into a matriarchal Middle East by Aryan invaders from the north, leading Stone to conclude, on page 127, that it was "ironic" that Hitler killed so many Jews, seeing as the Jews and the Nazis had so much in common.

As it so happens, Jewish descent has been reckoned in the maternal rather than the paternal line since about the middle of the 1st millenium BCE, but that is neither here nor there. The point is that you cannot effectively uphold democratic, secular and egalitarian values while at the same time demonizing the people who have done more than any other to promote those values. The reason why so many Jews have played such a prominent role in the progressive movements of modern times is because of the egalitarian values embedded in traditional Jewish culture, and the reason why those values are embedded there is because of the social revolution carried out by the Habiru. By the same token, it is because of the progressive character of

Jewish tradition that the state of Israel is so much more democratic, secular and egalitarian than any of its Arab and Muslim neighbors. Demonizing the Jews and demonizing Israel can serve no other purpose than to strengthen the hand of the alliance of autocratic states currently aligned against us. And conversely, adopting a positive attitude towards the Jewish people, including the Jewish state, is the key to freeing the progressive movement from the state of pathetic irrelevance in which we now find it.

Jewish Influence

Most people, including many Jews, know little or nothing about Jewish history and the little which they do know consists almost entirely of three components: the chronicles of the so-called "Old Testament", the fact that the Holocaust took place and the existence of the state of Israel. The 2000 years of Jewish history which separate the first of these components from the other two remain little known except to Jewish historians, and even among Jewish historians there is a strong tendency to minimize the significance of what happened during this period for anyone except the Jews themselves.

Looming over the historiography of the buried Jewish past are the ghetto walls of medieval Europe. These walls were erected for the specific purpose of preventing the Jews from influencing their neighbors, and they have succeeded so well that even now most Jewish historians cannot imagine the Jews of the past 2000 years as having influenced anyone except other Jews. This is unfortunate, for what it means among other things is that the origins of both Christianity and Islam will remain forever shrouded in mystery.

Ghettoization, whether official or unofficial, did eventually become the normal condition of Jewish life in the Diaspora prior to the modern era, but this did not happen immediately after the end of the "Biblical" period of Jewish history. It was only during the past 1000 years or so that the ghetto system was gradually imposed on the small and scattered Jewish communities which had managed to survive the rise of Christianity and Islam. At the time when first Christianity and then Islam actually took shape, the Jewish people was still a large and significant force in the politics of the Middle East and Mediterranean region. Once the extent and nature of this force is recognized, the origins of both Christianity and Islam appear in a whole new light.

Christianity

According to the census of the Roman empire conducted by the Romans in 42 CE, the empire had a total population of approximately 60 million people, of whom some 7 million were Jews. Jews therefore formed over 10% of the population of the entire empire, but as there were very few Jews living at that time in the western, Latin-speaking portion of the empire, Jews in the eastern, Greek-speaking part must have formed at least 20% of the population. Nicholas de Lange on page 25 of his authoritative *Atlas of the Jewish World* estimates that there were also approximately 1 million Jews living at that time in what is now Iraq, which was not under Roman rule, yielding a total of roughly 8 million Jews in the world 2000 years ago. The fact that there are only approximately 14 million Jews in the entire world today, some 2000 years later, speaks volumes about the genocidal pressures to which the Jewish people has been subjected throughout our history. Other nations and peoples have multiplied their population many times over during this time span, yet we who love children so much have had a hard time even maintaining our past numbers.

Of the 8 million Jews in the world 2000 years ago, historians estimate that there were at least 2 and perhaps 3 million in the land of Israel, plus roughly 1 million in each of the countries which are today Turkey, Syria, Iraq and Egypt. Jews were particularly numerous in the large Greek-speaking cities of the eastern Mediterranean region such as Alexandria, Antioch and Sardis. In these cities they must have formed considerably more than 20% of the population, since Jews were not heavily settled in the countryside at that time anywhere outside of the land of Israel. In short, far from constituting a small, ghettoized minority in the region where Christianity first arose and took shape, Jews formed a large and influential part of the population, one which came close to a majority in some cities.

The spread of Jewish influence in the Greco-Roman world of 2000 years ago was a direct consequence of the incorporation of the nation of Judah into the Roman empire. In 63 BCE a Roman army under the command of Pompey invaded the land of Israel and overthrew the Hasmonean dynasty which had ruled Judah for the previous 100 years. There ensued several decades of more or less continuous warfare between the Romans and the supporters of the Hasmoneans which ended in a kind of compromise in the time of Julius and Augustus Caesar. On the one hand the Jews accepted a puppet ruler, Herod, imposed on them by the Romans, but on the other hand Judaism was declared a "legal religion" by the Romans, thereby facilitating the growth of Jewish communities throughout the Greco-Roman world.

However, the more the Romans learned about Judaism, the less they liked it. In the first place, although the Roman empire was founded on the widespread exploitation of slave labor, Judaism had a fundamentally negative attitude towards slavery, as reflected in the injunction appearing in Chapter 23 of the *Book of Deuteronomy*:

> You shall not turn over to his master a slave who seeks refuge with you from his master. He may live with you in any place he may choose among the settlements in your midst, wherever he pleases; you must not ill-treat him.

And in the second place, Judaism prohibited the worship of idols, which meant that Jews had to refuse to take part in the ceremonies of emperor worship which became an increasingly important part of the religious program of the Caesars over the course of the 1st and 2nd centuries CE. From the point of view of the Roman ruling class, Judaism therefore came to appear as a subversive ideology, one which was essentially at odds with the autocratic principles on which the Roman empire was based.

What made Judaism particularly threatening in Roman eyes is that it not only implied an attitude of disapproval towards the Roman social order but also offered a clear alternative to that order. Although Jews were required to obey Roman law the same as all the other subjects of the empire, they also had their own Jewish law, which they followed as much as possible. Some of the provisions of Jewish law, such as the ban on work on the seventh day, proved popular even with non-Jews, giving rise to the complaint by the Roman philosopher Seneca, "The vanquished have given their laws to their victors." And although the nation of Judah may have lost its independence, it still retained much of its former power and prestige due to the presence in its midst of the Temple of Jerusalem. Greatly enlarged and refurbished during the reign of Herod, the Temple was considered one of the landmarks of the ancient world, a center of pilgrimage and devotion for Jews throughout the Mediterranean region.

However, in the year 70 CE the Temple was destroyed by the Romans towards the end of the so-called "First Jewish War", a genocidal campaign in which the Romans, according to the Jewish historian Josephus, killed more than 1 million Jews. This assault was followed by the "Second Jewish War", in the years 132-35 CE, in the course of which the Romans killed an additional 580,000 Jews according to the Roman historian Dio Cassius. And modern historians estimate that many hundreds of thousands of Jews were also killed by the Romans during the "Diaspora revolt" of 115-17 CE, which was touched off by a Roman invasion of Iraq and assault on the Jews there.

These mass murders and destruction of the Temple were accompanied by an attack on the nation of Judah as a political entity and Judaism as a religion. After first breaking up Herod's kingdom into smaller entities, the Romans eventually abolished it altogether and replaced it with a Roman province which they called "Palestine" in honor of the ancient Philistines. And at the start of the so-called "Second Jewish War" in 132 CE, the Romans issued a decree banning the practice of circumcision, which effectively banned Judaism as a religion. This decree was soon partially rescinded by a new decree permitting Jews to circumcise their male children, but it remained in effect for non-Jews, making conversion to Judaism an illegal act subject to the death penalty.

The cumulative effect of these measures was to sharply reduce the Jewish population of the Roman empire. Michael Avi-Yonah in *The Jews of Palestine* estimates that there were only 750,000 Jews remaining in the land of Israel at the end of the "Second Jewish War". Egypt and Syria had become almost completely Judenrein, and the Jewish population of Turkey was much smaller than it had previously been. It is impossible to judge precisely to what extent this process of depopulation was due to mass murder or rather to flight from the Romans, but it seems clear that something like 2 million Jews were killed by the Romans and their Greek allies during the course of the 1st and 2nd centuries CE. At the same time, the nation of Judah had officially ceased to exist and conversion to Judaism had been completely banned.

These facts are well attested, yet you will search in vain through the writings of the historians of classical antiquity for a recognition of the genocidal character of the Roman campaign against the Jews. To the contrary, the Romans are typically portrayed as "tolerant" and easy going in matters of religion but stirred to action by the "stubbornness" of the Jews. Each of the Roman assaults on the Jews is dealt with separately, often only in a few sentences, and the question of the actual number of Jewish deaths is never raised. The one detail that is always mentioned, the destruction of the Temple, is usually portrayed as a spur of the moment by-product of the Roman siege of Jerusalem and not as the end result of a conscious policy of suppressing Judaism. Yet Roman literature is full of anti-Semitic slurs against the Jews and the destruction of the Temple was preceded by a long series of attempts by the Romans to somehow introduce the practice of emperor worship into the Temple precincts.

The disinclination of historians of antiquity to recognize the true character and extent of the Roman campaign against the Jews has the effect, whether intended or unintended, of making it possible to attribute the origins of Christianity to the inspired guidance of a few remarkable individuals. Were historians to notice the mass murders carried out by the Romans against the Jews throughout the Roman empire during the 1st and 2nd centuries CE, they would also be compelled to notice the obvious connection between these mass murders and the emergence of a cult of a crucified Jew during precisely this same time period. And were historians to notice that conversion to Judaism was banned by the Romans on penalty of death in the early 2nd century CE, they would also be compelled to notice that Christianity functioned from this time forward as a kind of legal Judaism, one which preserved many Jewish beliefs and traditions but situated them within the framework of an anti-Semitic narrative that dovetailed neatly with the violently anti-Semitic culture of the Roman empire.

Moreover, the "New Testament" tale of how the Jews scorned

and rejected their one and only Messiah and then handed him over to the Romans to be killed was not the only anti-Semitic component of Christianity. Even more hostile in a way was the Christian treatment of Jesus himself. To be sure, he was worshipped as a god, but a very peculiar god, one whose outstanding characteristic was the willingness to be tortured, killed and eaten in effigy so that the Christians could live forever in a pleasant place in the sky. Pretending to eat the flesh and drink the blood of a Jewish man once a week effectively distanced Christianity from Judaism, and this same effect was also achieved by the explicit rejection of Jewish law as a code of conduct. Yet at the same time, the Christians preserved and disseminated a large quantity of Jewish literature in the form of the so-called "Old Testament" and upheld, in the name of the teachings of Jesus, a moral and ethical ideal which was a standard part of rabbinical Judaism.

In short, Christianity represented a compromise or synthesis between the pro-Jewish and anti-Jewish currents in Greco-Roman society. But what made this compromise or synthesis so popular and influential was the Roman campaign against the Jews. The murder of several million people, including many hundreds of thousands of residents of major Greco-Roman cities, had a profound effect on all concerned. On the one hand it tended to bring the autocratic values of the Roman empire into disrepute, but on the other hand it also eliminated Judaism as a likely alternative to Roman rule. The end result was a Christian empire, one which insisted on the supremacy of Greco-Roman culture yet sought to imbue this culture with attitudes and values more or less explicitly derived from Jewish tradition.

ISLAM

However, once Christianity became the official religion of the Roman empire in the 4th century CE, the legal position of the surviving Jews in the Roman world began to deteriorate rapidly. One consequence of the so-called "Jewish Wars" had been that the Roman Caesars ceased to view Judaism as a serious threat, so that there were no new persecutions or legal measures against Jews for a period of roughly 200 years following the end of the "Jewish Wars". But once the Christians came to power, a long series of anti-Jewish decrees followed which sharply restricted Jewish participation in public life, barred Jewish contact with Christians and imposed all kinds of new disabilities on the Jews. In the eyes of the Christian church, the very existence of the Jewish people constituted an implicit threat to the legitimacy of Christianity, and it therefore became the policy of the Christian empire to make life for the Jews so difficult that they would be forced to convert to Christianity.

The consequences of this policy were particularly severe for the surviving Jewish community of the land of Israel. The Christian rulers were determined to turn the land of Israel, which they called Palestine, into a Christian country, and they did everything in their power to encourage pious Christians to settle there. By the 5th century CE there was a Christian majority in the land of Israel, while the Jewish population had been greatly reduced. Michael Avi-Yonah in *The Jews of Palestine* estimates that there were only some 200,000 Jews remaining in the land of Israel by the 6th century CE, as opposed to perhaps 750,000 at the end of the "Jewish Wars". Christian harassment of the Jewish population of the land of Israel had touched off a Jewish revolt in 351 CE, and the Samaritans also rebelled against Christian rule in 484 and 529 CE, but all to no avail. By the end of the 6th century CE, Jews throughout the Greco-Roman world had been reduced to the position of a small, embattled minority numbering at most several million and Judaism had been denied the status of a "legal religion" in the authoritative law code of the 6th century Christian Caesar, Justinian.

Yet during this same period, from the 4th through the 6th century CE, large scale conversions to Judaism were taking place among the peoples established just to the south and east of the Greco-Roman world, in North Africa, Ethiopia and Arabia. Far from declining, the Jewish people was actually growing during this period, but you would never know it from standard histories of the ancient world. You will seek in vain through these works for even one word mentioning the mass conversions to Judaism on the fringes of the Greco-Roman world during the period of some 300 years preceding the rise of Islam. And even studies by Jewish historians, although they do document these conversions, treat each one individually and fail to take note of the obvious similarities between them. In this way the existence of a broadly based social movement in favor of Judaism is completely concealed from view, thereby creating a false and misleading impression of the historical background to the rise of Islam.

In North Africa, most of the Berber tribes living in the hill country just beyond the reach of the Romans on the coast converted to Judaism during this period. The Berbers were the indigenous people of what is called in Arabic the "Maghreb", the part of North Africa now forming the countries of Morocco, Algeria and Tunisia. In the area close to the Mediterranean coast, the Berbers were conquered and colonized by successive waves of invaders, beginning with the Phoenicians and continuing with the Romans, Byzantines and Vandals. Further inland the Berber tribes remained independent, and it was these independent tribes who began converting to Judaism in large numbers starting in the 2nd or 3rd centuries CE.

The story of the Berber Jews of North Africa is recounted by Andre Chouraqui in *Between East And West: A History of the Jews of North Africa*. Chouraqui on page 21 cites the Christian theologian Tertullian who "reported that the Berbers observed the Sabbath, the Jewish festivals and fasts, and the dietary laws". These tribes remained Jewish right up to the time of the Arab conquest of North Africa in the 7th century CE. In fact, the resistance to the Arab conquest in the Maghreb was led by the Jewish Berber tribes, and in particular by the Jerawa tribe, which was headed by Dahya al-Kahena, a Jewish priestess ("Kahena" means "priestess"). Chouraqui notes on page 35 that the forces under her command defeated an Arab army in 688 CE on the banks of the El Meskyana river, driving the Arabs back to Libya for a period of about 5 years. The Arabs subsequently returned in force and killed Dahya al-Kahena, opening the way to the conquest of the rest of the Maghreb. Many Berber Jews converted to Islam, but others remained Jewish. Of the approximately 500,000 Jews who were living in North Africa in modern times, Chouraqui estimates that approximately half were of Berber descent. Many were still Berber speaking, particularly in Morocco. According to Chouraqui, of the over 200,000 Jews living in Morocco in the early 20th century, 15% spoke only

Berber, 59% both Berber and Arabic, and 29% only Arabic.

In Ethiopia, the kingdom of Axum became Christian at some point in the 4th century CE, but there are many indications that before becoming Christian it had been Jewish. As is well known, the Ethiopians follow a form of Christianity that has strong Jewish overtones. They practice circumcision, follow the Jewish dietary laws, use the Star of David as an emblem and observe the Jewish Sabbath as well as the Christian Sunday. According to Christian Ethiopian tradition, this is because the Ethiopian monarchy was founded by a certain King Menelik, who was the descendant of the union of King Solomon with the Queen of Sheba. This legend, although widely believed, has been debunked by historians, who point out that Sheba was the Hebrew name for the ancient kingdom of Saba, which was located in Yemen, not Ethiopia. But why then did the Ethiopian Christian kings claim Jewish descent and promote Jewish practices? One possible reason is because the kingdom of Axum was first ruled by Jewish kings who subsequently converted to Christianity.

In any case there is no doubt that a mass conversion to Judaism took place in Ethiopia starting perhaps in the 3rd century CE. On page 3 of *The Falashas*, David Kessler states: "According to Ethiopian tradition half the population was Jewish before the country was converted to Christianity in the fourth century." This conclusion is borne out by the history of the "Falashas" or Ethiopian Jews, who once numbered in the millions. Until the 17th century, large portions of Ethiopia were under Falasha rule. The Falashas refused to accept the authority of the Christian kings, and in the 10th century CE they even attempted to seize control of the entire country under the leadership of a Jewish queen, called Judith or Esther in different sources. They were defeated, but Kessler states on page 93 that there were still as many as 500,000 Falashas living in Ethiopia in the 17th century, at which time their independence was drastically curtailed by the Christian kings with European military assistance. Persecution reduced their numbers considerably, but European travelers still reported close to 200,000 Falashas in Ethiopia in the mid-19th century.

In Arabia, the emergence of a Jewish community in Yemen starting in the 2nd century CE is described by Shlomo Goitein on page 47 of *Jews And Arabs.* Yemen was then as now the most populous part of Arabia and was the home of the rival kingdoms of Saba and Himyar. By the 4th century CE, the Jewish community in Yemen had grown through conversion to the point where it became a major factor in the politics of the region. The kingdom of Himyar was dominant at the start of the 4th century, but it was overthrown in 375 CE by the forces of As'ad Ab-Karib, who converted to Judaism and founded a new Sabaean kingdom. As'ad Ab-Karib, also called As'ad Kamil al-Tubba by later Arab historians, established Judaism as the state religion of the kingdom of Saba. This entire history is recounted in detail by Robert Stookey on page 20 of *Yemen.* Judaism remained the state religion of the kingdom of Saba for the next 150 years, until the overthrow of the rule of the Jewish king Joseph Dhu Nuwas by Christian Ethiopian invaders around 525 CE. Since Yemen was the only densely populated part of Arabia, it is very likely that a majority of Arabs were Jews during this period. Jewish communities also flourished in the caravan towns of northern Arabia. The town of Medina, to which Mohammed fled in 622 CE, was one third Jewish at the time.

If we put the pieces of the puzzle together, the picture which emerges is one of a mass movement in support of Judaism among the Middle Eastern peoples just out of reach of the Roman empire. At one time or another the Romans had in fact attempted to conquer the Berber tribes, Ethiopians and Arabs, but had found themselves unable to do so. Since the Jews were the most conspicuous victims of the Romans, conversion to Judaism by the Berbers, Ethiopians and Arabs clearly functioned as a way of affirming their desire to remain independent of Roman rule. At the same time, there was probably also an element of nation building involved, particularly among the Arabs and perhaps also the Ethiopians. With its written scriptures, monarchical history and long established religious practices, Judaism may have appealed to monarchical forces among these peoples as an appropriate royal ideology. But Judaism also had great popular appeal among these peoples, as shown by its survival in the Maghreb, Ethiopia and Yemen long after the monarchies associated with it had been overthrown.

In order to fully appreciate the significance of the mass conversions to Judaism during this period, it is necessary to remember that the one large Jewish community that had survived the "Jewish Wars" largely intact was the Jewish community of Iraq. Despite numerous invasions of Iraq, the Romans were never able to retain control of this area for very long. In the 3rd century CE, it came under the rule of a revived Persian empire, which remained in a more or less continual state of war with the Greco-Romans for the next 400 years. Although the Persians established Zoroastrianism as their state religion, they were not hostile to Judaism and the Jewish community of Iraq flourished under their rule. When the rabbinical Sanhedrin in the land of Israel was dissolved by Justinian in the 6th century CE, the rabbinical academies of Iraq replaced it as the authoritative interpreters of Jewish law in the eyes of the entire Jewish world. And since the Jews of Iraq were strong supporters of the Persian empire, which effectively protected them against Greco-Roman attack, conversion to Judaism during this period implied membership in a broad coalition of Middle Eastern peoples aligned with the Persians against the Greco-Romans.

The full meaning of this coalition became apparent at the beginning of the 7th century CE with the start of a major Persian offensive against the Greco-Roman (now called Byzantine) empire in Syria. In 614 CE, a Persian army entered Jerusalem. The Christians were driven from the city, their churches burned and control of Jerusalem placed in the hands of the Jews. Jewish detachments from Iraq had formed a part of the Persian army that conquered Jerusalem, and the surviving Jews of the land of Israel had also launched a revolt against the Byzantines as the Persian army approached. In liberated Jerusalem a Jewish government was constituted headed by a man called Nehemiah. A Jewish army was formed which joined the Persians in the siege of Tyre and other Byzantine strongholds in Lebanon. After hundreds of years of almost continuous struggle, the Zionist dream had finally come true. Jerusalem and the greater part of the land of Israel were once more under Jewish rule, whose legitimacy was formally recognized by the Persian king Chosroes in a triumphal visit to Jerusalem in 617 CE.

Unfortunately, soon afterward there took place a sudden shift in Persian policy. Persian support for the Jewish government in Jerusalem was abruptly withdrawn and a policy of alliance with the Christians of the land of Israel instituted instead. Avi-Yonah on page 268 of

The Jews of Palestine offers the following analysis of the change in Persian policy :

> Basically however there can be only one real reason for this sudden change in Persian policy. The Jews now suffered the common fate of revolutionaries after a successful revolution. While the fight was still going on, the Persians accepted Jewish aid because they were interested in upsetting the existing state of things...It seems, however, that the Persians quickly noticed that they were relying on only 10-15 per cent of the population, too weak a base for a permanent domination. As they got to know the situation on the spot, it became clearer every day that they would have to come to an agreement with the Christian majority.

The failure of the siege of Tyre seems to have been another factor which led the Persians to withdraw their support from the Jews. In any case, the Jewish government was driven from Jerusalem by Persian troops. Moreover, within a few years the fortunes of war shifted in favor of the Byzantines, and in 629 CE Byzantine troops reconquered Jerusalem. The Byzantine conquest was followed by massacres of Jews throughout the land of Israel, reducing the number of Jews remaining there to a small remnant. As Avi-Yonah succinctly puts it on page 269: "By betraying their Jewish allies the Persians put an end to the national hopes of the Jews for many centuries."

Although usually briefly mentioned in standard histories of the Jewish people, the formation of a Jewish government in Jerusalem in 614 CE is never alluded to in any other historical studies, and for one obvious reason. It was at just this time that an individual named Mohammed got up in the market at Mecca and began to preach a doctrine that called for observation of the Jewish dietary laws, prayer in the direction of Jerusalem and worship of the Jewish God, whom he called "Allah". However, after the Persians turned on the Jews, this same individual changed his tune and began to make hostile remarks about the Jews. Worse yet, once he got control of Medina, he attacked the Jews living there, exiled some, massacred others, and changed the direction of prayer from Jerusalem to Mecca. In this way there came into being a religion which, just like Christianity, synthesized pro-Jewish and anti-Jewish elements into one comprehensive package whose origins in a mass movement on behalf of Judaism were soon forgotten.

However, the pro-Jewish element in Islam was quite different from that in Christianity. Whereas Christianity created a kind of ideological affinity with Jewish tradition, if not the Jews themselves, through its canonization of the so-called "Old Testament", the Muslims paid little attention to this text and indeed accused the Jews of "falsifying the Scriptures". But unlike the Christians, the Muslims made a big point of their ethnic identity with the Jews by claiming descent from Abraham, practicing circumcision and following similar dietary laws. In this way, the Muslims sought to affirm a Middle Eastern cultural identity as a means of resistance to Greco-Roman cultural domination. But the reason why they chose this particular means of affirming their Middle Eastern identity is because this is precisely what a number of Middle Eastern peoples, including the Arabs, had already been doing in the name of Judaism for hundreds of years prior to the rise of Islam.

JUDAH

At the heart of Jewish influence is Judaism, and at the heart of Judaism is Judah. Judah is the standard English language version of the Hebrew word Yehudah, which appears in the Torah as the name of one of the twelve tribes of Israel. It is then commonly applied to the kingdom founded by David, who was a member of the tribe of Judah, around 1000 BCE. But when historians have to describe the country which the Romans invaded in 63 BCE, it suddenly ceases to be Judah and becomes "Palestine", or at best, "Judea" or "Judaea".

There was no "Palestine" before the Romans created this term in 135 CE, and there was no "Judea" or "Judaea" before the Romans began to use these terms for the country which they wished to turn into a province of their empire in the 1st century BCE. The term "Palestine" was derived from the geographical term "Philistia", the area on the southern coast of the land of Israel where the Philistines had once lived. And the terms "Judea" or "Judaea" were simply the Roman way of pronouncing "Yehudah", which initially they like everyone else regarded as the established name for the country which they invaded in 63 BCE. The Greeks called it "Ioudaia" and the Persians "Yahud", so if we are speaking English, the correct name for that country is Judah.

Judaism in its origins was nothing other than the veneration of the religion, language, laws and customs of the nation of Judah. This nation was founded by David, divided into the rival kingdoms of Judah and Israel after the death of Solomon, then overwhelmed by successive waves of Assyrian, Babylonian, Persian and Greek invaders, and finally restored to independence by the guerilla forces of Judah the Maccabee starting around 165 BCE. As a result of subsequent conquests by the Hasmonean (meaning Maccabean) kings, the nation of Judah at the time of the Roman invasion occupied roughly the same territory as had the ancient kingdom of David. And from that time to the present, the main goal of Judaism as a religion has been to restore the independence of the nation of Judah as a means of also restoring its original religion, language, laws and customs.

It is in its commitment to the restoration of Jewish national independence that Judaism differs most profoundly from both Christianity and Islam. Both of these religions were traditionally hostile to the idea of Jewish national independence for the simple reason that both came to function as the ideologies of great empires, the one initially Greco-Roman, the other initially Arab. It is in large part in order to denigrate the idea of Jewish national independence that both Christianity and Islam contain so many derogatory references to the Jews. Yet if the Jews had not fought to defend and revive the nation of Judah, there never would have been either a Christianity or an Islam. Such is the nature of Jewish influence, which more often than not is denied, concealed or rejected by the very ones most dependent on it.

What is needed today is the deghettoization of Jewish history and its inclusion in a mainstream narrative of world history. Jewish influence did not begin or end with Christianity and Islam. If the ideals of national self-determination, social equality and rational thought today form such an important part of modern culture, it is at least in part because of Jewish influence. It was precisely because of their adherence to these ideals that the Jews of Europe were slaughtered in the millions by the Nazis, yet today the United Nations that arose out of the defeat of the Nazis is consumed with hatred of the nation of Israel. It is high time that the world became aware of its own history and the progressive role which the Jewish people has played in it. Jewish histiory should not be confined to Jewish Studies but also treated as an integral part of the history of the entire world.

Calendar Wars

One of the most ancient and the most fundamental forms of ideological hegemony is control over the calendar. For example, by dividing all time into Before and After the alleged date of the birth of Jesus Christ, the Christian religion has succeeded in introducing its point of view into the heart of the so-called "civil calendar" now in use in the greater part of the world. But just what is this point of view? The so-called "civil calendar" comes in two versions, one "Julian" and the other "Gregorian", and the two have one thing in common: they are both Roman.

The Julian calendar is the calendar that was instituted by Julius Caesar a little more than 2000 years ago in conjunction with his efforts to become the undisputed ruler of Rome. It is a solar calendar consisting of 365 days plus a leap year every four years to account for the extra quarter day in the solar year. However, because the extra quarter day is actually slightly less than a quarter day, the Julian calendar very slowly drifted out of line with the seasons, leading the Roman Pope Gregory 13 to institute a slightly modified version of the Julian calendar a little more than 1600 years later. Despite Protestant resistance, this Gregorian calendar was eventually adopted, first by Europe and then by all the countries colonized by Europe, as the "civil calendar" of the entire world.

Conventional accounts of the history of the Julian and Gregorian calendars stress the superiority of the astronomical calculations on which they were based. Earlier solar calendars, such as the one adopted by the Egyptians over 4000 years ago, had taken no account of the extra quarter day in the solar year and therefore drifted out of line with the seasons much faster than the Julian calendar did. Nonetheless the question arises: is there no significance in the fact that both calendars were promulgated by rulers of Rome? And not just any old rulers either, but the original Caesar and the Pope of the Roman Catholic "counter-Reformation". who had a thanksgiving mass held in Rome to celebrate the massacre of French Protestants in Paris on Saint Bartholomew's Day some 10 years before he instituted the Gregorian calendar. Does not the power of the Julian and Gregorian calendars also say something about the power of Rome?

It's not as if the power of Rome were an arcane topic. For centuries much of the European continent was dominated by would be Caesars called Kaisers and Czars, testifying to the hold of the Roman empire on the European imagination long after the empire itself had been overthrown. Latin, the Roman language, remained the standard written language of European religion, philosophy and science for over 1000 years after the fall of the Roman empire. Entire libraries could be filled with books on Roman law, Roman architecture and Roman literature. Yet for some strange reason no one ever refers to the so-called "civil calendar" as the Roman calendar. Its Roman origins are not so much concealed as ignored, the better to present it as the natural and inevitable calendar for all peoples due to the accurate astronomical observations on which it is based.

But along with the observations comes an ideology, which is best described as a synthesis of the cult of Caesar and the cult of Christ. The most visible sign of the cult of Caesar in the Roman calendar is the fact that two months, July and August, are named after Julius Caesar and his heir, Augustus Caesar. As for the cult of Christ, it is of course clearly represented in the system of dividing all time into before and after Christ's birth, which has the effect of making it seem as if this were the most important event in world history. However, these visible signs of Caesar and Christ are only the tip of the iceberg. Like most solar calendars, the Roman calendar is associated with a religion of sun worship, a religion which was evolved under the Caesars and then given a Christian coloration by making December 25 the birthday of Christ and Sunday the day for worshipping him. The purpose of this article is to lay bare the origins, history and significance of the religion of sun worship which permeates the Roman calendar system.

Origins

The very first Roman calendar, the one which was in use at the time the city of Rome was founded, was a lunar calendar. Prior to recent centuries, most peoples around the world followed lunar calendars, but the original Roman lunar calendar was unusual in that it had only ten months.

Lunar calendars are much easier to formulate and follow than solar calendars. A solar calendar has to be perfect, or nearly so, in order to remain in line with the changing seasons, but lunar calendars can easily be adjusted so that the month associated with spring will actually arrive in the spring. The lunar cycle from new to crescent to full moon and back again lasts approximately 29 and a half days, so that lunar months are almost always regarded as consisting of either 29 or 30 days. Twelve lunar months therefore add up to approximately 354 days, which is short of a solar year, while thirteen lunar months add up to approximately 384 days, which is too long. However, if an extra month is added to a twelve month lunar calendar every two or three years, it will remain roughly in line with the seasons forever.

For this reason, most lunar calendars around the world consist of twelve months, plus an extra month held in reserve. It does not require precise astronomical observations to develop such a system, just an agreed upon basis for deciding if the time has come to add an extra month. In *The Lost Universe*, Gene Weltfish brings out how the Pawnee Indians of North America did it. Their traditional lunar calendar of twelve months began in the spring; a thirteenth month was added from time to time based on the overall climate at the time of the appearance of certain constellations of stars which a Pawnee "old man" described as "first one snake, then two ducks and then the real rattlesnakes". The ancient Romans could easily have developed a similar system, but for some strange reason they chose not to.

What makes their approach seem all the more mysterious is that they clearly wanted the calendar to begin in the spring. The first month, called March, was named after Mars, the chief god of all the Latin speaking peoples at that time, and the rites of Mars were supposed to be celebrated in the spring. Yet there was no way that a ten month lunar calendar could even approximate the cycle of the solar year, and the Romans must have known this. It would seem that they insisted upon the number ten for ideological reasons, because ten was an important number in their numerical system. Just in case anyone missed the point, the last six months had no names but only numbers, starting with Fifth and Sixth (eventually changed to July and August) and continuing with September, October, November and December, meaning Seventh, Eighth, Ninth and Tenth respectively. But in order to celebrate the month of March in the spring, what they would have had to do would be to count off an additional two or three lunar months after December, months that had no formal existence but which were nonetheless a necessary part of their calendar system. This taste for needless complexity in the service of ideological rigidity was to play an even more prominent part in their calendar system in the years to come.

However, at some point in the early history of Rome, two additional months were added to the calendar, transforming it into a normal lunar calendar. Roman tradition attributed this change to Numa Pompilius, the second king of Rome. His predecessor, Romulus, was said to have been fierce and warlike, while Numa Pompilius was thought to have been devoted to the arts of peace. In any case, the revised lunar calendar began with a month called January, named after the Roman god Janus, which was placed immediately after December, the last month of the old calendar. The effect of this change was to somewhat downgrade the rites of Mars. Although many Romans continued to celebrate March 1 as New Year's Day even after the institution of January as the first month, the rites of Mars no longer had quite the same official status as before. This change was in keeping with the image of Numa Pompilius as a wise and benevolent ruler.

Janus had a very different image from that of Mars. Mars was perhaps originally a god of virility, but after Jupiter replaced him as the chief god of the Romans during the era of the Roman monarchy, Mars came to be seen as the god of war. In later centuries the rites of Mars were celebrated by Roman aristocrats called "Salii" who gathered every March to dance about in a warlike manner and recite ancient prayers which were only half understood. Janus was a much

less important figure. He was considered the god of borders and begin-
nings, and he was represented in Roman art with two faces, one said to
be directed towards the past, the other towards the future. This made
him a kind of god of time, but whether these attributes preceded or
followed his elevation to the status of the god of the first month is not
clear. Originally only a small shrine was dedicated to him; its gates
were kept closed in times of peace, but opened in times of war. Since
the gates were usually open, Janus was actually associated with warfare
no less than Mars, but more in a juridical than a physical sense.

The modified lunar calendar attributed to Numa Pompilius
remained in use throughout the history of the Roman monarchy,
but at some point around the time of the rise of the Roman republic,
this calendar was modified still further, transforming it into one of
the strangest calendars ever devised. Historians generally call it "luni-
solar" for want of a better term, but actually it was neither lunar nor
solar. The months approximated lunar months, but they no longer
had any relationship to the actual cycle of the moon. Each month was
assigned a specific number of days as in a solar calendar, but instead of
adding up to a solar year, they added up to a lunar year, and an inexact
one at that. Strangest of all, whoever devised this calendar had what
amounts to a phobia against the use of even numbers.

This phobia manifested itself in a number of ways. Except for
February, the months were either 29 or 31 days in length, but there were
no months of 30 days. The months added up to a total of 355 days in
a normal year, even though the correct figure of 354 days was widely
known and used in their lunar calendars by all of Rome's neighbors,
especially the Greeks. Days of the month were reckoned by an elabo-
rate system of counting the number of days either before or after three
fixed points, the calends, the nones and the ides. The calends (from
which the word "calendar" is derived) came on the first of the month,
the nones on either the 5th or the 7th and the ides on either the 13th
or the 15th. It follows that none of the three fixed points in the month
could fall on an even numbered day. It is evident that these three fixed
points originated as the new moon, crescent moon and full moon of
the Roman lunar calendar, but in the system in use under the republic
they had no relationship to the actual lunar cycle and therefore could

be arbitrarily assigned to always fall on odd numbered days.

There is no doubt where this phobia against the use of even numbers came from. It came from the teachings of Pythagoras. In Roman eyes Pythagoras was the quintessential Greek philosopher, far more prestigious than either Plato or Aristotle. After traveling widely, he settled in Croton, a Greek colony in southern Italy, around the age of 50. His teachings soon gained a mass following in southern Italy right around the same time (about 450 years before the advent of Julius Caesar) that the Roman republic was founded. And in his book, *Pythagoras*, Peter Gorman reproduces, on page 141, a list of 10 pairs of "opposites" said to be drawn up by Pythagoras. One column is the "good" column; it includes "right", "male" and "odd". The other column is the "bad" column; it includes "left", "female" and "even". On page 139, Gorman explains that Pythagoras considered odd numbers "good" because they were derived from "the One", while "the dyad or two is the unevenness and inequality in the cosmos. Thus the dyad is the evil principle."

There was, however, one area of the calendar system of the Roman republic to which the ban on the use of even numbers did not apply. This was the method of keeping the calendar in line with the progression of the seasons. Even though it was not a true lunar calendar, it was still based on a 12 month lunar year, and therefore it could have been kept in line with the seasons by the normal method of adding an extra month of 29 or 30 days every two or three years. Instead, a method was devised to always add an extra month every two years. February was assigned 28 days in normal years, but every other year either 4 or 5 days were subtracted from February and added to a thirteenth month called Mercedonius which consisted of either 22 or 23 days. This meant that every other year February consisted of either 23 or 24 days, while Mercedonius, which followed February on the calendar, would always end up consisting of 27 days. It would seem that in this one area, the Roman taste for needless complexity won out over the Pythagorean aversion to even numbers.

What all this meant in practice was that under the calendar system of the Roman republic, years of 355 days alternated with years of either 377 or 378 days. This system implied an average year of a little over 366 days, a figure which was clearly intended to represent a solar year and therefore keep the calendar in line with the seasons without any need to figure out when to add the thirteenth month. The only fly in the ointment was that solar years do not in fact consist of a little over 366 days. Over time, the progression of the months inevitably drifted out of line with the progression of the seasons, until finally the Romans were forced to abandon the system of always adding an extra month every two years. Instead responsibility for deciding when to add the extra month was placed in the hands of the Pontifex Maximus, the High Priest of the Roman religion. But this system gave rise to constant quarrels and charges that certain parties bribed the Pontifex Maximus to lengthen the year when they were in power. In this way, the spirit of arbitrariness that had been inherent in the calendar system all along became manifest for all to see.

The question is: why did the transition from monarchy to republic give rise to such a complicated, wrong headed calendar when the Romans already had a perfectly good lunar calendar under the monarchy? The answer is far from obvious, but it must have had something to do with Pythagoras and the Greeks.

Ancient Rome was a Latin city situated between two powerful groups, the Etruscans to the north and the Greek colonists to the south. Etruscan influence was paramount under the monarchy. Several of the kings of Rome were of Etruscan descent, and many of the symbols of the Roman state that were adopted during this period were of Etruscan origin. These included the cult of Jupiter and the use of the "fasces", a double bladed axe bound with rods (from which the word "fascism" is derived) as an emblem of Roman military authority. But Etruscan influence was largely confined to the patrician class, and when the Roman plebeians overthrew the monarchy and established a republic, it was to the Greek colonists in the south that they looked for cultural inspiration. Adoption of the so-called "luni-solar" calendar of the republic, with its unmistakable Pythagorean bent, was only one aspect of a broader surge of Greek influence at this time which affected all classes of Roman society and the plebeians in particular.

The clearest expression of this trend was the construction by the plebeians of a temple dedicated to the goddess Ceres on the Aventine hill immediately following the establishment of the republic. The temple was built in the Greek style and the cult of Ceres was patterned after the cult of the Greek goddess Demeter. And just as Demeter was associated in Greek mythology with the figures of Dionysos and Persephone, so Ceres came to be associated with the Roman versions of these two figures, Liber and Libera. A new holiday was instituted in their honor, the Liberalia, which was celebrated beginning on March 17 on the new calendar. It featured orgiastic rites similar to those associated with the cult of Dionysos in Greece. All these innovations had the character of a response to the construction of a temple in the Etruscan style dedicated to Jupiter by the patricians shortly before the overthrow of the monarchy. The plebeian trinity of Ceres, Liber and Libera was intended as an alternative to and mockery of the patrician trinity of Jupiter, Juno and Minerva.

The adoption of a Pythagorean calendar fit in with the spread of Greek influence in Rome, but Pythagoreanism did not have the same plebeian character as the Liberalia. To the contrary, it was an elitist philosophy which taught that numbers were the basis of all things. In particular, the movement of the heavenly bodies was said to be governed by the same mathematical ratios as governed the intervals of the octave in music. There was a musical "harmony of the spheres" which Pythagoras claimed to be able to hear, and it is very likely that the complex numerical system of the new Roman calendar was intended to reflect an alleged harmony between the movement of the sun and the movement of the moon. Unfortunately no such harmony exists: there is no convenient mathematical ratio between the solar year of approximately 365 and a quarter days and the lunar month of approximately 29 and a half days. But it would have taken some time for the inaccuracy of the new calendar to become apparent, and in the meanwhile the Romans had evidently come to pride themselves on their commitment to the very last word in philosophic calendar design. So they continued to use their strange "luni-solar" calendar for some 450 years, but by the time of Julius Caesar, it was said to be about three months out of line with the actual solar year.

The thing about the calendar of the Roman republic is that it was lunar in form but solar in spirit. Its months approximated lunar months, they had the same names as the months of the Roman lunar calendar and they added up to a lunar year, but the entire structure was arbitrary and dogmatic. True lunar calendars are all pretty much the same because their months have to conform to the actual lunar cycle. But so long as the subdivisions of solar calendars add up to a solar year, there can be any number of them, of any length, and start on any day of the year. Some solar calendars around the world did have months, usually of 30 days, intended to approximate lunar months, but there is no inherent reason why this has to be so. The structure of a solar calendar has to be decreed, and hence there is greater scope for dogmatism in solar calendar design than there is in lunar calendar design. It was not for nothing that Pythagoras equated "the One", from whom odd numbers were said to be derived, with Apollo, the Greek god of the sun. For the "luni-solar" calendar of the Roman republic to be transformed into a true solar calendar, only one additional element was needed: knowledge of the extra quarter day in the solar year.

HISTORY

This knowledge eventually came to Rome from Egypt. After thousands of years of watching their 365 day solar calendar drift out of line with the seasons, the Egyptians were well aware of the fact that the solar year was not exactly 365 days in length. And Pythagoras, who had studied in Egypt before coming to southern Italy, was undoubtedly well aware of it too. But it was not until about 250 years after the time of Pythagoras that someone in Egypt came up with a figure of 365 and a quarter days for the solar year. That someone was probably Eratosthenes, the head of the library of Alexandria, who had not only figured out that the earth was round but calculated its circumference within a few hundred miles of the correct figure. In any case, the then ruler of Egypt, Ptolemy Euergetes 1, issued a decree, known as the "Decree of Canopus", declaring that henceforth an extra day should be added to the Egyptian solar calendar every four years in order to keep it in line with the progression of the seasons. The day was to be celebrated as the "Festival of the Benefactor Gods", a reference to Ptolemy himself and his family.

The Ptolemies were a Greek dynasty who became the rulers of Egypt in the wake of the conquests of Alexander of Macedon. Alexandria under their rule became the main center of mathematical and scientific knowledge in the entire Mediterranean area. However the Greeks were thin on the ground in Egypt, and the Decree of Canopus remained a dead letter so far as most Egyptians were concerned. The Ptolemies were also unsuccessful in their efforts to get the Egyptians to worship them as earthly incarnations of the god Sarapis, a god whom they had invented as a vaguely Egyptianized version of the Greek god Pluto. But in the Greek and Roman world, Alexandrian science and the religious ideas of the Ptolemies enjoyed immense prestige. The last of the Ptolemies was Cleopatra, and it was from her scientific adviser, Sosigenes, that Julius Caesar first learned that you could devise a pretty accurate 365 day solar calendar by adding an extra day every four years.

In conventional accounts of the career of Julius Caesar, he is credited with "reforming" the Roman calendar, but this achievement is not assigned all that much importance. Caesar was, among other things, Pontifex Maximus of the Roman religion, and therefore he was entitled, indeed expected, to fiddle with the calendar to keep it in line with the seasons. His new solar calendar did just that, and in some ways it was not very different from the calendar of the Roman republic. The months, at least initially, had the same names, and they were of approximately the same length, with only a day added here and there to make them add up to 365 days in the year. But although the calendar of the Roman republic may have been solar in spirit, it was not solar in form, and inasmuch as the idea for the leap year had come from Sosigenes and the Decree of Canopus, it was impossible to avoid noticing the link to the Egyptian solar calendar. What made this link significant was that the Egyptian solar calendar had always been associated with the idea of the ruler as a god. This had been true under the Pharaohs, and it was also true under the Ptolemies. For Caesar to institute a new solar calendar therefore had the inescapable implication that he aspired to the same status as the rulers of Egypt.

This brings us to the Ides of March. On the original 10 month lunar calendar of the Romans, the Ides of March would have coincided

with the full moon of the first month, the month dedicated to the rites
of Mars, which the aristocratic Salii were still celebrating in Caesar's
day. No better day could have been picked by Caesar's assassins to
emphasize their devotion to Roman tradition in the face of Caesar's
innovations and dictatorial ambitions. Had Brutus and Cassius won
the ensuing civil war, it is very likely that they would have abrogated
Caesar's solar calendar. And conversely, Caesar's heir, Octavian, the
future Augustus Caesar, demanded not only loyalty to the new calendar but acceptance of the notion that Caesar had in fact been a god.
On the eve of the outbreak of the civil war with the forces of Brutus
and Cassius, he convoked the Roman Senate, which was filled with his
own appointees. Ronald Syme, on page 202 of *The Roman Revolution*,
describes what happened next:

> On the first day of the new year Senate and magistrates took a sol-
> emn oath to maintain the acts of Caesar the Dictator. More than
> this, Caesar was enrolled among the gods of the Roman State. In
> the Forum a temple was to be built to the new deity, *Divus Julius*;
> and another law made provision for the cult in the towns of Italy.
> The young Caesar could now designate himself "Divi filius".

"Divi filius" means "son of god". Octavian was the adopted son
of Julius Caesar, who was now to be called "Divus Julius", "Julius the
god". Needless to say, all this took place on the first day of the new
year according to Caesar's calendar.

Over the course of the next 50 years or so there followed a concerted effort to portray the reign of Augustus Caesar, the "son of god",
as the advent of a "New Age", the "Golden Age" which everyone had
been waiting for. The promulgation of the Julian calendar throughout
the Roman empire was an integral part of this policy. And like the
Pharaohs of old, Augustus sought to identify himself with the sun
as a way of emphasizing his connection with the new solar calendar.
He proclaimed the Greek god of the sun, Apollo, as his own personal
god, and also sought to promote a cult of the Roman sun god, Sol,
who had previously played only a very minor role in Roman religion.
Gaston Halsberghe, on page 27 of *The Cult Of Sol Invictus*, notes that

sun worship was first popularized in Rome by Augustus, "who made it the very basis of his religious policy". But in the eyes of a majority of Romans, sun worship remained a foreign import, associated with the Greeks or the Egyptians, and therefore many of the Caesars who came after Augustus tried to find other gods with whom to identify themselves. What they needed was a popular religion of sun worship, but it took several hundred years for this to develop.

From the start, the popular celebration of Roman religion had always been centered in two months: March, the original first month, and December, which remained the last month throughout all the changes in the Roman calendar. Under the republic, the Liberalia became the big March festival, and it was followed by the Saturnalia in December. The Saturnalia began on December 17, precisely 9 months after the start of the Liberalia on March 17, and it had a similar plebeian tone. It was dedicated to the god Saturn, who was considered the Roman equivalent of the Greek god Cronos. Cronos in Greek mythology was the father of Zeus, whom Zeus overthrew in order to become king of the gods. The Roman plebeians seized upon this legend as the basis for an image of Saturn as the "Lord of the Golden Age", the ruler of mankind in the era before the advent of Jupiter. During the Saturnalia, the spirit of the "Golden Age" was supposed to be briefly revived. People wore special costumes in place of togas; slaves were allowed to talk back; everyone wore a "pileus", a woolen cap which was normally worn by emancipated slaves. Like the Liberalia, the Saturnalia had a riotous quality, but it was considered more serious and even aristocrats were expected to participate.

Although the literary proponents of the rule of Augustus sought to appropriate the concept of a revived "Golden Age" for their own use, the spirit of the Saturnalia was incompatible with the veiled dictatorship, military conquests and massive increase in the use of slave labor associated with the Augustan "New Age". On page 2 of the anthology, *Saturn from Antiquity to the Renaissance*, edited by Massimo Ciavolella and Amilcare Iannucci, appear the following lines from a poem by the Roman writer Tibullus, which sum up the image of Saturn in Roman tradition:

> How well man used to live with Saturn as king,
> Before the earth was laid open for faraway campaigns.

And the poem concludes:

> No armies, no rage to kill, no war existed;
> Nor had the cruel smith with brutal skill yet forged a sword.
> But now in the reign of Jove, slaughter and wounds are ever-present,
> Untimely Death comes now by sea, by a thousand other ways.

But already under the Roman republic, there was also another religious current developing, one which was to prove far more compatible with the rule of the Caesars than either the Liberalia or the Saturnalia. This was the current associated with the "mysteries".

The original mysteries were the mysteries of Eleusis, a small town situated not far from Athens. They were based on the legend of the abduction of Persephone, the daughter of the goddess Demeter, by Pluto, the Greek god of the underworld. In order to get her daughter back, Demeter, who was the goddess of grain and vegetation, blighted the earth, leading to a compromise whereby she had Persephone for six months, during which time plants grew, and Pluto for six, during which time they did not. After Athens got control of Eleusis, a new wrinkle was added to the traditional story, according to which following her abduction Persephone had a baby, the infant Dionysos, who was born to bring peace and joy into the world. Adulation of the baby Dionysos became the central ritual at Eleusis, and this rite was supposed to be kept a secret, hence the notion that what happened at Eleusis was a "mystery".

Some 500 years before the founding of the Roman empire, the legend of Eleusis underwent yet another permutation. The author of the new version was an Athenian named Onomacritos, the founder of what became known as the Orphic mysteries. According to this version, the father of the baby Dionysos was Zeus, not Pluto, and while still an infant, Dionysos had been killed and eaten by the evil Titans, whom Zeus then destroyed by fire, giving rise to the race of mortal men from their ashes. In order to atone for the sins of the Titans, it was necessary to partake in a ritual meal of bread and wine, symbolic of the flesh and blood of the baby Dionysos but expressing the transmutation of the primitive cannibal urge into civilized vegetarianism. Those who partook in this ritual would enjoy eternal life. These ideas formed the basis for a religious organization composed exclusively of men and claiming to live a pure, celibate life. The Orphic mysteries gradually spread from Greece to southern Italy, where they enjoyed considerable popularity. But although the central figures in the Roman Liberalia resembled Demeter, Persephone and Dionysos, there is no indication that the Liberalia had an Orphic component. Orphism was more of a middle class religion, and there was a persistent rumor that many of its initiates had a homosexual orientation.

Taken together, the mysteries of Eleusis and the Orphic mysteries came to constitute a kind of template for the mystery religions which swept the Roman world under the late republic and the empire. In Italy the themes of the Orphic mysteries were further popularized in a less elitist form by the Bacchic mysteries, Bacchus being the Roman name for Dionysos. In Egypt the Ptolemaic cult of Sarapis was associated with the mysteries of Isis and Osiris, which then spread from Egypt to Italy and Rome itself. And starting under the reign of the Roman Caesar Claudius about 50 years after the time of Augustus, the public celebration of the Phrygian mysteries was introduced into Rome with the intent of supplanting the Liberalia as the big March festival. It entailed the commemoration, on March 24 and 25, of the death and resurrection of Attis.

According to legend, Attis was a young man, the lover of the goddess Cybele, who was unfaithful to her. By way of punishment, she drove him insane, causing him to castrate himself and die. On March 24, the "Day of Blood", the priests of the Phrygian mysteries marched in procession in Rome, flagellating themselves for the sins of Attis. They carried a pine tree, symbol of the dead Attis. But the next day, Attis was resurrected in a ceremony enacted in the "Phrygianum", a temple devoted to the worship of Cybele. The main feature of the ceremony, notes Maarten Vermaseren on page 118 of *Cybele and Attis*, was a ritual meal, probably of bread and wine, which was said to confer immortality on the initiates. Vermaseren also points out, on page 46, that the Vatican was later built on the site of the Phrygianum.

The later mystery religions had certain themes in common which were ultimately derived from Eleusinian and Orphic tradition. Their central figures were goddesses, such as Isis or Cybele, whose worship was associated with the death and rebirth of an unfortunate young man, such as Osiris (who was torn apart in the Ptolemaic version of Egyptian mythology) or Attis. Initiates into the mysteries could attain eternal life by partaking in a ritual meal of bread and wine, symbolic of the flesh and blood of the resurrected young man. These religions presented themselves as an alternative to the worship of Jupiter or Caesar, but not a hostile alternative like the Liberalia or Saturnalia. The Golden Age was not to be had on earth but only in heaven in the form of individual immortality. These beliefs were entirely compatible with the rule of the Caesars and were actively promoted by many of them. It was therefore only natural that the Caesars should eventually come up with a mystery religion of their own, a mystery religion which was centered around the birth of the sun on December 25, exactly nine months after the resurrection of Attis on March 25.

The mystery religion of the Caesars was called Mithraism. Mithraism was a mystery religion in the same sense as the others in that it entailed a ritual meal of bread and wine which was said to confer immortality on the initiates. But the spirit of Mithraism was quite different from that of the other mystery religions. Mithra originated as the Persian god of the sun. Starting perhaps about 200 years after the time of Augustus, he was then taken over by the Romans, identified with the figure of Sol Invictus, "the invincible sun", and depicted as a mighty warrior. He was said to be born on December 25, the alleged date of the winter solstice, with only one purpose in mind, to kill a huge bull, the first animal ever created, from whose body all good things would flow. Franz Cumont, on page 136 of *The Mysteries of Mithra*, puts it this way:

> Then came an extraordinary prodigy to pass. From the body of the moribund victim sprang all the useful herbs and plants that cover the earth with their verdure. From the spinal cord of the animal sprang the wheat that gives us our bread, and from its blood the vine that produces the sacred drink of the Mysteries.

This legend in turn provided the rationale for the Mithraic ritual meal of bread and wine. Maarten Vermaseren, on page 47 of *Mithriaca I*, brings out the connection as follows:

> Many Mithraic monuments spread over the Roman Empire are worked on two sides, the obverse representing the bull-slaying and the reverse showing the sacred meal. These two scenes are intimately connected – the meal is only possible after the miraculous slaughter of the bull.

Killing the bull – an animal who was traditionally associated with Dionysos – also had the implication of a repudiation of sexual desire, and Mithraic initiates were expected to remain celibate.

Mithraism found its main base of support in the Roman army, and in conjunction with the cult of Sol Invictus, it became something like the official religion of the Roman empire during the period leading up to the conversion of the Roman Caesar Constantine to Christianity. Under Diocletian, Constantine's predecessor as Caesar, huge torchlit processions were held every December 25 in honor of Mithra. In Roman iconography, Mithra was invariably represented wearing a "Phrygian cap", a red cap which closely resembled the "pileus", the cap which Romans had been expected to wear during the Saturnalia and which was originally worn by liberated slaves. The Mithraic message was clear: freedom and immortality were to be attained through mastery of war. This was the direct opposite of the message of the other mystery religions, but Mithraism nonetheless closely resembled them in its negative attitude towards male sexuality and obsession with the flesh and blood of Dionysos, the divine figure lurking behind the Mithraic bull and all the dying and reborn gods of the mystery religions.

SIGNIFICANCE

Just where did this obsession come from? Prior to the introduction of the baby Dionysos at Eleusis, the rites of Dionysos were often associated with women called "maenads", who were said to go off into the hills, kill a goat or bull, symbolic of Dionysos, and eat its raw flesh. And since Dionysos was originally viewed as a god of sex, it is apparent that a negative attitude towards male sexuality was a key factor in motivating the activities of the maenads. Perhaps fear of pregnancy played a role here, and also resentment of male sexual aggression as symbolized by Pluto's rape of Persephone in the original legend of Eleusis. But there is no indication that eating Dionysos in the form of a goat or bull was associated in the minds of the maenads with achieving immortality. The promise of immortality was a kind of cover story introduced into the Eleusinian tradition by the Orphics in order to soften and rationalize the hostility to male sexuality that was at the heart of it. By the same token, eating Dionysos in the form of bread and wine had a much less aggresive image than eating raw flesh, and so it was that the Orphic ritual meal of bread and wine went on to become the characteristic rite of mystery religions that appealed to a broad spectrum of Greco-Roman society..

However, although there exists an extensive scholarly literature on the subject of the mystery religions, there is one feature of all of them that is hardly ever mentioned, and that is that nobody ate a god of their own nationality. Although Dionysos is generally pictured as a Greek god, the Greeks themselves viewed him as either Thracian or Phrygian, the confusion probably being due to the fact that the Phrygians were of Thracian origin. Likewise, the Romans never ate Liber, their own sex god, in effigy, but only Bacchus, their name for Dionysos and a name which was derived from Greek. In the Egyptian mysteries patronized by the Ptolemies, Osiris was eaten in effigy, but not by the Egyptians themselves, only by the Greeks and Romans. Attis too was eaten in effigy by the Romans but not by the Phrygians, from whose culture the legend of Cybele and Attis was derived. The obvious explanation for the reluctance of the Greeks and Romans to eat a god of their own nationality is that eating someone's flesh and blood, in however sedate, symbolic and spiritual a form, is nonetheless an aggressive act, one which they evidently felt more comforable visiting on others rather than on themselves.

It would seem that the mystery religions represented a convergence and synthesis of two distinct trends in Greco-Roman culture. On the one hand they were clearly a form of veiled protest against Greco-Roman militarism. The more militarist Greco-Roman society became, the greater the popularity of the mystery religions, which reached their peak under the rule of the Caesars. Yet at the same time, the mystery religions also represented a way of cannibalizing, in a somewhat literal sense, prestigious foreign cultures and assimilating them to the Greco-Roman way of life. The Egyptians and the Phrygians in particular were both viewed by the Greeks and Romans as bearers of ancient cultural traditions who were nonetheless no match for the Greco-Romans in the military arena and therefore treated with a mixture of respect and contempt perfectly symbolized in the rite of eating them in effigy. On the other hand, the Greco-Romans were never able to achieve a lasting conquest of the Persians, and therefore Mithra got to kill rather than be killed in Roman mythology. Only victim peoples were assigned victim gods, which brings us to the Jewish mysteries, also known as Christianity.

The historiography of the ancient world is seriously distorted by an all pervasive need to ignore, deny or minimize the fact that the Romans and their Greek allies murdered some 2 million Jews during the period of roughly 150 years following the establishment of the Roman empire. According to the figures given by Josephus in his account of the First Jewish War, the Romans killed a total of 1,356,460 Jews during the course of the war. The Roman historian Dio Cassius stated that the Romans killed 580,000 Jews during the Second Jewish War. Many hundreds of thousands of Jews were also killed by the Romans during the "Diaspora Revolt" of the Jewish communities in the eastern Mediterranean area who rose in protest against the massacre of Jews in Iraq carried out by the forces of the Roman Caesar Trajan. Egypt is thought to have been the home of some 1 million Jews at the start of this period, yet hardly any remained by the end of it. The large Jewish community in Syria was also totally wiped out, and that in Anatolia greatly reduced. The Jewish population of the land of Israel declined from perhaps 2 or 3 million to approximately 750,000. So even if the figures given by Josephus and Dio Cassius were somewhat exaggerated as many historians maintain, a figure of at least 2 million Jews killed by the Romans during the era of the Jewish Wars is still indicated by the evidence.

There are two main reasons why the Holocaust visited on the Jewish people by the Romans some 2000 years ago is so invisible in the historical literature. In the first place it puts the origins of Christianity in a whole new light. Christianity arose at the same time and in the same area where the massacres took place. It took one Jew out of the millions who had been massacred and made him the dying and reborn god of a mystery religion just like all the others, a mystery religion which promised eternal life to all who would eat of the symbolic flesh and drink of the symbolic blood of the dead Jew. Viewed in this light, Christianity appears less as a reflection of the wonderful message of Jesus and more as a result of the efforts of the survivors of the massacres to assimilate to Greco-Roman society. And in the second place, noticing the mass murders also has the effect of raising the question, just why did the Romans try to eradicate the Jewish people in such a brutal fashion? This question leads in turn to an examination of Jewish influence on the Greco-Roman world, which turns out to be far more extensive than is generally recognized.

According to the census of the population of the Roman empire conducted during the reign of the Caesar Claudius several decades before the outbreak of the First Jewish War, there were 6,944,000 Jews then living under Roman rule, which meant that Jews formed approximately 10% of the population of the Roman empire. And since there were very few Jews living in the western portion of the empire at that time, the Jewish population in the eastern Mediterranean region was probably closer to 20% of the total population of that area. Moreover, outside of the land of Israel, most Jews in the eastern Mediterranean region then lived in large Greek speaking cities like Alexandria, Antioch and Sardis, where they formed a minority which may have been even larger than 20% of the total. This minority had its own laws, which conflicted with Roman law on a number of key points. Jewish law frowned on slavery and mandated hospitality to runaway slaves (Deuteronomy, Chapter 23, Verse 16), whereas Roman law provided the death penalty for flight from slavery. Jewish law banned the worship of idols, whereas the Romans expected their subjects to worship statues of the Caesars as gods. Jewish law required Jews everywhere to contribute to the upkeep of the Temple in Jerusalem, making the Jews appear to the Romans as a state within a state, one which stood in blatant contradiction to the ideology of the Caesars. Moreover, Jewish beliefs and customs inevitably began to spread from this state within a state to the non-Jewish population, and of these beliefs and customs, none proved more popular than the legally mandated custom of abstaining from work every seventh day.

Historians have found it impossible to deny that the idea of resting on the seventh day originated with the Jews, but they have been extremely reluctant to accept the obvious corollary, namely that the Jews also popularized the concept of the week. To the contrary, insofar as they even raise the question of the origins of the week in Greco-Roman culture, their normal tendency is to present it as Babylonian in origin. According to the standard account, the ancient Babylonian astronomers believed that there were seven "planets", namely Mercury, Venus, Mars, Saturn and Jupiter, plus the sun and moon. This belief became the basis for an astrological cult according to which human destiny was ruled by the movements of the seven planets, which were actually divine entities. The practitioners of this cult, who became known as "Chaldeans", eventually introduced it to the Greco-Roman world, where it became the basis for the concept of the week. Proof that the Greco-Romans got their concept of the week from the Chaldeans and not the Jews is seen in the fact that they identified the days of the week with various divinities rather than simply numbering them as the Jews did.

However, there are several problems with this view. In the first place there is no evidence that either the Babylonians or the Chaldeans linked the idea of the seven planets to the concept of the week or themselves followed a seven day weekly cycle. And in the second place, there is conclusive evidence that the Greco-Roman concept of the week did not originate with the Chaldeans. In the Chaldean system, the planets were listed in order of decrease in the length of time it took for them to complete one full orbit in the sky: Saturn, Jupiter, Mars, Sun, Venus, Mercury, Moon. But the Greco-Roman days of the week follow a different order, and this point was commented on by the Greco-Romans themselves. As Eviatar Zerubavel brings out on page 15 of *The Seven*

Day Circle, the Greek writer Plutarch wrote a treatise, now lost, entitled: "Why Are The Days Named After The Planets Reckoned in a Different Order from the Actual Order?". By "Actual Order", Plutarch meant the Chaldean order. Plutarch wrote his treatise about 100 years after the time of Augustus; its title shows that the concept of the seven day week had taken hold in Greco-Roman society by that time and that it was linked in Plutarch's mind to the Chaldean planetary system but was seen as different from it.

Credit for figuring out the answer to Plutarch's question should go to the great classical scholar Franz Cumont, author of *Astrology and Religion among the Greeks and Romans*, first published in 1912. Working with original, unpublished manuscripts known as "Hermetic" literature, Cumont linked the origins of the planetary week to a specific astrological doctrine. This was the notion that every single hour of every single day was "ruled" in turn by one of the seven planets, which were listed for this purpose in the conventional Chaldean order. Starting with Saturn as the "ruler" of the first hour of the first day, this means that the "ruler" of the first hour of the second day will be the Sun. If the sequence is extended for seven days, the "rulers" of the first hour of each day will appear in the same sequence as the order of the days in the Greco-Roman planetary week: Saturn, Sun, Moon, Mars, Mercury, Jupiter and Venus.

Who wrote these "Hermetic" manuscripts? They were the work of Greek philosophers and mystics living in Alexandria during the period of Greek and Roman rule in Egypt. These writers proclaimed themselves the followers of "Hermes Trismegistus", "Thrice-greatest Hermes", a mythical figure combining features of the Greek god Hermes and the Egyptian god Thoth. They surrounded their activities with an aura of secrecy, an aura reflected in the connotations of the word "hermetic", meaning tightly sealed and therefore closed or hidden. And in fact, although these secretive mystics are known to have invented a version of the week which has now swept almost the entire world, their motives for doing so have remained a sealed book unto this day.

One thing is for sure: they were familiar with the Jewish concept of the week. Alexandria was the home of the largest Jewish community in the ancient world outside the land of Israel. That community produced an extensive Greek language literature directed in part towards familiarizing a non-Jewish Greek language audience with basic Jewish beliefs and concepts. As if in response to this literature, the Hermetic astrologers created an alternative to the Jewish concept of the week, one which was at odds with the Jewish concept in a number of ways. Their planetary week did not have a day of rest, and it asserted that human destiny was ruled by pagan divinities rather than the Jewish God. Moreover it contained an inherent tendency to exalt one day of the week over all the others, but this day was not the Jewish Sabbath but rather Sunday. Of all the seven planets, the sun is the only one which really does have a clear, obvious and significant effect upon human life. Originating in a country which had practiced sun worship for thousands of years, and created in a milieu not far removed from that which had supplied Julius Caesar with the basis for his solar calendar in the form of the concept of a leap year, the Hermetic concept of the week was a natural fit for the growing tendency of the Caesars to identify themselves with the sun and promote sun worship as the official religion of their empire.

A key question in this context is: just how did it happen that the Jewish Sabbath came to be equated with the Hermetic Saturday? In the Hermetic system, Saturday was the first day, whereas the Sabbath was of course the last day in the Jewish system. It would seem that the main reason for identifying the two was the perception of a certain similarity between Judaism and the Saturnalia. In particular, both Judaism and the Saturnalia were associated with a negative attitude towards the institution of slavery, which was the foundation on which the empire of the Caesars was built. But just as the Caesars sought to replace the Saturnalia with the celebration of the "birthday of the sun" on December 25 as the big December festival, so too did the Hermetic astrologers lay the basis for the replacement of the Jewish Sabbath with Sunday as the high point of the week. This change took place in conjunction with the elimination of the Jews themselves, whose community in Alexandria was devastated during the same period that the Hermetic concept of a planetary week took hold.

CONCLUSIONS

By the time of the conversion of Constantine to Christianity, the basic elements of the modern "civil calendar" were already in place. These included:

(1) The notion that the reign of Augustus marked the start of a new era, a "Golden Age" fundamentally different from everything that had gone before. This notion provided the basis for the subsequent Christian practice of dividing all time into Before and After the birth of Christ, which had taken place during the reign of Augustus.

(2) The notion that the birth of the new era took place on December 25, the birthday of the sun god with whom the Caesars identified themselves, which provided the basis for the subsequent Christian claim that Christ was born on this day.

(3) The notion that Sunday was a special day, more important than any of the other days of the week, which provided the basis for the subsequent Christian claim that Christ rose from the dead on a Sunday, which should therefore be the day on which Christians should gather to pretend to eat his flesh and drink his blood.

Through force and violence, first the Greco-Romans and then the Europeans have imposed this calendar system upon the greater part of the modern world. I leave it to the reader to decide whether the so-called "civil calendar" is really an appropriate basis for measuring time in a peaceful, united world.

ZION

For most people, Jewish history is something that begins with God and ends with Jesus. Even the historians tend to lose interest in the Jews once the miracles are over. If they mention us at all, it is to indicate that we wandered around for the next 1900 years, a despised and persecuted minority, until finally the Nazis put us in the ovens. Some profess regret at this history, others find reasons why we deserved it. To very few does it occur to credit us with any influence, and to even fewer with a positive influence. That we might have transformed the world in some ways does not occur to hardly anyone.

The other side of the coin of this massive indifference to post-Roman Jewish history is the obsessive mystification of the origins of the modern Jewish state of Israel. Israel is the one historical fact that would appear to indicate that the Jewish people has some influence. And since hardly anyone is interested in the possibility that this influence might have operated over time as a progressive political force, how tempting to conclude that this influence is of an occult, sinister nature. Israel must have been the product of a secret Jewish conspiracy operating in conjunction with British imperialism, American imperialism, international bankers, the Masons and possibly the KGB. Or if Israel was not the product of a conspiracy, then it was a kind of consolation prize handed to the Jewish people by the victorious Allies as a reward for being slaughtered by the Nazis. Anyone who studies Jewish history knows that the Jewish people has struggled for 2000 years to reverse the verdict of the "Jewish Wars"; but the world finds it very difficult to admit a connection between this struggle and the birth of Israel. To do so would be to recognize Israel as the outgrowth of a long historical process and the Jewish people as a progressive force in world history.

Many people imagine Zionism to be a recent phenomenon, dating back to the late 19th century, a by-product of European colonialism and European nationalism. Yet the longing to return to Zion is as old as the Babylonian captivity and probably older. And from the beginning, this longing had radical implications due to the radical traditions associated with Zion. During the Roman era, these traditions crystallized around the legend of the Messiah, and from this time forward, the dream of the Messiah and the dream of Zion were essentially the same dream. The task of the Messiah in Jewish tradition came to be seen as bringing about the ingathering of the exiles and the restoration of the Jewish nation in the land of Israel. For nearly 2000 years, Messianic movements continually arose in different parts of the Jewish world which sought to realize these goals by one means or another. None of these movements succeeded until modern times, but does this mean that they were without influence? To the contrary, they had a powerful influence not only on the Jewish people but also on non-Jews as well. They helped to give rise to a radical current within both Christianity and Islam and also to a wide range of other radical tendencies around the world. Yet their history is almost completely unknown, due primarily to the great reluctance of world opinion to credit the Jewish people with any positive achievements.

The movement to return to Zion was particularly broad based and influential during the first 500 years or so after the end of the "Jewish Wars" in 135 CE. Far from being destroyed by the "Jewish Wars", the Jewish people emerged from this ordeal in some ways stronger than ever. Even in the land of Israel, which had been thoroughly devastated by the Romans, there were still approximately 750,000 Jews remaining in 135 CE. And outside the Roman empire, the number of Jews rapidly increased, mainly through conversion, during the centuries immediately following the "Jewish Wars". Until the rise of Islam in the 7th century CE, there were still millions of Jews living in the Middle East, especially in Iraq, Iran, Arabia, Ethiopia and North Africa. These Jews actively pursued the dream of Zion through military campaigns directed against the Romans and their Byzantine successors. Neither the triumph of Christianity nor the origins of Islam can be understood without reference to this struggle. Yet standard histories of this period often make no mention whatsoever of the Jews; and if they do happen to mention us, it is invariably to indicate either that someone persecuted us or that some individual Jew did something disreputable.

What the historians are ignoring or concealing is the impact of the Zionist movement of this period on other movements for national liberation in the Middle East. Judaism appealed to the peoples of the Middle East because it offered a model of how national independence might be preserved and defended in the face of Roman and Byzantine imperialism. Conversion to Judaism did not require abandonment of the national traditions of the people who converted. They could remain Aramaeans, Arabs, Ethiopians or Berbers in language and culture yet adopt the Jewish religion and Jewish law. Under the influence of the many Jewish refugees who were forced to flee from the land of Israel during the era of the "Jewish Wars", large Jewish communities therefore emerged in the 2nd and 3rd centuries CE in all parts of the Middle East which stood outside the reach of the Roman army. In some areas, these communities even gave rise to Jewish kingdoms. This entire Middle Eastern Jewish world was united by opposition to Rome and dedication to the dream of Zion. Unearthing its buried history is the key to understanding how and why the Jewish radical tradition was able to transform the world.

ARAMAIC JUDAISM

The main link between the nation of Judah and other Middle Eastern nations was Aramaic Judaism. Over the course of the 1st millenium BCE, Aramaic gradually became the spoken language of the majority of people living in the area now consisting of the countries of Jordan, Syria, Iraq, Lebanon and Israel. By Roman times, most Jews living in this area spoke Aramaic rather than Hebrew. The Torah was translated into Aramaic and many Jewish texts, including portions of the scriptural books of Ezra and Daniel, were written in Aramaic. Since Hebrew and Aramaic are closely related languages, knowledge of Hebrew also remained common among Jews; but for most practical purposes, the Middle Eastern Jews of Roman and Byzantine times actually formed a part of a larger Aramaic nationality. They spoke the same language, shared the same material culture and had roughly the same physical appearance as the non-Jewish Aramaeans. Even Jewish religious services were conducted mainly in Aramaic, to the point where many prayers still recited to this day were composed in Aramaic rather than Hebrew. The Talmud was also written in Aramaic, yet despite the extensive evidence of a Jewish religious and secular culture in Aramaic, little or no attention has been directed by historians to the study of Aramaic nationality.

There do exist numerous studies of the Aramaic language but hardly anyone seems to think of the people who spoke this language as Aramaeans. One of the few scholarly works which does deal with Aramaic history is *Aram And Israel* by Emil Kraeling. However Kraeling is mainly concerned with the early phase of Aramaic history, the period in which the Aramaeans formed a number of small kingdoms centered around Harran and Damascus. This phase came to an end in 732 BCE with the conquest of Damascus by the Assyrians. But although the Aramaeans never regained their political independence, their cultural influence continued to grow, as manifested in the rapid spread of the Aramaic language under Assyrian, Babylonian and Persian rule. Kraeling's explanation for this development is completely unconvincing. He argues on page 139 that the Aramaeans were "great merchants" and therefore "their language had the opportunity of becoming a medium of exchange". He adds:

> Furthermore, the destruction of the Aramaic states separated this language from all national aspirations or religious propaganda, so that no prejudice against its use could arise.

This view of Aramaic culture as completely devoid of "national aspirations" or "religious propaganda" is characteristic of modern scholarship. Millions of people from the Euphrates to the Nile spoke and wrote in Aramaic for a period of well over 1000 years, yet we are supposed to believe that this was solely because Aramaic was a "medium of exchange" imposed on them by "great merchants".

One factor which certainly contributed to the spread of Aramaic was its adoption as the official language of the Persian empire in the area now consisting of Jordan, Syria, Iraq, Lebanon and Israel. Aramaic was written in an alphabetical script (from which the Hebrew script, "square Hebrew", still in use today, is derived) and was much easier to use as a written language than the Accadian cuneiform hieroglyphics preferred by the Assyrians and Babylonians. However, Aramaic was already spoken in Babylon itself even prior to the Persian conquest. The Persians aligned themselves with the Aramaic speaking element in the former Babylonian empire as a way of legitmizing their own rule. Their favorable attitude towards the Jewish exiles in Babylon was one facet of this policy. And the returning exiles in their turn accepted Persian rule and discouraged all talk of restoring the Jewish monarchy in the land of Israel so long as the Persian empire survived. The Aramaic language and culture thus became the common ground between the Persians on the one hand and the Jews on the other. As a result, a popular Aramaic language religious culture gradually emerged in which themes from the Zoroastrian religion of the Persians, the Hebrew language religion of the Jews and the pagan beliefs of the ancient kingdoms of Aram all played a part.

Characteristic of this religious culture was a belief in a benevolent Supreme Being who would resurrect the dead and send them to either Heaven or Hell on a final Day of Judgment. A tendency to proliferate hierarchies of angels and demons also formed a part of this set of beliefs. Rabbinic Judaism was to a large extent rooted in this belief system, which differed significantly from the religion of the early Hebrews in its stress on the fate of the soul in an afterlife. The rabbis justified these innovations on the grounds that they constituted part of the so-called "oral Torah", beliefs said to be transmitted by Moses to his followers but not included in the written Torah. This "oral Torah" could also be viewed as a code word for Aramaic religious culture. The rabbis who elaborated this doctrine were active throughout the area where Aramaic was spoken. Hillel, who is viewed by many as the founder of rabbinic Judaism, was born and educated in what is now Iraq; and in later centuries, the greater part of the Talmud was also composed in what is now Iraq. Unfortunately, most of the area where Aramaic was spoken was well within the reach of the Roman army, whose genocidal assault on the nation of Judah was coupled with the systematic denigration and suppression of all forms of Aramaic culture.

Roman policy in this area was symbolized by the temple dedicated to "Jupiter Heliopolitan" which the Romans erected at Baalbek – today a part of Lebanon – in the 1st century CE. The statue of Jupiter inside the temple, described by Friedrich Ragette on page 20 of *Baalbek*, depicted him with a whip in one hand and a thunderbolt in the other. Hundreds of thousands of Jews in the area of Lebanon and Syria were slaughtered by the Romans in the 1st and 2nd centuries CE at the same time as they devastated the land of Israel. However, the area of Iraq remained under Parthian control for most of this period, despite periodic invasions by the Romans. Nissim Rejwan on page 29 of *The Jews of Iraq* estimates that there were approximately 2 million Jews living in this area by 200 CE. "The most important and commonest occupation of the Babylonian Jews was agriculture", notes Rejwan on page 24. They constituted "the only major Jewish community not under Roman rule" at this time. Perhaps for this reason, the Romans launched a massive invasion of Iraq in 194 CE under the command of the Caesar Septimus Severus. The area was devastated but the Romans were finally driven off by the Parthians.

Freya Stark in *Rome on the Euphrates* sees this invasion as precipitating the revival of the Persian empire at the start of the 3rd century CE. Parthian rule was overthrown by the Persians, led by the Sasanian dynasty, and a much more aggressive anti-Roman policy was instituted. Stark notes on page 262 that the coins of the first Sasanian ruler, Ardashir 1, were issued in Aramaic rather than Greek, which had been used by the Parthians. This signaled a desire on the part of the Sasanian kings to liberate the entire Aramaic speaking region from the Romans. By the middle of the 3rd century CE the Persians were on the offensive, and in 260 CE they captured the Roman Caesar Valerian, who died in captivity. However the Persians proved unable to drive the Romans out of Syria and a see-saw battle ensued, lasting for literally hundreds of years, with the Aramaic speaking region of Syria and Iraq as the main battlefield between the Persians on the one hand and the Romans and Byzantines on the other. This was the context in which the Jewish Messianic movement, quiescent after the defeat of the Jewish forces in the "Second Jewish War", revived once more throughout the Aramaic speaking world.

Michael Avi-Yonah in *The Jews of Palestine* describes in detail the

revival of Messianic agitation among Jews in Roman Palestine during
the 3rd century CE. He states on page 131:

> Hatred of Rome and the Messianic idea combined into one
> vision of redemption and vengeance. According to Rabbi Levi
> the Messiah from the House of Joseph will, after rebuilding the
> Temple, march upon Rome and conquer it as Joshua conquered
> Jericho; for "Our father Jacob foresaw that the descendants of
> Esau shall be delivered into the hands of the descendants of
> Joseph".

Similar views also became current among the Jews of Iraq during
this same period. Many Jews from this area served in the Persian army
with the expectation that after the Persians defeated the Romans the
Jews would be permitted to return to the land of Israel and rebuild
the Temple. For their part the Jews of Palestine, who still numbered
perhaps half a million people in the 3rd and 4th centuries CE, were
not content to passively await the Persians. In 351 CE, encouraged by
reports of a new Persian offensive, the Jews seized control of the towns
of Tiberias, Sepphoris and Lydda in Galilee and proclaimed "a kind
of kingdom" as the Romans put it. However the revolt was suppressed
by the Roman Caesar Gallus and from this time forward the Jewish
population of Palestine entered a period of steady decline.

In the Middle East, the military conflict between the Romans and
Persians also assumed the form of a cultural conflict between Greek
and Aramaic. In this area the Romans were too thin on the ground to
impose the Latin language and culture on their subjects. They therefore
adopted Greek as the official language of their administration while
the Persians continued to rely on Aramaic. The rise of Christianity to
the position of the official religion of the Roman empire during the
3rd and 4th centuries CE must be seen in this context. Christianity was
essentially a Greek language adaptation of religious beliefs which were
not only Jewish but also Aramaic. The belief in the Last Judgment
and Heaven and Hell entered Christianity from the same source as it
entered Judaism, Aramaic popular culture. The only original feature
of Christianity from an Aramaic point of view was the association of

these beliefs with a cannibalistic rite of pretending to eat the flesh and drink the blood of the Messiah of the Jews. This rite, which was derived from the Greco-Roman mystery religions, imbued Christianity with a profound anti-Semitic bias, a bias which made it an appropriate official religion for the Roman empire in the Middle East. In response to the Persian offensive and upsurge of Jewish Messianism, Christianity provided the Romans and their Byzantine successors with a way of asserting Greek cultural hegemony over the Aramaic speaking peoples in a pseudo-Aramaic, anti-Jewish form.

The real meaning of Christianity was particularly apparent in Palestine, where its adoption as the official religion of Rome signaled the start of a concerted effort to stamp out Judaism altogether in the land of its birth. The main reason for the decline of the Jewish population of Palestine after the unsuccessful revolt of 351 CE was the growth of the Christian population. From the middle of the 4th century onwards, Greek-speaking Christian monks and missionaries began to flock to Palestine from Egypt and Syria. By the 5th century CE there was a Christian majority in Palestine. The Christians utilized their position of power to burn and loot synagogues and implement the numerous anti-Jewish decrees issued by the Christian Caesars in Constantinople. The pagan Romans had permitted the Jews of Palestine a certain degree of autonomy, symbolized by the institution of the Sanhedrin, a body of rabbis with limited judicial powers. Early in the 5th century the Christians abolished the Sanhedrin, which resulted in the transfer of formal authority over the Jewish world from the rabbis of Palestine to the rabbis of Iraq. Although several hundred thousand Jews still remained in Palestine after this time, their influence was greatly diminished.

In the area of Syria and Lebanon, most Jews had been killed by the Romans and their Greek allies at the time of the "Jewish Wars". Nonetheless, the efforts of the Byzantine empire to impose Greek language Christianity on the Aramaeans of this region proved largely unsuccessful. Resistance to anything Greek was so strong that the Christians were compelled to begin translating their literature into Aramaic. By the 4th century CE, Aramaic language Christian churches had come into being throughout this area. These churches were viewed by the "Greek Orthodox" authorities as "heretical" because they were more open to Jewish practices and traditions than the Greeks. At the council of Ephesus in 431 CE, the Aramaic language churches were formally expelled from the "Greek Orthodox" church on the grounds that their views resembled those of a Greek speaking Christian, Nestorius, who had supposedly denied that Jesus was the son of God. The so-called "Nestorians" were forced to flee to Iraq and Iran, from where they gradually built up a string of Nestorian congregations throughout Central Asia. A small number of Aramaic language Christian congregations also survived in Lebanon and Syria under the name of Jacobites. Despite the retention of certain Jewish practices, the teachings of the Nestorians and Jacobites did not greatly differ from those of the "Orthodox" Christians; but the mere fact that they were couched in Aramaic rather than Greek was enough to assure their eventual condemnation.

Although Aramaic was of course the language of Jesus Christ, the prejudice against it in the Greek and Roman world was so intense that even the Aramaic speaking Ebionites, who were composed of the friends and relatives of Jesus himself, were also condemned as "heretics". It is this same prejudice which is clearly responsible for the complete disinterest of modern scholars in the history of Aramaic nationality. Adhering to the principle of "divide and conquer", the scholars never speak of Aramaeans as a group but only of "Babylonians", "Syrians" and "Jews", all of whom coincidentally spoke the same language and shared many of the same beliefs and cultural traits. An important component of this culture was Aramaic Judaism, which combined elements of Aramaic popular culture with traditional Jewish beliefs in a form that was widely disseminated throughout the Aramaic speaking world. It was largely through the vehicle of Aramaic Judaism that Jewish beliefs and practices were introduced to other Middle Eastern peoples on the fringes of the Roman empire. Inspired by the heroic struggle of the Jews against Greco-Roman imperialism, these peoples began to convert to Judaism in large numbers from the 3rd century CE onwards. Chief among them were the Arabs, Ethiopians and Berbers, all of whom first became Jews before they subsequently became Christians or Muslims.

THE SPREAD OF JUDAISM

The spread of Judaism in the centuries following the "Jewish Wars" is a well attested historic fact, yet it has been systematically ignored in all standard histories of this period. A simple exposition of the facts will indicate just how complete and shocking this suppression of the Jewish role in world history has been,

Shlomo Goitein starting on page 47 of *Jews And Arabs* describes the movement of Jews into the Arabian peninsula, resulting in the emergence of a Jewish community in Yemen by the 2nd century CE. Yemen was then as now the most populous part of Arabia and was the home of the rival kingdoms of Saba and Himyar. By the 4th century CE, the Jewish community in Yemen had grown through conversion to the point where it became a major factor in the politics of the region. The kingdom of Himyar was dominant at the start of the 4th century, but it was overthrown in 375 CE by the forces of As'ad Ab-Karib, who converted to Judaism and founded a new Sabaean kingdom. As'ad Ab-Karib, also called As'ad Kamil al-Tubba by later Arab historians, established Judaism as the state religion of the kingdom of Saba. This entire incident is recounted in detail by Robert Stookey on page 20 of *Yemen*. Judaism remained the state religion of the kingdom of Saba for the next 150 years, until the overthrow of the rule of the Jewish king Joseph Dhu Nuwas by Christian Ethiopian invaders around 525 CE. Since Yemen was the only densely populated part of Arabia, it is very likely that a majority of Arabs were Jews during this period. Jewish communities also flourished in the caravan towns of northern Arabia. The town of Medina, to which Mohammed fled in 622 CE, was one third Jewish at the time.

The Ethiopian monarchy that overthrew the rule of Joseph Dhu Nuwas had been Christian since the 4th century CE. As is well known, the Ethiopians followed a form of Christianity that had strong Jewish overtones. They practiced circumcision, followed the Jewish dietary laws, used the Star of David as an emblem and observed the Jewish Sabbath as well as the Christian Sunday. According to Christian Ethiopian tradition, this was because the Ethiopian monarchy had been founded by a certain King Menelik, who was the descendant of the union of King Solomon with the Queen of Sheba. This legend, although widely believed, has been debunked by historians, who point out that Sheba was the Hebrew name for Saba, which is located in Yemen, not Ethiopia. But why then did the Ethiopian Christian kings claim Jewish descent and promote Jewish practices? The probable reason is because the monarchy was founded by Jewish kings, who subsequently converted to Christianity.

There is no evidence whatsoever of an Ethiopian kingdom of any kind prior to the 1st century CE, when references first appear to a kingdom of Axum. It was the rulers of Axum who converted to Christianity in the 4th century CE and composed the national epic, the "Kebra Nagest", claiming descent from Solomon, who had lived some 1300 years earlier. However, on page 3 of *The Falashas*, David Kessler states: "According to Ethiopian tradition half the population was Jewish before the country was converted to Christianity in the fourth century." This conclusion is borne out by the history of the "Falashas" or Ethiopian Jews, who once numbered in the millions. Until the 17th century, large portions of Ethiopia were under Falasha rule. The Falashas refused to accept the authority of the Christian kings, who had stigmatized them as "enemies of God" in the "Kebra Nagest". In the 10th century CE, the Falashas even attempted to seize control of the entire country under the leadership of a Jewish queen, called Judith or Esther in different sources. Kessler states on page 81:

> One of the few documents of the period of Queen Judith is a letter written shortly after 979 by the Abyssinian king to his Christian contemporary, King George of Nubia, asking for assistance to counteract the persecution of Christians by a queen who had usurped his throne.

Kessler also states on page 93 that were still as many 500,000 Falashas living in Ethiopia in the 17th century, at which time their independence was drastically curtailed by the Christian kings with European military assistance. Persecution reduced their numbers considerably, but European travelers still reported close to 200,000 Falashas in Ethiopia in the mid-19th century. By modern times the number had shrunk to around 30,000, most of whom emigrated to Israel in recent decades.

The story of the Berber Jews of North Africa is recounted by Andre Chouraqui in *Between East And West: A History of the Jews of North Africa*. Until the era of the "Jewish Wars", there were large Jewish communities in Egypt and Libya. Most historians estimate that there were something like 1 million Jews in Egypt alone at the time of the "Jewish Wars". Josephus thought that there were also approximately 500,000 Jews in Libya, which was called Cyrenaica at that time. However almost all of the Jews of Egypt and Libya were killed or dispersed during the "Jewish Wars", so that there is hardly any mention of Jews living in these countries from the 2nd century CE onwards. But starting in the 2nd century CE references begin to appear to the conversion of Berber tribes to Judaism in the area of modern Tunisia, Algeria and Morocco. The Berbers are the indigeneous people of what Arabs call "the Maghreb", the coastal region of North Africa. In the area close to the coast, the Berbers were conquered and colonized by successive waves of invaders, beginning with the Phoenicians and continuing with the Greeks and Romans. Further inland the Berber tribes remained independent, and it was these independent tribes who began converting to Judaism in large numbers in the 2nd century CE.

By the 3rd century CE, most Berber tribes living outside the Roman-dominated cities of the coast had become Jewish. Chouraqui on page 21 cites the Christian theologian Tertullian who "reported that the Berbers observed the Sabbath, the Jewish festivals and fasts, and the dietary laws". These tribes remained Jewish right up to the time of the Arab conquest of North Africa in the 7th century CE. In fact, the resistance to the Arab conquest in the Maghreb was led by the Jewish Berber tribes, and in particular by the Jerawa tribe, which was headed by Dahya al-Kahena, a Jewish priestess ("Kahena" means "priestess"). Chouraqui notes on page 35 that the forces under her command defeated an Arab army in 688 CE on the banks of the El Meskyana river, driving the Arabs back to Libya for a period of about 5 years. The Arabs subsequently returned in force and killed Dahya al-Kahena, opening the way to the conquest of the rest of the Maghreb. Many Berber Jews converted to Islam, but others remained Jewish.

Of the approximately 500,000 Jews who were living in North Africa in modern times, Chouraqui estimates that approximately half were of Berber descent. Many were still Berber speaking, particularly in Morocco. According to Chouraqui, of the over 200,000 Jews living in Morocco in the early 20th century, 15% spoke only Berber, 59% both Berber and Arabic, and 29% only Arabic.

The Arab, Ethiopian and Berber converts to Judaism of the period from the 3rd to the 6th century CE all had certain traits in common. For one thing they lived just outside the reach of the Roman army. The Romans conquered the Arab kingdom of Nabatea in the area of modern Jordan but their one attempt to invade Yemen proved unsuccessful. South of Egypt the Romans penetrated as far as Nubia but were unable to reach Ethiopia. Likewise in the Maghreb they were content to dominate the rich coastal plain and ignored the nomadic tribes of the interior. These Berber tribes lived mainly by herding, as did many Arabs and Ethiopians. In Yemen and Ethiopia Jewish converts also practiced settled agriculture, but in none of these areas were there any large, wealthy cities. With its egalitarian legal system and long history of opposition to foreign conquest, Judaism must have appealed to these peoples as a way of resisting Rome. It cannot have been a complete coincidence that the net effect of their conversion was to create a loose network of Jewish tribes and kingdoms which confronted the Romans across a long frontier stretching from Morocco in the west all the way to Arabia in the east. And if the Jewish community of Iraq, which was the largest Jewish community in the world at that time, is included in the picture, an image emerges of a Jewish Afro-Asian resistance to European imperialism which was very clearly the predecessor and model for the rise of Islam.

The main weapon of the Romans in their struggle with this resistance proved to be Christianity. It was through Christian influence that the Jewish kingdoms in both Ethiopia and Yemen were overthrown. Christianity resembled Judaism in many respects but was associated with a pro-Roman political orientation. However, the further from the Roman empire Christianity traveled, the more "heretical" it appeared. This was because it was compelled to adapt itself to to the pro-Jewish political climate which existed virtually everywhere on the fringes of

the Roman empire. Even in northern Europe, where direct Jewish
influence was not very strong, the Teutonic tribes who dominated the
area surrounding the Roman frontier began converting to a "heretical"
form of Christianity known as Arianism. In *The Arians of the Fourth
Century*, written by a prominent 19th century English Catholic writer
named John Newman, the Arian "heresy" is traced to the teachings of
Paul of Samosata, the Christian bishop of Palmyra in the 3rd century
CE. Palmyra was an Aramaic speaking city in the area of Iraq noted
for its pro-Jewish sympathies; Newman, on page 5, calls the teachings
of Paul of Samosata "a kind of Judaism in doctrine". He characterizes Arianism as follows on page 18:

> I will not say that the Arian doctrine is the direct result of a juda-
> izing practice, but it deserves consideration whether a tendency
> to derogate from the honour due to Christ, was not created by an
> observance of the Jewish rites, and much more, by that carnal,
> self-indulgent religion, which seems at that time to have prevailed
> in the rejected nation.

Although it originated in the Middle East, Arianism eventually found its main support among the Goths, who overran southern
Europe and Rome itself in the 5th century CE.

All forms of Christianity, whether "Orthodox", "Catholic" or
"heretical", adopted a two-faced attitude in relation to Judaism and
the Jewish people. On the one hand, Christianity was itself a manifestation of the spread of Judaism. The Christians venerated the Jewish
Scriptures and helped to spread them to areas which the Jews themselves did not reach. But on the other hand, Chrtistian editions of the
Jewish Scriptures were always accompanied by the New Testament, a
violently anti-Semitic tract which stigmatized the Jews for the death of
Jesus Christ as part of the rationale for eating him in effigy. Where the
orthodox Christians and the heretics differed was where to draw the
line between the pro-Jewish and anti-Jewish sides of Christianity. The
closer to the fringes of the Roman empire and the further down on
the social scale within the empire, the more pro-Jewish the Christian
doctrine became. The closer to the centers of Roman power, the more

anti-Jewish the doctrine. A kind of spectrum thus evolved, with the "Orthodox" and "Catholic" Christians defending the empire, the "heretics" vacillating on the fringes and the outright "Judaizers" testifying to their rejection of the empire by converting to Judaism.

On the extreme left of this entire spectrum were the Jews themselves. It was the struggle of the Jewish people, first to defend and then to restore the nation of Judah, which was ultimately responsible for the spread of Judaism in all its manifestations. A strange dynamic was set in motion by the "Jewish Wars": the greater the losses suffered by the Jewish people in the land of Israel and the surrounding Aramaic speaking area, the greater the political appeal of Judaism over a much wider area that included the entire Middle East plus large portions of Europe, Africa and Asia. This dynamic resulted in the emergence, first of Christianity and then of Islam, and also in the transformation of the ethnic character of the Jewish people. A predominantly Semitic people up to the time of the "Jewish Wars", the Jewish people in the next 500 years became through conversion, flight and intermarriage a world people with predominantly Middle Eastern ethnic characteristics. This world people exercised a radical influence throughout the Old World, but nowhere was this influence more intense than in the heartland of the post-Roman Jewish community, the Persian empire.

JEWS AND ZOROASTRIANS

The spread of Judaism helped to create favorable conditions for the realization of the Zionist dream, but the bottom line was military. So long as the Greco-Romans retained physical control of the land of Israel, which they called Palestine, the nation of Judah could not be reborn. Christianity made the situation in Palestine worse, not better, from a Jewish point of view, because it imbued the Greco-Romans with the conviction that they were the "true Jews" and therefore entitled to suppress Judaism altogether. For all practical purposes, Jewish hopes for a return to Zion therefore rested on the expectation of a Persian victory in the endless war between the Persians and the Greco-Romans. This was not an unrealistic expectation. The Persians generally held Iraq; their forces had only to move a short distance in order to drive the Greco-Romans out of the land of Israel. The prior history of Persian support for the nation of Judah, the influence and prestige of the large Jewish community of Iraq, the existence of other Jewish communities scattered throughout Persian territory: all these factors tended to support the view that the Persians would indeed look favorably on the restoration of Judah if they were to gain physical control of Palestine. Underlying all these factors, moreover, was a long history of convergence between Judaism and Zoroastrianism.

This history began at the time of the founding of the Persian empire in the late 6th century BCE. The early Persian kings of the Achaemenian dynasty made two fateful decisions: to adopt Zoroastrianism as the official religion of their empire, and to permit the Jewish exiles in Babylon to return to the land of Israel and rebuild the Temple. Although direct evidence is lacking, it seems likely that there was some connection between these two decisions. R. Ghirshman states on page 204 of *Iran*: "Tolerant in religious matters and themselves inclining towards monotheism, the Achaemenians were particularly well disposed towards monotheistic peoples, above all the Jews." Monotheism was not the only feature which Zoroastrianism and Judaism had in common. George Carter published an entire book, *Zoroastrianism And Judaism*, describing the similarities between the two religions. The most fundamental similarity of all was a strong sense of identification with those who were oppressed and downtrodden. In *Priests, Warriors And Cattle*, Bruce Lincoln shows that this spirit of identification with the oppressed was at the heart of Zoroastrianism from the very start. He states on page 162:

> For contrary to the usually held opinion, the struggle in which Zarathustra was involved was not one of settled agriculturalist against nomad or one in which tribal or cultic rivalries were at stake. Rather, as Barr's research has shown, this was a class struggle in which warriors were pitted against priests and in which the priests under Zarathustra's leadership sought the support of the class of commoners. His polemic against the warriors emphasizes all their misdeeds: *haoma* intoxication, furor and violence, stealing

of cattle, eating of meat to produce furor, and lastly, refusal to pay the sacrificial stipends they had promised.

Zoroaster, also called Zarathustra, is thought to have lived in the early 6th century BCE. His teachings became popular in Iran, but since the Zoroastrian liturgy was entirely in Persian, the Persian kings made little effort to impose Zoroastrianism outside of Iran. It would appear that they saw Judaism as a religion similar to Zoroastrianism which was appropriate for their non-Persian subjects, particularly those who spoke Aramaic.

By the time of the revival of the Persian empire by the Sasanian dynasty in the 3rd century CE, Judaism had absorbed a whole set of ideas relating to the Last Judgment from Zoroastrianism via Aramaic popular culture. At the same time, Zoroastrianism had become more radical. Characteristic of the Sasanian period was the emergence of a wide range of "heretical" Zoroastrian tendencies in which the spirit of class war already implicit in Zoroaster's original teachings became much more explicit and pronounced. The best known of these radical "heresies" were the teachings of Mazdak, who lived around 500 CE. On page 998 of Volume 3 of *The Cambridge History of Iran* appears the following description of the teachings of Mazdak by the Muslim historian Tha'alibi:

> Mazdak declared that God placed the means of subsistence on earth so that people divide them among themselves equally, in a manner that no one of them could have more than his share; but people wronged one another and sought domination over one another; the strong defeated the weak and took exclusive possession of livelihood and property. It is absolutely necessary that one take from the rich for giving to the poor, so that all become equal in wealth. Whoever possesses an excess of property, women or goods he has no more right to it than another.

Incredibly, Mazdak and his teachings were protected by the Sasanian ruler Kavad, but after Kavad's death Mazdakism was declared a "heresy" and suppressed. *The Cambridge History of Iran* notes that among the demands of the Mazdakists were "the breaking up of large estates, prohibition of hoarding, adjustment of landlords' shares from crops, lowering of class distinctions, and instituting public foundations for the benefit of the needy". These demands were similar to those associated with a Zoroastrian sect founded by a "heretic" named Zaradusht during the early Sasanian period.

Another "heretical" tendency which became widespread under the Sasanians was Zurvanism. Orthodox Zoroastrianism taught that the world was the theater of a war between Ahura Mazda, the "Wise Lord", and Ahriman, the Devil, for the possession of the human soul. This war would continue until the final victory of Ahura Mazda at the time of the Last Judgment. But according to the Zurvanites, both Ahura Mazda and Ahriman were actually but emanations of Zurvan, "Infinite Time", who was beyond all personifications and moral distinctions. R.C. Zaehner states in *The Dawn and Twilight of Zoroastrianism* that many Zurvanites were "materialists" who saw infinite, eternal, uncreated space-time as the true basis of the universe. Zurvanites who held this view were called Zandiks. Zurvanism was favored by many Sasanian rulers, including Shapur 1, the Persian king whose forces defeated and captured the Roman Caesar Valerian. Other Sasanian rulers persecuted the Zurvanites, particularly the Zandiks, who were viewed as outright atheists. It is worth noting that ideas very similar to those of the Zandiks later became prominent in Judaism under the name of Kabbalah. Whether these ideas were already popular among Jews in the Persian empire during the Sasanian period is hard to say, but Mazdakism certainly closely resembled the views of the Jewish Messianists of Roman times.

Contacts between Jews and Zoroastrians under the Sassanians were not limited to the Aramaic speaking part of the Persian empire. There was a steady movement of Jews into Iran and beyond during this period, probably motivated in large part by the frequent Roman assaults on the region of Iraq. This movement resulted in the formation of large Jewish communities in the major Iranian cities and also in the area north and east of Iran, particularly the Caucasus mountains. Jews throughout Iran and the surrounding area became fluent in Persian, which they continued to speak right down to modern times in the form of a dialect called Judeo-Persian. Relations with the Zoroastrians were generally cordial, although there were certain instances of attacks on Judaism by the orthodox Zoroastrians. Sustained clashes were averted, first by the growing convergence between Judaism and Zoroastrianism, second by the convergence of the Zionist dream and the military ambitions of the Persian empire. The orthodox Zoroastrians were clearly worried by the more radical implications of Jewish thought, but their influence was counter-balanced by that of the Sasanian kings, many of whom were attracted to "heretical" ideas, which were generally associated with a militant anti-Roman and anti-Byzantine outlook.

This outlook reached its height at the beginning of the 7th century CE with the start of a major Persian offensive against the Byzantines in the area of Syria and Palestine. This offensive led to one of the least mentioned important events in world history, the Persian conquest of Jerusalem in 614 CE. The Christians were driven from the city, their churches burned and control of Jerusalem placed in the hands of the Jews. Jewish detachments formed a part of the Persian army that conquered Jerusalem, and the conquest was also facilitated by a revolt of the remaining Jews of Palestine against the Byzantines as the Persian army approached. Avi-Yonah, on page 262 of *The Jews of Palestine*, cites the following hostile description by the Armenian historian Sebaeus of the Jewish revolt:

> When the Persians approached the Holy Land the remains of the Hebrew nation rose against the Christians. They committed great crimes out of national zeal and did many wrongs to the Christian community. They went and joined the Persians and made common cause with them.

In liberated Jerusalem a Jewish government was constituted headed by a man called Nehemiah. A Jewish army was formed which joined the Persians in the siege of Tyre and other Byzantine strongholds in Lebanon. After hundreds of years of almost continuous warfare, the Zionist dream had finally come true. Jerusalem and the greater part of the land of Israel were once more under Jewish rule, whose legitimacy was formally recognized by the Persian king Chosroes, who made a triumphal visit to Jerusalem in 617 CE.

Unfortunately, just at this time there took place a sudden shift in Persian policy. Persian support for the Jewish government in Jerusalem was abruptly withdrawn and a policy of alliance with the Christians of Palestine instituted instead. Avi-Yonah offers the following analysis of the change in Persian policy on page 268:

> Basically however there can be only one real reason for this sudden change in Persian policy. The Jews now suffered the common fate of revolutionaries after a successful revolution. While the fight was still going on, the Persians accepted Jewish aid because they were interested in upsetting the existing state of things...It seems, however, that the Persians quickly noticed that they were relying on only 10-15 per cent of the population, too weak a base for a permanent domination. As they got to know the situation on the spot, it became clearer every day that they would have to come to an agreement with the Christian majority.

The failure of the siege of Tyre seems to have been another factor which led the Persians to withdraw their support from the Jews. In any case, the Jewish government was driven from Jerusalem by Persian troops. Moreover, within a few years the fortunes of war shifted in favor of the Byzantines, and in 629 Byzantine troops reconquered Jerusalem. The Byzantine conquest was followed by massacres of Jews throughout Palestine, reducing the number of Jews in the land of Israel to a small remnant. As Avi-Yonah succinctly puts it on page 269: "By betraying their Jewish allies the Persians put an end to the national hopes of the Jews for many centuries."

Although systematically ignored by later historians in both the Christian and Muslim worlds, the brief restoration of Jewish rule in Jerusalem was long remembered in Jewish tradition due to its description in literary form in the *Book of Zerubabbel*. Thought to have been written in the decade of the 630s, the entire text of the *Book of Zerubabbel* appears in English translation starting on page 157 of *Wars Of The Jews,* published in 1990 by Monroe Rosenthal and Isaac Mozeson. The authors state on page 155:

The strange and mystical apocalypse, the Book of Zerubabbel, is a most important work, yet it has never before been translated into English. For the 1,000-year period from approximately 650 C.E. to the 17th century it was one of the most popular books of the Jewish people, both Sephardi and Ashkenazi.

In the *Book of Zerubabbel*, Nehemiah, the head of the Jewish government instituted in 614 CE, is hailed as the "Messiah ben Joseph", whose defeat and death will be followed by the triumph of the "Messiah ben David" who is yet to come. The triumph of the "Messiah ben David" will require the defeat of ten hostile kings, of whom the ninth will be "Cheroui king of Persia" and the tenth "Armilus son of Satan", the king of Rome. These hopes and dreams were the legacy of the massive Zionist movement of the period prior to 614 CE to the much weaker and more isolated Zionist movement of later centuries.

Reliance on Persian aid proved to be the Achilles heel of the early Zionist movement. Despite the convergence of Persian and Jewish ideology, the fact remained that the Persians were the rulers of a large empire while the Jews were associated with the claims to national self-determination of a small and embattled people. The Persians were generally tolerant of Jewish claims because they did not aspire to impose their own Persian language Zoroastrian culture on other peoples. Nonetheless the Persians were no more prepared to accept a completely independent Judah than the Egyptians, Assyrians, Babylonians, Greeks, Romans and Byzantines had been. They too feared the effect of Jewish independence on the other peoples under their rule, and it was perhaps ultimately for this reason that no sooner did the Jews achieve their independence than the Persians hastened to put them back in their place. The Persians could accept High Priests in Jerusalem but not kings. All the same, the liberation of Jerusalem in 614 CE was an event of world historic significance. It sent shock waves throughout the surrounding area, and not the least of these was felt in Arabia. At precisely the same time as the Persians approached Palestine and the Jews there rose in rebellion, an individual named Mohammed began to preach a doctrine closely resembling Judaism in a place called Mecca.

ISLAM

Conventional histories of Islam almost completely ignore the impact of the early Zionist movement on Mohammed and the early Muslims. The Jewish influence on Mohammed cannot be entirely ignored since Islam resembles Judaism in so many ways; but this influence is normally explained by saying that Mohammed met some Jews during his travels and was therefore familiar with their teachings. These incidental contacts were supposedly sufficient to induce Mohammed to claim to worship the same God as the Jews, to promote the same dietary laws, to teach his early followers to pray in the direction of Jerusalem and to assert that the entire Arab nation was descended from Abraham, a Hebrew. This belief was not original with Mohammed; it was derived from a Jewish tradition that the Arabs were descended from Ishmael, the son of Abraham and Hagar. Invariably missing from conventional accounts of the origins of Islam are the fact that Jews constituted a large proportion of the population of Arabia at the time of Mohammed's birth and the fact that Mohammed's decision to begin preaching his version of Judaism in Mecca coincided with the apparent triumph of the Jewish Zionist movement.

A partial exception to the conventional practice of distancing Islam from Judaism is a book by Patricia Crone and Michael Cook called *Hagarism: The Making of the Islamic World*. This book caused quite a stir when it was published in 1977 because it portrayed Islam as an outgrowth of "Jewish Messianism". While standard accounts of the life of Mohammed stress the hostility between him and the large Jewish community of Medina, the authors of *Hagarism* state on page 7:

> In contrast to the standard Islamic account of the relations between Muhammad and the Jewish tribes of Medina, the Jews appear in the document known as the "Constitution of Medina" as forming one community (*umma*) with the believers despite the retention of their own religion, and are distributed nameless among a number of Arab tribes.

However, just like all the others, Crone and Cook paid little attention to the actual Jewish Messianic movement of Mohammed's day, preferring to trace Mohammed's beliefs to his own internal thought processes. The liberation of Jerusalem in 614 CE is not even mentioned. The tone of the book, as shown by the title, is disrespectful of both Judaism and Islam; whether this is an improvement on the normal practice of being disrespectful only of Judaism is not clear.

Mohammed's career can be divided into two phases, one pro-Jewish, the other anti-Jewish. Mohammed was born in 570 CE, the same year in which an Ethiopian Christian invasion of Mecca and northern Arabia was turned back. He came from a prestigious family but was orphaned at an early age and spent the first forty years of his life in relative obscurity. Around 610 CE, just as the Persian offensive was achieving its first major successes, Mohammed began preaching in the market place in Mecca. For the next twelve years, while the Jews fought for, liberated and struggled to regain Jerusalem, Mohammed preached his version of Judaism to the people of Mecca. When he was driven from Mecca in 622 CE, Mohammed fled to Medina, where he enjoyed good relations with the Jewish community. But around 624 CE, as the tide of battle to the north turned in favor of the Byzantines and the Jewish situation in Palestine became increasingly desperate, Mohammed broke with the Jews. He and his followers killed or enslaved the Jews of Medina and the other towns of northern Arabia, and denunciations of the Jews began to appear in his speeches. This betrayal of the Jewish cause was accompanied by flattering remarks concerning the Christians, whom Mohammed now began to woo just as the Persians had done. When the Muslims took control of Yemen in southern Arabia, they tried unsuccessfully to force the entire Jewish population to convert to Islam. Many did, but a large number refused, constituting the basis for a sizeable Jewish community which survived in Yemen right down to modern times.

Mohammed's break with the Jews was foreshadowed by the one clearly non-Jewish element in his early teachings, his insistence on giving God an Arabic rather than a Hebrew name, "Allah" instead of "El". Mohammed appealed to the national pride of the Arabs, declaring that he was the prophet sent especially to them just as Moses had been sent especially to the Hebrews. When it became apparent that the Jews were going to be defeated once again, Mohammed was therefore well positioned to turn on them in the name of Allah and Arab unity. For centuries, the Arab world had been divided between contending Jewish and Christian factions, the one supported by the Persians, the other by the Byzantines and Ethiopians. So long as it appeared that the Jewish faction was going to win, Mohammed sided with them, but breaking with them had the great advantage of enabling him to transcend the conflict between Christians and Jews and unify the Arabs around his own teachings. Following Mohammed's death in 632 CE, the Muslim forces were therefore large enough to move north and embark on an invasion of the entire Middle East. The success of Mohammed's policies sealed the fate of the Jews, reducing them to a small minority despised and reviled in both the New Testament and the Koran.

From a Jewish point of view, the closest parallels to Mohammed in world history are Luther and Stalin. All three of these figures helped and harmed the Jewish people to an equally high degree. Mohammed was responsible for the destruction of the greater part of the Jewish community of Arabia and the vilification of the Jewish people in the Koran; but at the same time, the Muslim invasion of the Middle East may well have saved the Jewish people from complete destruction. As might be expected, the reaction of the Byzantines to the liberation of Jerusalem was to completely outlaw Judaism throughout their empire and even write to neighboring kingdoms asking them to do the same. Negative as it was, Muslim policy towards the Jews was still far more tolerant than Christian policy. Under Muslim rule, the Jewish communities of the Middle East were permitted to survive, greatly diminished in size and prestige to be sure, but still formally recognized as "People of the Book" and entitled to a certain measure of protection from Christian persecution. Moreover, since Islam was so clearly derived from Judaism, its triumph did enhance the prestige, if not of the Jews themselves, then at least of Jewish thought. Mohammed thus helped to create a strange situation in which a large part of the Old World paid homage to Jewish ideas in a Christian or Muslim garb while the Jews themselves were reduced to the position of a small and inconsequential minority.

Basically what happened is that Islam replaced Judaism as the ideology of the Middle Eastern coalition which stood opposed to Greco-Roman imperialism. The reason was simple: it took an empire to defeat an empire. Despite its alliance with the Persian empire, Judaism was fundamentally hostile to all forms of imperialism because it was based on the demand for national self-determination of the Jewish people. Judaism sought to oppose Greco-Roman imperialism with a coalition of independent nations led by the Persians; but the events of the early 7th century – the liberation of Jerusalem followed by the Persian betrayal and Byzantine revival – had the effect of discrediting this strategy once and for all. Islam differed from Judaism in that it was based on a people, the Arabs, who stood ready and willing to impose their will on the Middle East by force. They did so in the name of Jewish ideas, but the Jewish idea of national self-determination they completely rejected. Wherever the Arabs went they sought to impose their religion and language on the people whom they conquered. Islam was therefore less radical and idealistic but more successful than Judaism. Like Christianity before it, it became the ideology of empire, and between them the Christian and Muslim empires dominated the greater part of the Old World. Judaism was all but forgotten, yet even under these adverse conditions Jewish tradition continued to function as a powerful force in world history.

THE SELEUCID ERA

My attention was first drawn to the subject of the Seleucid Era by reading the recent biography of Maimonides by Joel Kraemer. In the course of his narrative, Kraemer had occasion to cite many documents written by Maimonides and his contemporaries, and I noticed that quite a few of these documents were dated according to the Seleucid Era. "That's odd", I thought to myself, "why is Maimonides using the Seleucid dating system more than 1000 years after the Seleucid empire was overthrown?"

Kraemer himself did not raise this question. All he had to say on the subject of the Seleucid Era appears in a footnote on page 485 of *Maimonides*: "The Seleucid era, which began in 312/311 B.C.E., was used mainly on legal documents." Used by whom, and for what reason, and for how long? Kraemer did not say, but as I was soon to discover, he was actually more forthcoming than most.

One source which did prove helpful was Wikipedia, the on line encyclopedia. In the entry under "Seleucid era" I found the following concise description of the origins of the Seleucid Era:

> The Seleucid era was a system of numbering years in use by the Seleucid Empire and other countries among the ancient Hellenistic civilizations. The era dates from the return of Seleucus 1 Nicator to Babylon in 311 BC after his exile in Ptolemaic Egypt, considered by Seleucus and his court to mark the foundation of the Seleucid Empire. The introduction of the new era is mentioned in one of the Babylonian Chronicles, the Chronicle of the Diadochi.

Wikipedia also provided a few details regarding the continued use of the Seleucid Era system even after the complete collapse of the Seleucid empire during the 1st century BCE:

The Seleucid era was used as late as the 6th century CE, for instance in the Zebed inscription in Syria, dated the 24th of Gorpiaios, 823 (24 September, 512 CE). It was also used by Yemenite Jews until modern times.

But instead of clearing up the mystery, this information only deepened it. Why would anyone want to count the years starting with the foundation of the Seleucid empire long after this empire had not only been overthrown but largely forgotten? And why would Jews, of all people, want to do this, seeing as one of the key events in Jewish history was the successful rebellion led by the Maccabees against the Seleucid ruler Antiochus Epiphanes? Moreover, Yemen had not even been a part of the Seleucid empire, nor had Egypt, where Maimonides composed most of the letters cited by Kraemer.

Nonetheless Wikipedia was right about the Jews of Yemen as I was able to verify by consulting *From The Land Of Sheba*, a collection of documents from different periods in the history of the Jews of Yemen edited by S.D. Goitein. In one document describing a severe persecution of the Jews of Yemen during the 17th century, the chronicler stated that this persecution began "in the year 1988, shortly before the Passover feast". In a footnote Goitein explained that this date was "according to the Seleucid reckoning" and corresponded to the year 1677 on the Gregorian calendar.

Goitein was a prominent Jewish scholar best known for his work with the thousands of documents unearthed in the "Geniza" (storeroom) of a Jewish synagogue in Old Cairo and dating from the 9th through the 13th centuries. In the year 2008 a massive collection of documents from the Cairo Geniza was published under the title, *India Traders of the Middle Ages*. Goitein and Mordechai Akiva Friedman were credited as the editors, but since Goitein died in 1985, I assume that it was Friedman who put the collection together. In any case, it occurred to me that by checking out the many letters and contracts contained in this collection, I could form a good idea of just how common was the use of the Seleucid dating system during this period and precisely who was using it. But to my dismay, I discovered that every time a letter or contract began with a date, the year had been changed by the editor into its Gregorian equivalent, making it impossible to determine what system of numbering the years had been used in the original document.

Since it would not have been difficult to give both the original date and its Gregorian equivalent, it seems to me that the failure to do so betrays an indifference to, verging on denial of, the significance of calendar systems as a repository of competing ideological values. And the more I began to research the subject of the Seleucid Era, the more pervasive I found this attitude to be. Few historians took note of the remarkable persistence of the Seleucid Era, basically because they did not attach much importance to the calendar system which a given culture might choose to use. To cite just one example, F.E. Peters wrote an entire book, widely circulated, entitled *The Harvest of Hellenism*, containing a detailed description of the cultural legacy of the Hellenistic monarchies formed in the wake of the conquests of Alexander of Macedon. The Seleucid empire was by far the largest of these monarchies, and Peters goes into its cultural history at considerable length, yet he does not even mention the existence of the Seleucid calendar system. In a book devoted to the exposition of the long term legacy of Hellenism, this was an astonishing omission.

A useful corrective to the prevailing view of the insignificance of calendar systems may be found in *Calendar and Community* by Sacha Stern. Stern states:

> Calendar reckoning is not just a technical pursuit: it is fundamental to social interaction and communal life. The calendar provides an essential point of reference for interpersonal relations and time-bound communal activity. It determines how time is lived and utilized in the community, and sometimes shapes the community's distinctive identity. The calendar is also a way of conceptualizing the dimension of time, and hence, of 'making sense' of an important facet of human lived experience.

Just so, and I would add that calendar systems also have an ideological dimension which typically affirms certain values at the expense of others. The purpose of this article is to demonstrate the truth of this assertion in the context of an in depth study of the history of the Seleucid Era.

SELEUCUS NICATOR

Seleucus Nicator means "Seleucus the Victorious", and Seleucus was in fact quite successful both as a military commander and as an empire builder. Yet little is known about him as an individual, and his public image entirely lacked that legendary quality so prominent in the case of Alexander of Macedon. Cold and calculating, Seleucus was in some ways an unlikely candidate for the role of founder of a new era in human history.

He first rose to prominence as one of Alexander's subordinates in the army that overthrew the Persian empire. Seleucus was the commander of Alexander's bodyguard, the "Shield-bearers", a relatively small force of no more than 6000 men who also served as a kind of military police, rooting out dissidents and trouble makers. This force was composed mainly of Macedonians, whereas Alexander's army also included large numbers of Greeks, Persians and others arrayed around a Macedonian core. Seleucus evidently enjoyed Alexander's trust, but he did not have a power base of his own apart from the "Shield-bearers", and when Alexander died under mysterious circumstances in Babylon in 323 BCE, Seleucus played only a minor role in the initial stages of the power struggle that soon broke out among Alexander's subordinates.

The struggle went on for decades, during the course of which Seleucus gradually improved his position, until he finally emerged around 300 BCE as the ruler of the greater part of the former Persian empire. It appears to me that the key to his success was his insistent claim to authority over Babylon and the region of Babylonia. His very first move in the power struggle among the "Diadochi", the would be "Successors" to Alexander, was to demand the title of "Satrap" (meaning Governor) of Babylon. Babylon was a large and famous city that had at one time ruled over an empire of its own, and even after the Persians overthrew that empire, they still treated Babylon as their administrative capital. Alexander had declared his intention to make

Babylon his capital as well, and by insisting that he be recognized as the governor of Babylon, Seleucus was in effect advancing a claim to be regarded as the true successor to Alexander. Although he was repeatedly driven from the city during the wars of the Diadochi, Seleucus always managed to return, and it was his return in 312/311 BCE that was eventually adopted as the starting point of the Seleucid Era.

However, Babylon was so devastated and depopulated by the battles that were fought over it that Seleucus founded a new city, Seleucia-on-the-Tigris, to serve as his capital. But although it had ceased to function as a major administrative or commercial center, Babylon was still treated by Seleucus, and also his son and heir, Antiochus, as a holy city whose religious traditions and institutions were worthy of the utmost respect. F.E. Peters on page 234 of *The Harvest of Hellenism* described this aspect of Seleucid religious policy as follows:

> Babylon in particular was the recipient of a great deal of Seleucid patronage. The temple of Marduk in Babylon, that of Anu in Orchoi, earlier known as Uruk, and of Nabu in Borsippa were all reconstructed and readorned under Seleucid auspices.

Peters saw patronage of Babylonian religion by the Seleucids as intended to endow them with "the same kind of legitimacy as successors of the Babylonian divinely inspired kings that prompted Alexander to choose Babylon as the center of his embryonic empire." But what Peters chose not to notice was that Seleucid identification with Babylonian religion was also a fundamental component of the Seleucid calendar system.

Seleucus was assassinated in 281 BCE, but by this time his empire was well established. He devoted the last twenty years or so of his life to founding cities which were populated with colonists from Greece. A little more than ten years before his death he entrusted his son Antiochus with responsibility for the administration of the eastern portion of his empire, and Antiochus had no difficulty gaining control of the entire empire, which stretched from Turkey to Afghanistan, after his father's death. It would appear that it was Antiochus who instituted the Seleucid Era. At that time it was the normal practice, not only in the Middle East but in many other parts of the world, to number the years based on the starting date of the reign of each successive king. But rather than number the years from the start of his own reign, Antiochus chose to continue to number the years based on the starting point of the reign of his father, which had been somewhat arbitrarily designated as what would now be called 312/311 BCE.

Just why did he do this? For one thing Antiochus had already acted as ruler of a large part of the empire during his father's lifetime, so it was only natural for him to stress the continuity between the two reigns. But the main reason for numbering the years in this way was undoubtedly to enhance the prestige of Seleucus, to present him as a great conqueror whose empire was destined to last forever and ever. Glorifying Seleucus also had the effect of glorifying the dynasty which he founded, and therefore the successors to Antiochus continued the practice of numbering the years based on the purported starting point of the reign of Seleucus. In this way the concept of a Seleucid Era was born, but what few historians appear to understand is that the Seleucid Era was only one part of a comprehensive calendar system which was put into effect, probably by Antiochus, in the early 3rd century BCE. It was the popularity of this entire calendar system, and not merely one part of it, which accounts for the fact that the Seleucid Era was not forgotten after the Seleucid empire disappeared from sight.

THE SELEUCID CALENDAR

The Seleucid calendar was a lunar calendar of the type sometimes called "luni-solar", meaning that it had an established method of keeping the progression of the lunar months roughly in line with the changing seasons of the solar year. Actually most ancient lunar calendars everywhere in the world were of this type, because most peoples wanted to make sure that the month of the big spring festival actually arrived in the spring, the month of the big fall festival in the fall, and so forth and so on.

Lunar months are 29 or 30 days in length, meaning that 12 lunar months will add up to 354 days, and 13 lunar months to 384 days. And since the solar year is roughly 365 days in length, lunar calendars will not remain in line with the progression of the seasons without some special device to bring this about. The typical, normal device adopted by most peoples everywhere in the world was to add a thirteenth month to a twelve month lunar calendar every few years. At first they decided when to do this based on criteria such as the position of the sun and stars, but eventually some peoples, especially those that had a writing system, tried to develop a fixed schedule for when to add the thirteenth month.

This proved to be a difficult task. The big problem with calendar science in general is that almost perfect is not good enough. For example, some peoples independently developed a solar calendar of 365 days in length, but because the solar year is actually closer to 365 and a quarter days in length, all of these calendars gradually drifted out of line with the seasons, rendering them useless for scheduling seasonal events. By the same token, a number of Greek city-states developed a system of adding a thirteenth month to their lunar calendars three times in eight years. This system seemed to work well at first, but eventually it became clear that it was deviating too far from the progression of the seasons. Finally one group of experts devised a perfect system, one which consisted of adding a thirteenth month seven times in nineteen years. That group consisted of the priests and astronomers of Babylon.

Religion and astronomy were traditionally closely linked in most if not all cultures due to the fact that one of the main functions of early calendars was to set the date for religious ceremonies. However religion and astronomy seem to have been even more closely linked in Babylonian culture than was usually the case elsewhere. S. Langdon in *Babylonian Menologies and the Semitic Calendars* argued that the Babylonians inherited from the Sumerians a belief that the constellations formed by the stars had a religious significance. As he put it on page 10: "A striking aspect of Sumero-Babylonian religion is the association of myths with each of the months and the attempt to find in the regnal constellations of the months figures which correspond to the ideas involved in the monthly myths." These myths in turn provided the basis for monthly religious festivals. Whether for this reason or some other, the Babylonian priests and astronomers began at an early date to compile extensive written records dealing with every aspect of the movement of the heavenly bodies.

The fruit of these labors was the discovery of the so-called Metonic cycle. Meton was a Greek astronomer who introduced the idea of intercalating an extra month seven times in nineteen years to the Greeks, but it seems likely that Meton got this idea from the Babylonians. Meton introduced his cycle to the Athenians in 432 BCE, but as John Britton points out in his article, "Calendars, Intercalations and Year-Lengths in Mesopotamian Astronomy", appearing in John Steele's anthology, *Calendars and Years*, use of the nineteen year cycle had already become official in Babylon by 483 BCE. Steele also brings out that by the 6th century BCE the Babylonians had recognized that the solar year was a little more than 365 days in length, but they had no interest in replacing their lunar calendar with a solar one based on their estimates of 365.14 or 365.16 days in the solar year. The nineteen year cycle was good enough for them and could in fact be used for thousands of years without requiring any change or adjustment.

When the Seleucids came to power they found the Babylonian calendar in use throughout a large part of the former Persian empire. The spread of this calendar from Babylon to the surrounding region had begun in the days of the Babylonian empire and was if anything accelerated by the advent of Persian rule. The adoption of the nineteen year cycle by the Babylonians took place a short time after the Persian conquest, making available to the Persians a standarized calendar system that specified in advance the years in which to add an extra month.. The Persians had their own calendar, which they used in Iran, but they did not seek to impose it on the rest of their empire, preferring to adopt the Babylonian calendar for administrative purposes outside Iran. As a result the Persians ended up spreading the Babylonian calendar to areas in the eastern part of their empire that had not been a part of the former Babylonian empire.

The Seleucids had little choice but to follow in the footsteps of the Persians and adopt the Babylonian calendar for administrative purposes. It was already well established throughout most of their empire and was in any case one of the most reliable calendar systems then available anywhere in Europe or the Middle East. But also not unlike the Persians, the Seleucids had no desire to follow the Babylonian calendar themselves. Seleucus and his immediate entourage were almost all Macedonians, and they continued to follow the Macedonian lunar calendar after coming to power. What is more, they expected the Greek colonists who populated the cities which they founded to do the same. In practice the Seleucid calendar system therefore came to consist of two overlapping systems, one Babylonian, the other Macedonian, but both lunar, both utilizing the nineteen year cycle and both counting the years from the date of the triumphant return to Babylon of Seleucus Nicator.

However there was a slight difference in this date as defined by the Macedonian calendar and as defined by the Babylonian calendar. The Macedonian calendar began in the fall, and whether for this reason or because Seleucus had actually returned in the fall, the starting point of the Seleucid Era in the Macedonian version was in the fall of 312 BCE. But it was decided that in the Babylonian calendar, the starting point of the Seleucid Era should coincide with the Babylonian New Year, and as this came in the spring, the Seleucid Era in the Babylonian version began in the spring of 311 BCE. Of course it is only because the Gregorian calendar begins in the winter that the two starting dates now appear to be in different years rather than simply some months apart. The discrepancy between them would not have been much of a problem at the time because everyone writing in Greek used the Macedonian version and everyone writing in Aramaic used the Babylonian version.

The key question is why it was decided to start the Seleucid Era with the Babylonian New Year in the Babylonian version. The Babylonian New Year was not just any old New Year; it was the start of the Akitu festival, the most important festival in the Babylonian religious calendar. And the main concern of the Akitu was to affirm the relationship between the king of Babylon and the chief god of the Babylonian pantheon, Marduk. Viewed in the context of Seleucid patronage of Babylonian religion in general and the temple of Marduk in Babylon in particular, there can be little doubt that the choice of the Babylonian New Year as the starting point of the Seleucid Era in the Babylonian version was consciously intended to present Seleucus as the legitimate heir of the Babylonian kings and the chosen one of Marduk.

As it so happens, here too the Persians had done something similar. E. A. Wallis Budge, on page 47 of *Babylonian Life and History*, reproduces the following astonishing declaration by Cyrus, the conqueror of Babylon and founder of the Persian empire:

> When I had entered Babylon, I entered under favorable auspices; I made my abode in the Royal Palace, a splendid building, amid shouts of gladness and cries of joy. Marduk, the great lord, the darling god of the Babylonians, inclined graciously to me, and daily did I duly worship him.

It goes without saying that Cyrus was no more sincere than Seleucus in his devotion to Marduk. Both conquerors were simply trying to identify themselves with the great prestige of Babylonian religious culture, a prestige that was derived in large part from the prestige of Babylonian astronomy. As Budge puts it on page 168:

> The Babylonians studied the heavens diligently, not so much to increase their knowledge of astronomy as to learn from the stars, which they regarded as gods, the will of heaven in respect of their king, their country, and themselves, and so became the founders of the science of Astrology.

Astrological doctrines were also embedded in the Babylonian calendar, whose month names were evocative of religious festivals associated with the various constellations visible in the sky at different times of the year.

Leaving no stone unturned, the Seleucids also claimed for the benefit of their Greek subjects that Seleucus was actually the son of Apollo and hence a god or demi-god in his own right. It is hard to say to what extent these claims were linked to the Macedonian calendar, about which little is known apart from the names of the months. But since lunar months are defined by the phases of the moon, they necessarily begin and end at approximately the same time in every lunar calendar. It is therefore easy to equate one lunar calendar system with another, and this is what the Seleucids did. Sacha Stern summed up their system and its legacy as follows on page 28 of *Calendar and Community*:

> Macedonian and Babylonian months were formally equated by the Seleucids not later than 245 BCE. Macedonian names of months were used in Greek, and Babylonian names in Aramaic. The Babylonian calendar was thus maintained in the Near East, and eventually outlived the disintegration of the Seleucid Empire.

Indeed, all of the components of the Seleucid calendar system, including the Seleucid Era in both its Macedonian and Babylonian versions, survived the collapse of the Seleucid empire. Just what was it about this system that made it so influential even without the backing of the imperial dynasty which it was originally intended to serve?

Whatever the secret of its success, one thing that it wasn't was veneration of the Seleucids. The term, "Seleucid Era", is a creation of modern historians. It is an apt description of the Seleucid method of numbering the years, but no one used this term prior to modern times. The closest equivalents that I was able to find were "the era of the Greek kings" or "year of the kingdom of the Greeks". According to E.J. Bickerman in *Chronology Of The Ancient World*, the Jewish and Syrian subjects of the Seleucids actually referred to it as "the years of the Greek domination". But probably the most common designation for the Seleucid Era, still used by some modern historians, was "the era of Alexander".

In terms of literal fact this was a complete misnomer. Alexander died more than ten years before the starting point of the Seleucid Era and he had nothing to do with its creation, which took place some 40 years after his death.. But it was called "the era of Alexander" in large part because Alexander was remembered while Seleucus was forgotten. All the efforts of the Seleucids to confer some kind of divine status on themselves were not very successful during the lifetime of the dynasty, and once it was overthrown, only a hazy memory remained of its very existence. Alexander was remembered because he was an egomaniac who wanted to make a name for himself and was able to defeat every army that faced him in one battle after another. He did not found a dynasty or establish an empire, but his name eclipsed that of the man who did because he achieved his ambition of making himself famous. And there was also a subtle difference in the image of Alexander as compared with the image of Seleucus, a difference which may help to explain why the Seleucid Era came to be known as "the era of Alexander".

THE ERA OF ALEXANDER

There was, after all, a good reason why the Seleucid dynasty was identified with the Greeks in the minds of its subjects. Although it was founded by Macedonians and made use of the Babylonian calendar and the Aramaic language, its main base of support was always in the Greek cities founded by Seleucus and his succesors. To be sure, a few historians, most notably Susan Sherwin-White and Amelie Kuhrt in *From Samarkand to Sardis*, have argued that the Seleucid empire was more multi-cultural than is generally recognized. They claim that the Greek cities were not given preferential treatment and that there were only a few attempts at forced Hellenization of older cities by Seleucid rulers. Be that as it may, the fact remains that the language of the court was Greek, the gods with whom the later Seleucid rulers sought to identify themselves were Greek and the core of their army was formed by Greeks. In the eyes of their subjects, Seleucid rule meant Greek rule, and to the extent that this was unpopular, so too were the Seleucids.

The thing about the Hellenistic monarchies in general is that they were somewhat more exploitative than the Persian empire which they supplanted. Greek rule meant more taxation, an increase in the number of slaves and also an increase in the number of large estates worked by tenant farmers who no longer held title to the land. Peter Green on page 76 of *The Hellenistic Age* notes that in treaties of the Hellenistic League "we already find what seems to have been a regular clause requiring members to cooperate in suppressing any movement that involved debt cancellation, the redistribution or confiscation of land and other property, or the freeing of slaves to implement such 'revolutionary' policies." All those who benefited from the exploitative methods of the Hellenistic monarchies tended to identify as Greeks

regardless of their ethnic origin, while the majority of the population, which was Aramaic speaking in the heartland of the Seleucid
empire, developed a negative attitude towards "the years of the Greek
domination".

Alexander was probably more responsible than anyone for bringing about this state of affairs, but that is not necessarily how he was
viewed by posterity. In his capacity as king of Macedonia he had suppressed a revolt by the Greek city of Thebes against Macedonian rule
and massacred a large part of the population to teach them a lesson.
As a result he had difficulty getting Greek recruits for his campaign
against the Persians; the Greeks, notes Green on page 15, "simply had
no enthusasism for in any way aiding the hated figure who had conquered and brutalized them". Following his initial victories against
the Persians, Alexander therefore began an intensive effort to recruit
Persian troops to replace his Greek levies, whom he did not trust. To
this end he presented himself to the Persians as aiming at a kind of
fusion with them, and he made all kinds of symbolic gestures in this
direction. Had he lived and founded a dynasty it would undoubtedly
have evolved in precisely the same way as the Hellenistic kingdoms of
the Diadochi, but since he died young, it was possible to view him as
seeking something other than an empire of the Greeks.

In a formal sense the Seleucid empire came to an end during the
2nd and 1st centuries BCE due to the conquests of the Romans in the
west and the Parthians in the east. The Seleucid empire was attacked
by both: the Romans drove the Seleucids out of Turkey in the early
2nd century BCE, and the Parthians drove them out of Iran and the
surrounding region later in that same century. Syria, the last bastion of
the Seleucids, was conquered by the Romans in the middle of the 1st
century BCE. But although the Greeks lost their empire, they remained
a powerful force throughout the Middle East due to the popularity of
the Greek language and culture among the upper classes. Both the
Romans and the Parthians treated the Greeks as allies and made little
or no attempt to supplant Greek culture with their own. Yet at the
same time, they also intended that the taxes and other benefits which
had formerly accrued to the Greek rulers should now accrue to them.
These were the considerations that determined the Parthian attitude

towards the Seleucid Era, which they simultaneously perpetuated and sought to replace.

The Parthians were a nomadic people of uncertain origin who established themselves in the region of Parthia in eastern Iran during the 3rd century BCE. Little is known of their original language and culture but they eventually came under both Persian and Greek influence. At some point in the late 3rd century BCE they decided to proclaim what is now known as the "Arsacid Era", which they dated from the establishment of the Parthian monarchy by a ruler named Arsaces in 247 BCE. The Arsacid Era was clearly intended as a rival dating system to the Seleucid Era, but once the Parthians gained control of the greater part of the Seleucid empire, they also made use of the Seleucid Era on coins intended for use in the Greek cities. Indeed, according to Sherwin-White and Kuhrt in *From Samarkand to Sardis*, there is even a Babylonian text dating from 141 BCE which used both the Arsacid and the Seleucid year dates side by side. Jamshedji Maneckji Unvala on page 15 of *Observations on the Religion of the Parthians* sums up the Parthian approach to numbering the years as follows: "Thus it seems that only for political reasons the Parthian kings employed always the Seleucid era on their coins, whereas the Arsacid era was at the same time in general use among the Parthians, and was very seldom mentioned in the Parthian records."

Yet another approach to the simultaneous perpetuation and replacement of the Seleucid Era was adopted after the overthrow of Parthian rule in Iran by the Sasanian dynasty in the early 3rd century CE. Zoroastrianism was the official religion of the Sasanian dynasty, which was of Persian origin, and the Zoroastrian priests developed a system according to which the Sasanian dynasty came to power in the year 3538 of the "era of Zoroaster". They arrived at this figure by taking the year 538, which was the starting point of Sasanian rule according to the Seleucid Era, and adding to it 3000 years, which were said to have elapsed following the advent of Zoroaster. According to Volume 3 of *The Cambridge History of Iran*, the Sasanians "had no recollection of the Seleucids", and believed that Parthian rule, which they reckoned had lasted 266 years, "began immediately after Alexander". However the Zoroastrian system of using the Seleucid Era plus 3000 to date the years proved too cumbersome for the Sasanian monarchs, who clung to the traditional method of counting the years from the accession of each individual monarch.

All the same, the main trend during the period following the decline and fall of the Seleucid empire was in the direction of a growth in popularity of the very idea of counting the years on the basis of an "era". The rulers of Pontus, a Greek kingdom in northern Turkey, also adopted an "era" at this time. In the late 3rd century CE, the Romans began to date the years from the reign of Diocletian, and the "era of Diocletian" survived in Roman and Byzantine usage for many centuries thereafter. The bottom line was that the method of counting the years on the basis of an "era" was on the whole easier and more convenient than dating the years from the accession of each individual ruler. Yet at the same time, the use of an "era" system also raised the issue of precisely when and how the "era" was supposed to begin. And as the oldest and best established "era" system, the one on which all the others were modeled, the Seleucid Era outlasted its rivals, mainly under the name of "the era of Alexander".

Identifying the Seleucid Era with Alexander made it more prestigious and at the same time not quite so closely identified with Greek rule. But the main reason for the persistence of the Seleucid Era was simply that it formed an integral part of an entire calendar system which remained in use without interruption in Syria and Iraq for approximately 1000 years, from the establishment of the Seleucid empire in the 3rd century BCE down to the Arab conquest in the 7th century CE. Throughout this period, Aramaic and Greek remained the main languages of the population of Syria and Iraq, and both the Babylonian and Macedonian versions of the Seleucid calendar therefore remained in use as well. Bickerman in *Chronology Of The Ancient World* puts it this way: "In fact, it was not the solar year of the Caesars but the Islamic, purely lunar, calendar which ended the use of the cyclical (Babylonian, Seleucid) time-measurement in the Near East." However, Bickerman was wrong about one thing. There was one group of people in the "Near East" whose use of the Seleucid calendar did not end with the Arab conquest. That group of people was the Jews.

THE JEWISH CALENDAR

Bickerman was an outstanding scholar, one who wrote extensively on both ancient chronology and ancient Jewish history, but his understanding of the evolution of the Jewish calendar was hampered by his acceptance of the belief that the Jews adopted the Babylonian month names for their calendar during the Babylonian captivity in the 6th century BCE. He makes this claim on page 24 of *Chronology Of The Ancient World* but cites no evidence in support of it apart from noting that "the ancient rabbis already stated" as much. He might have added that not only the ancient rabbis but also every modern historian who has touched on this subject have all claimed the same thing, yet it is clear to me that they are mistaken. In point of fact the evidence is overwhelming that the Jews did not adopt the Babylonian month names until the 2nd century BCE, and the reason why they did so is because they adopted the entire Seleucid calendar, including the Seleucid Era in its Babylonian form, at this time.

The Jewish calendar as it exists today is a lunar calendar consisting of twelve lunar months with an extra month added seven times in nineteen years just like the Seleucid calendar. The names of the months are also identical to those of the Seleucid calendar in its Babylonian version. But according to the standard version of the history of the Jewish calendar, the Jews became accustomed to using the Babylonian month names during the Babylonian captivity, and they continued to do so after returning to the land of Israel in the late 6th century BCE. As for Jewish use of the same nineteen year cycle as found in the Seleucid calendar, it is often asserted or even more often implied that the Jews discovered this cycle independently. In practice the standard version of the history of the Jewish calendar therefore denies any connection between that calendar and the Seleucid calendar, despite the close resemblance between them. However, it does not make this denial openly, but covertly, by avoiding any discussion of the resemblance between the two and in particular by maintaining a kind of conspiracy of silence regarding Jewish use of the Seleucid Era. It was this silence that drew me to the topic of the Seleucid Era in the first place, but fortunately I was able to discover enough exceptions to the rule to piece together the long and complex history of Jewish use of the Seleucid calendar.

The main source for the early history of the Jewish calendar is the so-called Old Testament, known in Hebrew as Tanach. In the books of Tanach, the months are almost invariably referred to solely by number, such as "the first month", "the second month", and so forth. However there are a few indications that at one time the months also had names. The first month, called Nisan in the Babylonian calendar, is referred to a few times in Tanach as Aviv, meaning "Spring". Three other months are also referred to once or twice by name, but it is apparent that at the time the books of Tanach were written, this system of month names was no longer in general use. Identifying the months solely by number was probably somehow connected with the Jewish concept of the week, because the days of the week were also identified solely by number, except for the seventh day, which was called Shabbat.

Had the Jews adopted the Babylonian month names during the Babylonian captivity, you would expect that the Babylonian month names would appear in the books of Tanach written during or after that time, but for the most part this is not the case. The Book of Ezekiel, which was written during the Babylonian captivity, and the Books of Ezra and Nehemiah, which were written some time after, continue to identify the months solely by number. There is only one book of Tanach in which the Babylonian month names appear, and that is the Book of Esther. This book purports to provide a contemporary account of events in the Persian empire during the 5th century BCE, and therefore it would seem to constitute proof that the Babylonian month names were in fact adopted during the Babylonian captivity, which immediately preceded the establishment of the Persian empire. However, there is every indication that the Book of Esther was actually written not earlier than the latter part of the 2nd century BCE, following the Jewish adoption of the Seleucid calendar at the beginning of that century.

The authenticity of the Book of Esther as a historical narrative is thrown into doubt by many details. In the first place there is no evidence whatsoever that the Persian rulers ever contemplated a massacre of the Jews under their rule such as is alleged by the Book of

Esther. To the contrary, Persian policy was generally favorable to the Jews, as is attested by many sources. In the second place, the names of the chief protagonists, Mordechai and Esther, are not Jewish names but are derived from the names of the Babylonian deities Marduk and Ishtar, suggesting that some kind of parody is intended. And in fact Jewish tradition has always treated the recital of the Book of Esther at Purim as the occasion for all kinds of parodies, masquerades and satires. But most important of all, the celebration of Purim on the 14th of Adar follows one day after a festival celebrated on the 13th of Adar in Maccabean times known as Nicanor Day. And the theme of Nicanor Day was the defeat and death of the Seleucid general Nicanor at the hands of the forces of Judah the Maccabee after Nicanor had vowed to exterminate the entire Jewish people.

It seems apparent that Purim was originally intended as a substitute for Nicanor Day, which the author of the Book of Esther clearly did not like. As if to underline this point, the 13th of Adar, the day on which Nicanor Day was celebrated in Maccabean times, is treated by the celebrants of Purim as a fast day, the "Fast of Esther", whereas Nicanor Day was officially regarded as a day for feasting and rejoicing. Purim and Nicanor Day both have the same basic theme, the defeat and death of an anti-Semite at the hands of the Jews, but in the Purim story this goal is accomplished by deception and persuasion, whereas in the case of Nicanor Day it was accomplished by military force. And since we know that Nicanor Day was instituted by the Maccabees as a holiday not earlier than 160 BCE, this means that the Book of Esther could not have been written until after that date. It uses the Babylonian month names for the same reason as the First and Second Book of Maccabees also use them, because they were adopted by the Jewish people following the Seleucid conquest of the land of Israel around 200 BCE.

The land of Israel was seized by the Seleucid king Antiochus 3, called by his followers "Antiochus the Great", from the Ptolemaic dynasty of Egypt, which had gained control of the land of Israel during the wars of the Diadochi. Victor Tcherikover presents a detailed narrative in *Hellenistic Civilization and the Jews* showing that the weight of Jewish opinion at this time was in favor of Seleucid as opposed to Ptolemaic rule. There were many reasons for this, such as: resentment against the autocratic rule of the Ptolemies; a series of pro-Jewish gestures on the part of Antiochus 3; and above all the perception that the Seleucids were stronger than the Ptolemies and therefore it would be more advantageous to side with them. No doubt independence from both dynasties would have been the preferred alternative of most Jews, but at the time this did not appear to be a realistic option. It seems clear from Tcherikover's analysis that Seleucid rule was initially preferred by the Jewish people over Ptolemaic rule, and Jewish adoption of the Seleucid calendar system would not be all that surprising in this context.

There is ample proof that the entire Seleucid calendar system, and not just the Babylonian month names, was in fact adopted not long after 200 BCE. For example, in the First Book of Maccabees, written in the latter part of the 2nd century BCE, Chapter 13, Verse 41 states: "Thus the yoke of the heathen was taken away from Israel in the hundred and seventieth year." The reference is to the election of the Maccabean leader Simon as High Priest, which took place in 141 BCE, which is the equivalent of the year 170 of the Seleucid Era. Likewise, in the Second Book of Maccabees, written not long after 100 BCE, in Chapter 1, Verse 10, there is a reference to a letter from the Jews of Jerusalem to the Jews of Egypt written "in the year one hundred and eighty-eight", which is the Seleucid equivalent of the Gregorian year 123 BCE. By the way, the Second Book of Maccabees, in Chapter 15, Verse 37, also contains a reference to Nicanor Day, which is to be celebrated "on the thirteenth day of the twelfth month, which in the Syrian tongue is called Adar". Second Maccabees was originally written in Greek; hence the explanation that the twelfth month was called Adar "in the Syrian tongue", meaning Aramaic.

By the second century BCE Aramaic had replaced Hebrew as the spoken language of most Jews in the land of Israel, and the fact that the Seleucid calendar system was available in an Aramaic language format was undoubtedly a major factor in its acceptance. But it is worth noting that the Babylonian month names did not at first entirely replace the traditional system of designating the months solely by number. In the First and Second Books of the Maccabees, and also in the Book of Esther, the months were described both by name and by number, so that someone unfamiliar with the Babylonian month names could still follow the story. Moreover, in the Dead Sea scrolls, which date from the 2nd or 1st century BCE, the Babylonian month names are only used on one scroll, while all the rest designate the months solely by number. This seems a clear indication that the sect which wrote the Dead Sea scrolls was hostile to the use of the Babylonian month names, which it undoubtedly regarded as a foreign importation. Yet over time whatever opposition there may have been to this foreign importation gradually subsided, to the point where designating the months by number went out of style and only the Babylonian month names were used.

However, continued use of the Seleucid Era encountered much stronger opposition. The fact that the Seleucid Era was used in the First and Second Books of Maccabees has to be seen in the context of efforts by the various Maccabean rulers to win formal Seleucid acceptance of their authority and independence. Once the Seleucids were completely overthrown, use of the Seleucid Era became a much less attractive option. Already in the passage from the First Book of Maccabees cited above, after the people acclaimed Simon as the High Priest, the next line reads: "Then the people of Israel began to write in their instruments and contracts, In the first year of Simon the high priest, the governor and leader of the Jews." Since the author of First Maccabees nonetheless dates this event as occurring "in the hundred and seventieth year", it would seem that substituting Simon for Seleucus did not set a precedent, but it suggests that the Seleucid Era was not a popular concept, linked as it was to the efforts of the Seleucid ruler Antiochus Epiphanes to destroy the Jewish people.

Josephus, in *Jewish Antiquities*, written in the late 1st century CE, also describes the acclamation of Simon as High Priest, and the way he does is very revealing. Clearly drawing on First Maccabees as his source, in Book 13, Chapter 6 he states:

But Simon, who was made high priest by the multitude, on the very first year of his high priesthood set his people free from their slavery to the Macedonians, and permitted them to pay tribute to them no longer; which liberty and freedom from tribute they obtained after a hundred and seventy years of the kingdom of the

Assyrians, which was after Seleucus, who was called Nicator, got
the dominion over Syria.

Josephus got the figure of "a hundred and seventy years" from
First Maccabees, but whereas First Maccabees had treated this date as
self explanatory, Josephus felt he had to explain it to his readers, who
may not have been familiar with the Seleucid Era. By "Assyrians" he
seems to have meant "Syrians", but why he didn't say "kingdom of the
Greeks" like everyone else is not clear. In any case, his treatment of the
Seleucid Era appears to reflect a situation in which it was still in use
but no longer standard.

Evidence of Jewish opposition to the use of the Seleucid Era
appears on page 29 of *Holidays, History, and Halakhah* by Eliezer
Segal. Segal states that in the Mishnah, which dates from the 3rd century CE, various options for dating legal documents are discussed, but
the Mishnah "evidently permits only those that refer to the year in
the term of the reigning king". This injunction notwithstanding, some
indication of continued Jewish use of the Seleucid Era after the time
of the Mishnah can be found. Lee Levine on page 240 of *The Ancient
Synagogue* describes a synagogue excavated at Apamea in Syria which
contains an inscription dating from "the year 703" of the Seleucid Era,
which Levine equates to 391 CE. And on page 349 Levine provides the
following instructive summary of the different types of dating systems
used in inscriptions in synagogues in and around the land of Israel in
late antiquity:

> Precious, though rare, are inscriptions which mention the date of
> a building's construction or renovation. Such pieces of informa-
> tion have been retrieved from the synagogues of Nabratein, Bet
> Alpha, Ashkelon, and Gaza in Palestine and Stobi and Dura in
> the Diaspora. The various eras invoked might include the reign
> of a given emperor (Dura, Bet Alpha), a municipal era (Gaza,
> Ashkelon), a famous event, such as the battle of Actium (Stobi),
> the Seleucid era (Dura), creation of the world (Susiya, Bet Alpha),
> sabbatical years (Susiya), and the time since the Temple's destruc-
> tion (Nevoraya).

In short, it is evident that use of the Seleucid Era, although not completely discontinued, was not popular among Jews in and around the land of Israel throughout the period from the disappearance of the Seleucid empire in the 1st century BCE to the Arab conqest in the 7th century CE. As Levine shows, there was no standard method of counting the years in use during this period but rather a wide variety of different systems, one of which was the Seleucid Era.

Yet following the Arab conquest, there took place a major change in the status of the Seleucid Era among Jews everywhere. By the 9th century CE, it was in general use in Jewish communities throughout the entire Mediterranean region and beyond. The Arabs themselves showed no interest in the Seleucid Era and soon adopted an era system of their own based on the date of Mohammed's flight from Mecca to Medina. They did nothing to encourage use of the Seleucid Era among Jews, and yet this use became standard in precisely those areas, from Spain to Iran, that had been conquered by the Arabs. This is a historical development that cries out for explanation, yet it has been completely ignored by the great majority of Jewish historians. It's not as if the explanation were all that difficult to find either; once you look for it, it soon becomes apparent. The reason why it has been ignored is because of the light which it sheds, not just on Jewish history, but also on the relationship of Jewish history to the history of Christianity and Islam.

THE ERA OF THE DOCUMENTS

In Jewish texts which date from the period after the Arab conquest, the Seleucid Era is typically referred to as "the era of the documents". For example, Erich Brauer in *The Jews of Kurdistan* describes numerous inscriptions dating from the 13th century in synagogues in Kurdistan which make reference to "the era of the documents". Brauer states, on page 250: "The year such-and-such of the documents refers to the Seleucid Era, which was the basis of reckoning years during the Second Temple period and remained in use in some Jewish communities down to modern times." The Kurdish Jewish community may have been one of these communities, as was the Jewish community of Yemen. By the way, Brauer also brings out that in one inscription, the name of Alexander also appears. He describes an inscription in a synagogue which reads: "The beginning of its building was in 1549 of the documents of Alexander; forty years later, they built the galleries." Brauer adds: "It is interesting to note that in folk memory Alexander the Great was substituted for Seleucus I Nicator as the conqueror to whose name is tied the era of the documents." But most Jewish references to the Seleucid Era, both in Kurdistan and elsewhere, from the 8th century onwards, simply characterize it as "the era of the documents".

Just which documents were indicated here? Kraemer, in his biography of Maimonides that first alerted me to the potential importance of the Seleucid Era, said that it "was used mainly on legal documents", but this turns out to be slightly misleading. The Seleucid Era was indeed used on Jewish legal documents, but also on many other kinds of documents as well. In the Introduction to the 1956 Dover edition of *The Guide For The Perplexed* by Maimonides, there is an excerpt from a "note" which Maimonides appended to his *Commentary on the Mishnah* and which states, with reference to this commentary, "I, Moses, the son of Maimon, commenced it when I was twenty-three years old, and finished it in Egypt, at the age of thirty [-three years], in the year 1479 Sel. (1168)." Needless to say, the Gregorian date 1168 would not have appeared in the original "note", but only the Seleucid date 1479, which would not have been described as "Sel." either. But the important point is that Maimonides himself used the Seleucid Era in a number of different contexts, as did many others.

What Kraemer should have said is that the use of the Seleucid Era by a large part of the Jewish community in the period following the Arab conquest originated with legal documents and was then extended to other kinds of documents (or inscriptions) as well. The legal documents in question were exclusively Jewish legal documents because Jews were virtually the only people in the world who continued to use the Seleucid Era for a long time after the Arab conquest. Credit for knowing just which legal documents were originally involved must go to Eliezer Segal, author of *Holidays, History, and Halakhah*. Of the few authors who even bothered to notice the existence of the "era of the documents", Segal was the only one I could find who knew where the term came from. On page 30 he stated: "Throughout the medieval era, the Seleucid system remained the only officially sanctioned manner for recording dates in legal deeds among the communities that followed the Babylonian rite, and hence it was standardly designated as *minyan ha-shetarot*, the 'documentary reckoning'." Amazing as it seems, the Seleucid Era had come full circle. Originating in the Seleucid cult of Babylon, it ended up as an expression of the religious authority of the Jewish community of Babylonia.

In Jewish circles, the region which the Europeans called Mesopotamia and the Arabs called Iraq was known as Babylonia, and it retained this name even after the city of Babylon itself had fallen into ruins and disappeared from sight. The Jewish community of Babylonia is thought to date from the time of the Babylonian captivity; by the end of the Second Temple period it numbered around one million people. And because Babylonia was largely spared the devastation wreaked on the Jewish communities of the Mediterranean region by the Romans and their Greek allies, the Jewish community of Babylonia emerged from the time of the so-called "Jewish Wars" as the largest and most prosperous Jewish community anywhere in the world. It was saved from the Romans by the fact that Babylonia remained under first Parthian and then Sasanian rule throughout the period from the 2nd century BCE to the 7th century CE. But for much of this period, the Jewish community of the land of Israel, although greatly reduced in numbers as a result of the "Jewish Wars", still retained its traditional position as the supreme authority on all questions relating to Jewish law and the Jewish religion.

The turning point in the relative status of the rabbinical authorities of the two communities came with the compilation of the Babylonian Talmud. Opinions differ among Jewish scholars just when this compilation was completed; various dates from 400 to 600 CE have been proposed. In any case, the Babylonian Talmud was essentially a record of the deliberations of the rabbinical academies of Babylonia commenting and elaborating on the compendium of Jewish "oral law" contained in the Mishnah. The Mishnah, which dated from around 200 CE, was compiled by the rabbinical Sanhedrin of the land of Israel, and the Sanhedrin also later produced a "Talmud of the land of Israel" commenting on the Mishnah, but this Talmud had little influence or authority. As commonly used, the term "Talmud" refers only to the Babylonian Talmud, which eventually achieved canonical status throughout the Jewish world. And since it was the Babylonian rabbinical academies that had produced the Talmud, it became the standard practice of Jews elsewhere to turn to those same academies for elucidation of the fine points of Jewish law.

The elevation of the rabbinical academies of Babylonia to the position of supreme authorities on Jewish law was further aided by the Arab conquest. The Abbasid Caliphs, who were based in Baghdad, recognized the "Exilarch", or head of the Jewish community of Babylonia, as the official head of the entire Jewish community then under their rule, which included perhaps 90% of all the Jews in the world. The Exilarch was more like a secular prince than a religious scholar, but his authority naturally tended to enhance the authority of the rabbinical academies of Babylonia as well. Those academies received a steady stream of letters from all over the Jewish world asking them for their opinion on this or that point of Jewish law. To these letters they replied with the famous "responsa", letters written in Aramaic, Hebrew or Arabic, depending on the language in which the request for information was written, and containing the answers to the questions asked of them. And since the rabbinical academies of Babylonia all used the Seleucid Era whenever a specific year had to be indicated, whether on a legal document or any other, their prestige and authority resulted in the adoption of the Seleucid Era as the standard method for counting the years throughout a large part of the Jewish world.

By the time of the Arab conquest, the Seleucid Era had been in more or less continuous use in the region of Babylonia for nearly 1000 years. Whatever they may have done elsewhere, it does not appear that either the Parthian or the Sasanian empires made any attempt to replace it in Babylonia with the "Arsacid era" or the "era of Zoroaster". Moreover, even if some dim memories of the association of the Seleucid Era with "the kings of Greece" or Alexander may have persisted, there is every indication that the "era of the documents" was generally viewed in Jewish circles as a well established, objective way of recording dates. Its adoption by most of the Jewish communities of the Mediterranean region was not a political statement on behalf of Greek rule but simply a recognition of the authority of the Babylonian rabbinical academies, who in turn derived their use of the Seleucid Era from the fact that it was the established method of counting the years in Babylonia.

A good example of the way in which use of the Seleucid Era was spread from the Jews of Babylonia to Jews elsewhere is provided by a letter written by the Babylonian rabbi Hai ben Sherira Gaon to the Jewish community of Kairouan in the late 10th century. Kairouan was located in Tunisia and was a major center of Jewish scholarship in North Africa. The letter is discussed by Robert Brody in *The Geonim of Babylonia and the Shaping of Medieval Jewish Cuulture*. The letter was written in reply to a request by the Jews of Kairouan for information regarding the history of Talmudic scholarship in Babylonia. Hai Gaon replied at length, giving dates for the work of various Babylonian religious scholars and even subdividing their history into centuries, all "according to the Seleucid Era", as Brody notes on page 24. The letter presupposed a knowledge and understanding of the use of the Seleucid Era, and since Tunisia had never been a part of the Seleucid empire, this knowledge must have come to Kairouan from Babylonia.

The influence of the Babylonian rabbinical academies over the Jewish world reached its peak in the 10th century in connection with the spread of the writings of Saadiah Gaon. "Gaon" was an honorary title applied to the heads of the Babylonian rabbinical academies. It literally means "genius" but is usually translated as "Excellency" or something of the sort. Saadiah became head of the academy of Sura in 928 CE; he really was a genius whose literary output ranks in stature with that of Maimonides in the shaping of Jewish religious philosophy. His *Book of Beliefs and Opinions* was "the first systematic presentation of Judaism as a rational body of beliefs" according to the Introduction to the 1948 New Haven edition. Saadiah also translated Tanach into Arabic and played a key role in establishing the authority of the Babylonian academies over the Jewish calendar as superior to that of the rabbis of the land of Israel. Although the issue which Saadiah resolved in favor of the Babylonian academies did not relate to the counting of the years, the fact that the Babylonian version was accepted throughout the Jewish world could not help but reinforce the authority of the Seleucid Era as well.

Yet although the Seleucid Era remained in use in the time of Maimonides, who lived in the 12th century, it was no longer the standard method of measuring the passage of the years in Jewish circles. An alternative system had gradually come into use, one which utilized as its starting date the purported date of the creation of the universe by God as described in the Book of Genesis. By the 13th or 14th century this alternative system had completely supplanted the Seleucid Era throughout the Jewish world with the exception of Yemen and perhaps a few places in or around Iran. This alternative system is still in use today and is utilized by orthodox Jews alongside or even in preference to the Gregorian calendar. But precisely why did this system supplant the Seleucid Era, which had seemed so well established in the time of Saadiah Gaon? You will seek in vain through most treatments of the history of the Jewish calendar for an answer to this question. Only by probing the ideological implications of the two competing systems will the reasons for the replacement of the one by the other become apparent.

THE ERA OF THE CREATION

The original source of the idea of counting the years from the alleged date of Creation is well known; it is a text called the Seder Olam probably dating from the 2nd century CE and written by a rabbi in the land of Israel. "Seder" means "order" or "sequence"; "Olam" is a term difficult to translate. It can mean "universe" or "world", but also "eternity". The Seder Olam was intended as a history of the world, or at least the Jewish world, beginning with the Creation and then assigning precise dates to the events described in Tanach based on the author's estimate of how many years must have passed between one event and another. Utilizing methods of this kind, the author of the Seder Olam arrived at a date of Creation equivalent to the year 3760 BCE on the Gregorian calendar.

Many studies of the Jewish calendar attempt to give the impression that the chronology of the Seder Olam soon came into general use for the purpose of counting the years on the calendar. For example,

Wikipedia in its article on the Seder Olam Rabbah (the earliest version of the Seder Olam) states: "The author probably designed the work for calendrical purposes, to determine the era of the Creation; his system, adopted as early as the 3rd century, is still followed." But in the list of inscriptions found in synagogues in and around the land of Israel dating from late antiquity and listed by Lee Levine on page 240 of *The Ancient Synagogue*, only two used the era of the Creation to record dates, as against eight that used different systems, including one that used the Seleucid Era. Nor is there any evidence of Jewish use of the era of the Creation "for calendrical purposes" at all comparable to the range and scope of the use of the Seleucid Era during the heyday of the rabbinical academies of Babylonia. It was only after these academies began to decline in influence, starting in the 11th century, that the era of the Creation began to supplant the Seleucid Era throughout most of the Jewish world.

This is not to say that the Seder Olam was ignored prior to this time. To the contrary, it was discussed in the Talmud and widely circulated among Jewish scholars everywhere. Its method of computing the time of Creation was generally accepted as valid, but for a long time there was no agreement as to its precise implications. Some argued that the count of the years in the Seder Olam was not entirely accurate, and there were also differences over whether the count of the years should begin before, during or after the seven days of Creation described in the Book of Genesis. Saadiah Gaon contended in one of his works that the Seder Olam had not included the year of the Deluge in its calculations and was therefore one year off. There was no easy way of resolving these disputes, since one arbitrary date was as good as another, and therefore the era of the Creation was not generally used to record dates on documents so long as the Seleucid Era remained in force.

However, on a conceptual level the notion of an era of Creation became popular among Jewish scholars even before it was integrated into the calendar system. Saadiah Gaon used the Seleucid Era in his writings but this didn't mean that he rejected the idea of an era of Creation. In *The Book of Beliefs and Opinions* he listed a whole series of arguments that could be advanced against the belief in the creation of the universe by God and then sought to refute each one. One argument was simply: "Now perhaps someone will say, 'How can it be acceptable that the world has been in existence only 4693 years?'." Saadiah replied that even if it didn't seem obvious, it was true nonetheless, showing that he was in complete agreement with the basic approach of the Seder Olam. No one knows exactly when Saadiah wrote these lines, but in a footnote the editor indicated that it must have been in 933 CE, a figure he arrived at by subtracting the date of Creation of the Seder Olam, the equivalent of 3760 BCE, from 4693.

It would appear that one reason for the subsequent decline in use of the Seleucid Era was the decline of the Abbasid caliphate. By the 11th century Spain and Egypt were under the rule of rival caliphates and Baghdad itself was controlled by the Seljuk Turks. Although the Abbasid caliphs still claimed authority over the Muslim world, they had little real power, and therefore their recognition of the Exilarch as the head of the entire Jewish community under their rule no longer carried much weight. The rabbinical academies of Babylonia likewise declined in prestige, and their authority in Babylonia itself was challenged by the rise of the Karaite movement, which treated both the Mishnah and the Talmud as null and void. And as Salo Wittmayer Baron brings out in Volume 8 of *A Social and Religious History of the Jews*, it was around this same time that a standard version of the era of the Creation took shape, putting to an end the disputes which had previously restricted its application to the Jewish calendar. So well established did the standard version become that when the rabbi Azariah de Rossi of Mantua wrote a critique of the Seder Olam in the 16th century, his book was ordered banned by the leading rabbinical scholar of the day, Joseph Caro.

Baron observed that the standardization of the era of the Creation went hand in hand with its growing popularity in Jewish circles. He put it this way, on page 204:

> Once most Jews had begun to date their business documents, funeral inscriptions, and historical records by the new era – a practice which may indeed have become prevalent first in Italy, as suggested by Bernstein – the system of dating accepted by Shabtai

Donnelo, Hai Gaon, and Savasorda, in agreement with that previously recorded in the Venosa inscriptions and elsewhere, became uniform throughout the Jewish world.

On the other hand, Eliezer Segal on page 31 of *Holidays, History, and Halakhah* stressed political factors as mainly responsible for the spread of the new system:

> Although Jews who were politically subject to the Baghdadi Caliphate (and hence, religiously, to the Babylonian *Ga'on*) continued to follow the talmudic convention of dating according to the "Greek kings", those communities that continued to accept the authority of the Palestinian leadership – primarily in Egypt and southern Italy, as well as in the Holy Land itself – took the *Seder Olam* chronology as their norm in legal documents, which they dated from the alleged creation of the world.

It is significant that in the 11th century both Egypt and the land of Israel were under the rule of the Fatimid caliphate, which repudiated the authority of the Abbasid caliphate and recognized the rabbis of the land of Israel rather than those of Babylonia as the official leaders of the Jewish community. And since the rabbis of the land of Israel had never liked the Seleucid Era in the first place, the system of the Seder Olam, which had originated in the land of Israel, was the logical choice to supplant the Seleucid Era both in the land of Israel and also wherever the authority of the Abbasid caliphate was no longer recotgnized.

However, during the 11th and 12th centuries the Seleucid Era was still used to some extent even in those communities which had begun to switch over to the new system. Robert Brody. on page 12 of *The Geonim of Babylonia and the Shaping of Medieval Jewish Culture*, cites a passage from the Book of Tradition of Abraham Ibn Daud, which was written in Spain in 1161 CE, in which the two systems are used side by side. According to Ibn Daud, Hai Gaon was the last of the Geonim of Babylonia, and he died in "the year 1349 of the Seleucid era, which is equivalent to 4798 (Anno Mundi)". That would place his death in the year 1038 of the Gregorian calendar. The purpose of Ibn Daud's book was to provide a historical sketch demonstrating a transition of rabbinical authority from Babylonia to Spain. No doubt he considered a transition from the Seleucid Era to the era of the Creation to be part of this process, but he evidently did not feel comfortable omitting it entirely from his account. By "Anno Mundi" Ibn Daud, or more precisely the translator of this passage, meant the era of the Creation. But just why did the translator use a Latin term for a Jewish concept?

ANNO MUNDI

Many scholars, especially non-Jewish but also Jewish, use the term "Anno Mundi", frequently abbreviated as "AM", to denote the era of the Creation. Anno Mundi means "the year of the world" in Latin. And the reason why a Latin term is often used to denote the era of the Creation is that the Christians had their own era of the Creation, which they used for many hundreds of years prior to switching over to the era of Christ, which they called Anno Domini.

The first Christian chronographer who sought to outline an era of the Creation was Sextus Julius Africanus, "who lived in Palestine and Syria in the second half of the second and the first half of the third century" according to Georges Declereq on page 27 of *Anno Domini*. Although Declereq doesn't mention it, that would put him in the same place and the same time frame as the author of the Seder Olam. The Seder Olam is thought to have been written around 160 CE, which would make it a little earlier than the work of Africanus. Whether the latter was familiar with the Seder Olam is unclear; in any case Africanus ended up with a completely different date of Creation, which he assigned to the equivalent of 5500 BCE on the Gregorian calendar. Perhaps one reason for the discrepancy was that Africanus used Greek as well as Jewish records in making his computations.

During the next few centuries a number of similar works appeared, of which the most popular was an account by the Christian theologian and historian Eusebius. Most came up with dates for the Creation similar to that of Africanus. One said 5492, another 5508, and so forth. Eusebius calculated 2242 years from Adam to the Flood, 942 years from the Flood to Abraham, and 1240 years from Abraham to the birth of Christ, which would yield a date for the Creation equivalent to 4424 BCE on the Gregorian calendar. By the 9th century a date equivalent to 5508 BCE had become standard throughout the Byzantine world, but in the 10th century this was officially changed to 5509 BCE, "in order to adjust the year of the world to the Byzantine civil year, which began on 1 September", according to Declereq. He added, on page 39, that "the Byzantine era dating the creation of the world in 5508/9 BC, was generally accepted throughout the Byzantine world, where it remained the official reckoning of the Empire and the Church until the fall of Constantinople."

Perhaps due to the popularity of the era of Diocletian in the western Roman empire, the Byzantine dates were not regarded as authoritative in the Latin world. In the 6th century a Byzantine monk named Dionysius Exiguus, in a treatise on the date of Easter intended for the use of the Latin church, suggested replacing the era of Diocletian with an era of Christ for calendrical purposes. He calculated that the year 248 of the era of Diocletian should become the year 532 of the era of Christ. His suggestion was then taken up by the Latin church, first in Spain, then in England, and finally in the Carolingian empire, eventually resulting in the establishment of the era of Christ as standard throughout Europe. But even if it did not become a part of the calendar in the West, the concept of an era of Creation remained popular throughout the entire Christian world, and official in the Byzantine part of that world, at precisely the same time as this same concept was being integrated into the calendar in the Jewish world.

Was there no connection between the two belief systems? Both Baron and Segal pinpointed Italy as one of the first places where the era of the Creation became standard in Jewish circles. The Jewish community there was small and subject to intense Christian influence. Also, Baron mentioned Savasorda as one of the key figures involved in the standardization of the era of the Creation for use in the Jewish calendar. Savasorda was the nickname of Abraham Bar Hiyya, a 12th century Jewish astronomer and theologian, who wrote extensively on the subject of the calendar. In one of his books he described the different eras used by various peoples for reckoning time and provided formulas for the conversion of other eras into the era of the Creation. Savasorda lived in Barcelona, which was by his time already under Christian rule, and he was the first prominent Jewish writer in Spain who did not write in Arabic but solely in Hebrew.

Julius Guttman, on page 114 of *Philosophies of Judaism*, noted that Savasorda's philosophy of history "is founded upon the idea of an exact correspondence between world eras and the days of creation", and saw this as "the first instance of Christian speculation exerting a direct influence upon Jewish philosophy in the Middle Ages." And in fact Africanus had followed a similar scheme, arguing that each of the seven days of Creation stood for an era of 1000 years of world history. His date for the Creation of 5500 BCE was intended to represent the advent of Christ as coming at the precise midpoint of the 6th millenium, which was the equivalent of the 6th day of Creation, to be followed by a 7th millenium, which would be the equivalent of the Sabbath. In Savasorda's scheme, the 7th millenium would witness the advent of the Messiah. With reference to Savasorda, Guttman also stated: "The extent to which his philosophy of history is based on Christian models is shown by the fact that it even contains an analogy for the Christian doctrine of original sin."

It would seem that the Jewish and Christian versions of the era of the Creation mutually reinforced one another. Even though they ended up with different dates, and argued over which was the correct date, they both took essentially the same approach to computing the time of Creation. This approach entailed insisting on the literal truth not only of the account of Creation in the Book of Genesis but also of all the other events described in Tanach on which they based their computations. Moreover, in order to come up with a standard version of the date of Creation, which was done by the Byzantine church as well as the Jewish scholars, they had to close ranks in favor of one arbitrary date as opposed to another. All this implied a high degree of respect for authority, or dogmatism, such as is generally associated with the religious climate of the Middle Ages. And in particular it amounted to a virtual polemic on behalf of Creationism, which became a major article of faith in both the Jewish and Christian worlds.

To be sure, the description of the seven days of Creation in the

Book of Genesis had long been an accepted part of Judaism, if for no other reason than that it provided the theological basis for the institution of the Sabbath. But integrating this description into the calendar marked a new level of insistence on its importance, and it does not seem to have been a coincidence that this happened when and where it did. As is well known, starting with the 8th century and the emergence of the Abbasid caliphate, there developed a lengthy philosophical and theological dispute in the Arab world over the proper place of Reason under the rule of Islam. This dispute also spilled over into the Jewish world, leading to a long series of works by Jewish scholars living under Muslim rule and seeking to achieve the proper balance between Reason and Jewish religious belief. Saadia Gaon's *Book of Beliefs and Opinions* is often characterized as the first of these works, and the writings of Maimonides are generally thought to represent the culmination and crowning achievement of the debate over Jewish religious philosophy stretching from the 9th to the 13th century. It was this same period that witnessed a gradual transition from the Seleucid Era to the era of the Creation in the Jewish calendar. And as it so happened, the question of the validity of Creationism from the standpoint of Reason was the central issue in the entire debate.

REASON

"Reason" in the language of medieval theology was essentially a code word for Greek philosophy. As the works of Plato and Aristotle began to be available in Arabic translation, both Muslim and Jewish theologians were confronted with a serious dilemma. On the one hand, both Plato and Aristotle could be seen as affirming the concept of God, Plato in the form of "the Good", Aristotle in the form of "the Unmoved Mover". The works of the leading Greek philosophers could therefore be used to prove that the existence of God was so self evident that even Reason unaided by Revelation would inevitably affirm it. Yet on the other hand, neither Plato nor Aristotle believed in the creation of the universe but rather tended towards the view that it was eternal. There was evidently a conflict between Reason and Revelation, and the theologians had to find a way of resolving this conflict if they wanted to use Greek philosophy to buttress their religious beliefs.

Quite a few Muslim writers sought to resolve this dilemma by affirming the existence of God but denying the validity of the account of Creation in the Book of Genesis. They were aided in this stance by the fact that the Koran does not have much to say on the subject of the origin of the universe but simply asserts Allah's sovereignty over man and nature. In *A History of Islamic Philosophy*, Majid Fakhry cites the following convoluted argument on behalf of the eternity of matter advanced by the 10th century Muslim writer, Al-Razi:

> The eternity of matter is demonstrated in two ways. Creation, the act of "in-forming" matter, presupposes not only a Creator who has preceded it, but also a substratum of matter in which this act inheres. Moreover, the very concept of creation *ex nihilo* is logically untenable, for if God had been able to create *anything* out of nothing, He would have been bound to create *everything* out of nothing, since this is the simplest and readiest mode of production. But since this is far from being the case, the world must be said to have been created out of a formless matter, which has preceded it since all time.

Similar views were held by the most famous Muslim theologian, Averroes, who lived in the 12th century in Spain. Averroes lived much of his life under the rule of the crusading Muslim sect known as the Almohads, yet he was not persecuted for affirming the eternity of matter, a view that was essentially banned in the Christian world.

Actually, denial of Creation "ex nihilo" was only the tip of the iceberg of a much more radical current of thought which was prevalent in Muslim circles under the Abbasid caliphate. Guttman on page 53 of *Philosophies of Judaism* refers to a "well known report from the end of the tenth century on the friendly discussions concerning religions held in Bagdad between members of various religions." He continues:

> The participants agreed upon absolute tolerance toward one another; when their various faiths were being discussed, any dogmatic appeal to authority was ruled out. The only source upon

which one could rely in the search for the true religion was the "human intellect". Reason, instead of authority, thus became the criterion for religious truth.

And Guttman adds:

This new rationalism was in many cases definitely antagonistic to religion. Participants in the above-mentioned philosophic discussion included "materialists", and the polemics of Islamic and Jewish scholars mention the Dahriya, a sect which denied the existence of a divine Being, as taking part in the disputations.

Likewise, Fakhry on page 107 of *A History of Islamic Philosophy* describes an 11th century Muslim writer named al-Mu'aari who adopted "an agnostic posture" in "matters of religious belief". He went so far as to divide mankind into two groups: "those who possess reason but no religion, and those who possess religion but no reason".

Given the strength of the rationalist current in the Muslim world, it was only natural that this current should spill over into the Jewish world. Guttman on page 57 describes the views of "the Jewish heretic Hiwi of Balkh" who wrote a book in the second half of the 9th century containing 200 "objections to the Bible". The book was suppressed, but its contents are known through a lengthy polemic against it by Saadiah Gaon. Guttman adds that Saadiah also wrote critiques of a number of Jewish thinkers who rejected the doctrine of Creation "ex nihilo" and "took the view that God created the world out of a pre-existent primary matter, and actually sought to read this idea into the biblical text". It is also significant that the entire body of work of Averroes was translated from Arabic into Hebrew and widely discussed by the Jewish philosophers of the late Middle Ages. The views of Averroes on the eternity of matter were accepted by the 14th century Jewish writer, Gersonides.

But due to the importance of the Book of Genesis in Jewish tradition, there was no way that a denial of the Creation "ex nihilo" could become the mainstream Jewish position. The Book of Genesis seemed to say that God did indeed create the universe out of nothing, and the mainstream Jewish position, as represented by both Saadiah Gaon and Maimonides, was that since that was what the Book of Genesis said, it had to be true. However, they added that this position was not inconsistent with Reason, because the notion of the eternity of matter was not susceptible of rational proof. But there was a subtle difference in the way that Saadiah Gaon and Maimonides formulated this position. Saadiah Gaon argued that all the proofs that had been advanced in favor of the idea of eternity of matter were false and he could demonstrate precisely what was wrong with each of them. On the other hand, Maimonides conceded that he could not actually disprove the thesis that matter was eternal, but he maintained that the arguments of those who had tried to prove that it was were not conclusive either. In short, the issue could not be resolved by Reason, and therefore it was necessary to be guided by Revelation, which came down on the side of Creationism.

From the acceptance of Creationism in theory to the acceptance of its insertion into the calendar was not a difficult transition to make. Maimonides used the era of the Creation as well as the Seleucid Era in his writings, which dated from a time when the Babylonian rabbinate no longer exercised much authority over the Jewish world. In the absence of that authority, there was no particular reason why most Jews should feel a strong sense of loyalty to the Seleucid Era. The extent to which use of the Seleucid Era was bound up with the authority of the Babylonian rabbinate is also shown by the exception that proves the rule, the continued use of the Seleucid Era by the Jews of Yemen. Reuben Ahroni in *Yemenite Jewry* shows that there existed particularly close ties between the Jews of Yemen and the Jews of Babylonia. He notes on page 67 that the Geniza documents show "that the Yemenite Jews not only maintained strong ties with the Jewish centers in Babylon, but even supported them financially." And on page 75, with reference to the interaction between the two communities, he states:

> Such interaction is also evidenced by the fact that the Yemenite Jews were the only Jewish community which unceasingly adhered to the system of dating events in accordance with the "era of the contracts" (Seleucid). Thus, for example, the dating of epitaphs in

the old cemetery in Aden by means of this system certainly points to the Yemenite ties with the Babylonian schools.

But even in Yemen, the era of the Creation was also used to some extent.

Acceptance of the era of the Creation had the effect of placing the Jewish people in the same camp as the followers of all the other "monotheistic" religions. By the time that this era was adopted, there was already an era of Christ, an era of Mohammed, a Christian era of the Creation and an era of Zoroaster. It could be argued that all of these eras were ultimately modeled on the Seleucid Era, but in a world dominated by religious belief, the Seleucid Era had the serious drawback of being secular. It is true that the Seleucids did try to create a religious foundation for their rule, but this effort, never very successful, had been long forgotten by the time that the Babylonian academies popularized the Seleucid Era among Jews everywhere. If anything was remembered of the origins of the "era of the documents", it was that it was somehow connected with the Greeks. But this was significant, because as S.D. Goitein notes in his Introduction to one of his books, *Jews and Arabs*, much of early Islamic culture was "largely secular, (meaning, derived from the pagan Greek world.)" Jewish use of the Seleucid Era fit well into this larger pattern of Islamic tolerance of Greek secularism, but the less secular Islamic culture became during the course of the Middle Ages, the stronger the inclination of Jews to follow a religious era of their own.

In general it would seem that the integration of the era of the Creation into the Jewish calendar was linked to the development of a negative attitude towards secular Greek philosophy. A connection of this kind can definitely be seen in the work of Savasorda, a key figure in facilitating the transition from the Seleucid Era to the era of the Creation. On page 219 *of Judaism As A Philosophy*, Leon Stitskin cites Savasorda as declaring, with reference to the Greek philosophers, that "all their great thoughts" were "taken from the words of the Torah", which was the true "fountain of wisdom" in this world. The argument that Greek philosophy was but a pale imitation of Jewish doctrine was one which had already been advanced by a number of both Jewish

and Christian writers. Savasorda also contended that every word of
Scripture was literally true regardless of whether or not it appeared
to be consistent with Reason. This stance was commonplace in the
Christian world, under whose rule Savasorda lived.

THE END OF AN ERA

The disappearance of the Seleucid Era from most Jewish texts by
the late Middle Ages marked the end of an era, but it is important
to understand just what era. Despite its Babylonian roots and Greek
veneer, the Seleucid Era was first and foremost a part of Aramaic
language culture, and it rose and fell with the rise and fall of that
culture.

Aramaic was in its origins the language of the kingdom of Aram, a
Syrian kingdom bordering on the rival kingdoms of Judah and Israel.
All three kingdoms shared the same fate, which was to be conquered by
the empires of Assyria and Babylon. But for some strange reason, the
language of the kingdom of Aram conquered its conquerors and by
the middle of the 1st millenium BCE it had become the main spoken
language of both Babylonia and Assyria. I have never seen a convincing explanation of this development, which was also paralleled by the
expansion of spoken Aramaic into the land of Israel. The emergence
of Aramaic as the main spoken language of the entire region bordering on Syria was further amplified by its adoption as the official written language of the Persian empire. So influential did written Aramaic
become that the Jews under Persian rule adopted a modified form of
the Aramaic script to replace their traditional Hebrew script. The new
script is now known as "square Hebrew" and is still in use today.

Further evidence of the prominence of written Aramaic is provided by the fact that it was subsequently used as an administrative language to one extent or another by the Seleucid, Parthian and Sasanian
empires in turn. Yet although there exists a voluminous Aramaic
language literature of both Jewish and Christian origin, virtually nothing has been written by scholars on the subject of Aramaic language
culture as a distinct culture in its own right. It is as if the Aramaic
language were a neutral vehicle that could express Greek or Persian

administrative needs and Jewish or Christian religious beliefs without imparting to its users anything of its own. This assumption seems inherently implausible and is rendered even more unlikely by the fact that Judaism, Zoroastrianism, Christianity and Islam all share certain beliefs which circulated for centuries in an Aramaic language setting. In particular the notion of the resurrection of the dead at the time of the Last Judgment may well have originated with Zoroastrianism and then been spread to Judaism and Christianity and ultimately to Islam through its dissemination in a popular Aramaic language form.

In the final analysis, the lack of scholarly interest in the subject of Aramaic culture appears to reflect a certain prejudice that can be traced back to the era of the Greek conquest of the Middle East. This prejudice persisted in a Christian guise, as shown by the following remarks appearing on page 96 of the anthology, *Languages of Iraq, Ancient and Modern*, edited by J.N. Postgate:

> The Aramaic speaking Christians preferred to designate themselves as "Syrians", a term used by the Greeks to designate the inhabitants of the Fertile Crescent, rather than the term "Aramaeans", which had come to be used in the sense of "pagans". The Aramaic word *suryaya* or *suraya* eventually came to have the sense of "Christian", as is the case in the modern Aramaic dialects.

For their part the Greek speaking Christians looked down on their Aramaic speaking brethren, regarding them as heretics, and defined their alleged heresy as "Nestorianism" despite the fact that Nestorius was a Greek speaking Christian who had never had any connection with the Aramaic speaking Christians. In a vain search for respectability in Greek eyes the latter dubbed their written language, which was a dialect of Aramaic, as "Syriac".

The dialect of Aramaic which became known as Syriac was the one spoken in the city of Edessa, the first major center of the so-called Nestorian church. In the 9th century CE a Byzantine chronographer named George Synkellos attempted to write a history of the world starting with the Creation, and on page 398 of the 2002 Oxford edition he stated: "The first king of Syria and Babylonia and the interior

regions was Seleukos Nikator." He went on to give the date of the
start of his reign as 5171 Anno Mundi. Since Synkellos believed that
the world was created 5501 years before the birth of Christ, this would
yield a slightly erroneous figure of 330 BCE for the start of the Seleucid
Era. He added "The Edessenes calculate their chronology from that
point." Whether the early Aramaic speaking Christians did the same
is unclear, but there can be no doubt that it was because Edessa was
an important center of Aramaic language culture that it continued to
follow the Seleucid Era even though it was under Muslim rule at the
time that Synkellos wrote his chronography.

Use of the Seleucid Era and attachment to Aramaic language
culture were also closely linked in the Jewish centers of Babylonia.
Aramaic remained the main spoken and written language of the Jews
of Babylonia for at least two centuries after the Arab conquest. One
reason for this was that the Jewish population of Babylonia was not
exclusively urban but included a substantial proportion who lived
in the countryside. The prestigious rabbinical academies of Sura,
Nehardea and Pumbeditha were all located in rural areas, where
the transition from Aramaic to Arabic was much slower than in the
cities. But around the end of the 9th century the academies of Sura
and Pumbeditha moved to Baghdad, suggesting a greater reliance on
Arabic than previously. Even so, it was not until the 11th century that
the Babylonian rabbis stopped writing in Aramaic. And of course they,
along with Jewish scholars everywhere, continued to learn Aramaic as
a literary language, because the Talmud and many other Jewish texts
were written in Aramaic.

Just what the connection was between the views of the rabbinical
academies of Babylonia and Aramaic popular culture is difficult to
say. However, it is probably significant that the Babylonian academies
played a major role in the establishment of belief in the "End of Days"
as an article of faith in orthodox Judaism. Here as elsewhere Saadiah
Gaon was a key figure in the delineation of the orthodox position. In
The Book of Beliefs and Opinions he asserted that "all Jews" believed
that the resurrection of the dead at the End of Days would coincide
with the "redemption" of the Jewish people, the ingathering of the
exiles in the land of Israel and the establishment of the rule of the

Messiah over the entire world. The redemption of Israel would take place whether the Jews merited it or not, but they could hasten the advent of the Messiah by meriting it. Saadiah's view of redemption as coinciding with the End of Days was later questioned by Maimonides, who saw the ingathering of the exiles in much more secular terms, but in orthodox Jewish circles it was Saadiah's view that prevailed.

It is also worth noting that although Aramaic gradually ceased to be spoken by the Jews of Babylonia, it did not entirely die out as a spoken language among Jews. Erich Brauer in *The Jews of Kurdistan* brings out that small Jewish communities survived in mountainous regions of Kurdistan right down to modern times speaking a dialect of Aramaic which they called "Targum". According to Brauer, Targum had a "neo-Aramaic base" with admixtures of Kurdish, Turkish, Old Aramaic and Hebrew words. Brauer also shows that the Jews of Kurdistan were still using the Seleucid Era in the late 13th century, but his account does not make it clear how long they continued to use it after then. It may well have been for a long time, as these Jewish communities were located in the Zagros mountains, an area difficult of access by outsiders. After pointing this out, Brauer states on page 51: "Hence, this area is a classical example of a place of retreat in which remnants of different people and tribes have survived for centuries." Perhaps there were a few more such places of retreat for Aramaic speaking Jews in the region of Iran, but for the most part the spread of Arabic as a spoken language in Syria and Iraq marked the end of an era for Aramaic language culture in the Middle East. And once it no longer had the support of a large Aramaic speaking community, the Seleucid Era came to an end at the same time.

THE SECRET OF INTERCALATION

There remains the larger question of the relationship between the Jewish calendar and the Seleucid calendar. And in particular, how much significance should be assigned to the fact that the two calendars not only had the same month names but used the identical system of intercalation?

"Intercalation" is the technical term used to describe the insertion of an extra month from time to time in lunar calendars. Elias
Bickerman, on page 74 of his article "Notes on Seleucid and Parthian
Chronology", appearing in *Berytus*, Volume 8, Part 2 (1944), states
that the Seleucid calendar used the same system of intercalation as the
Babylonian calendar. This system is well known; it was based on the
addition of an extra month 7 times in 19 years. The Jewish calendar
still in use today uses this same system, and what is more, it adds the
extra month in precisely the same years as the Babylonians did, namely
the years 3, 6, 8, 11, 14, 17 and 19 of the cycle. This same sequence of
years was also used in the Athenian calendar inspired by the Greek
astronomer Meton. Wikipedia, the on line encyclopedia, notes in its
article on the "Metonic cycle" that the Babylonians, Athenians and
Jews all intercalated using this same sequence of years, but draws no
conclusions from this fact.

According to the standard version of the history of the Jewish calendar, intercalation was originally based on direct observation of the
changing seasons. When it seemed that Pesach would arrive too early,
an extra month was added. Deciding when to add the extra month was
originally the responsibility of the priesthood, but during the Second
Temple period it came to be vested in the Sanhedrin, a deliberative
body that eventually also included rabbis. After the destruction of the
Temple, the Sanhedrin came to be exclusively composed of rabbis, who
continued to decide when to intercalate based on direct observation.
However, by the mid-4th century CE, Byzantine persecution had made
it difficult or impossible for the Sanhedrin to meet. The head of the
Sanhedrin, the rabbi Hillel II, therefore decided to reveal the "secret
of intercalation" (the "sod ha'ibbur") to the Jewish world, so that it
would no longer be necessary to rely on the Sanhedrin to know when
to intercalate. The secret of intercalation was that you should intercalate 7 times in 19 years. It seems the rabbis had known this for some
time but kept it a secret, using it only to check the results which they
arrived at by direct observation.

Although the story of the revelation of the secret of intercalation
by Hillel II is repeated in virtually every account of the history of the
Jewish calendar, the first mention of this story in rabbinic literature

was by the Babylonian rabbi Hai Gaon, who lived in the late 10th and early 11th century, over 600 years after the time of Hillel II. Sacha Stern, in *Calendar and Community*, thinks that the adoption of the Metonic cycle by the rabbis did in fact occur around the time of Hillel II, but perhaps the change was slower and more informal than the standard version would have us believe. Stern also suggests that pressure from the Babylonian rabbis played a role in the decision to adopt a fixed system of intercalation. The new system was adopted, states Stern on page 256, "so as to ensure that Babylonian rabbis were able to observe the same calendar as in the land of Israel." Stern's book is subtitled "A History of the Jewish Calendar Second Century BCE – Tenth Century CE" and is by far the most comprehensive, detailed and scholarly treatment of this subject available in print.

As it so happens, the period covered by Stern's book is also the period of the heyday of the Seleucid calendar, but aside from one mention of the use of the Macedonian month names in the writings of Josephus, Stern shows no interest whatsoever in the relationship between the Jewish calendar and the Seleucid calendar. And no wonder, because if the Jews adopted the Seleucid calendar following the Seleucid conquest of the land of Israel around 200 BCE, then the standard history of intercalation in the Jewish calendar must be revised. The thing about intercalation is that even if the deliberations leading up to it remain secret, intercalation itself is a public act. We know that the Seleucid calendar intercalated in the years 3, 6, 8, 11, 14, 17 and 19 of the Metonic cycle, and over time anyone who used or saw others use that calendar would know it too. It is simply not plausible that the Jews adopted the Seleucid month names, followed the Seleucid Era to at least some extent but for centuries intercalated in different years than those in which the Seleucid calendar, predictably, did. They may have begun by doing this, but since the results of using the Seleucid system could be verified by direct observation, there is every reason to assume that the Sanhedrin adopted the Metonic cycle much earlier than the standard account would have it.

The standard account seems particularly implausible if we consider the situation of the Jews of Babylonia, whose involvement with the Seleucid calendar was earlier and more complete than that of the

Jews of the land of Israel. The Babylonian Jews had every reason to intercalate at the same time as everyone else in Babylonia considering that they were using the same calendar in every other respect. Yet in theory they were supposed to follow the lead of the Sanhedrin, which in theory was supposed to intercalate based solely on direct observation. This situation had to give rise to a constant pressure on the Sanhedrin by the Jews of Babylonia to follow the Metonic cycle in practice while continuing to depend on direct observation in theory. And the standard account can be read as implying that the Sanhedrin did just that, only the likelihood is that it began to do it long before the time of Hillel II. What may well have changed around that time is that henceforth it was the Babylonian rabbis who assumed actual responsibility for deciding when to intercalate. Perhaps the point of Hai Gaon's story about Hillel II was to show that the Sanhedrin had agreed to this change.

Hai Gaon would have had a strong motive to make this point, because once it became public knowledge that the Babylonian rabbis were in charge of a system of intercalating based on the Metonic cycle, the Karaites in Babylonia attacked this practice as an unwarranted deviation from Jewish tradition. The Karaite movement originated in the 7th and 8th centuries as a loose coalition of Jewish groups who were critical of the beliefs and policies of the rabbinical academies of Babylonia. By the 10th or 11th centuries they had coalesced into a sect, one of whose distinguishing characteristics was the assertion that all decisions regarding the Jewish calendar, including when to start the lunar month as well as when to intercalate, should be based solely on direct observation. There was probably a connection between this stance and another doctrine of theirs, namely that Jews should not wait for redemption at the End of Days but should settle immediately in the land of Israel. In their mind the primacy of the land of Israel and the control of the calendar by direct observation were related, whereas Hai Gaon was saying that the Sanhedrin itself had instituted the system of reliance on the Metonic cycle.

In the *Karaite Anthology* edited by Leon Nemoy there is a passage from the writings of the Karaite author Daniel al-Kumisi which may have a bearing on this point. After asserting that observance of the

Law required settlement in the land of Israel, al-Kumisi continued as
follows on page 38:

> You will have no valid excuse before the Lord if you do not return
> today to the Law of the Lord and to His ordinances as prescribed
> in it, because since the beginning of the Exile, in the days of
> the kingdom of the Greeks, the Romans, and the Magians, the
> Rabbanites held the offices of princes and judges, and those who
> sought the Law could not even open their mouths in behalf of the
> ordinances of the Lord in fear of the Rabbanites who were [ruling
> over them]. Upon the arrival of the kingdom of Ishmael, however,
> matters improved, for the Ishmaelites always help the Karaites to
> observe the true faith as set forth in the Law of Moses, and we
> must bless them for it. Now you are living in the midst of the
> kingdom of Ishmael, which loves those who fix the new moon by
> direct observation.

"Rabbanites" was the Karaite term for the rabbis. Reading between
the lines, al-Kumisi appears to be saying that the rabbis, with their
Seleucid calendar, were actually acting as agents of "the Greeks, the
Romans, and the Magians", but under the rule of the Arabs things
would be different because the Arabs did not follow the Seleucid calendar and relied on direct observation of the new moon to start the
lunar month. However, as it turned out, the Karaites were eventually
forced to relocate to the Byzantine empire, and there they adopted the
rabbinical calendar in its entirety, including the era of the Creation.

Whatever the precise details, it appears to me incontestable that the
Jewish calendar as it exists today is basically derived from the Seleucid
calendar and differs from it only in that the era of the Creation has
come to replace the Seleucid Era as a way of counting the years. Even
this change only happened after some 1000 years in which the Seleucid
Era was the main way in which most Jews in most places counted the
years. Starting as an expression of Greek (and Macedonian) domination, the Seleucid Era evolved into a secular method of counting the
years rooted in the Aramaic language culture of a good part of the
Middle East. Its replacement by competing era systems based on the

teachings of the Christian, Muslim and Jewish religions was an expression both of the decline of Aramaic language culture and the growing religiosity of Middle Eastern and European culture in the era of the Crusades. Perhaps some day a new secular method of counting the years will be adopted in keeping with the realization that no religion can provide an objective basis for chronology on a world scale.

JEWISH IDEAS

Up to the time of the emergence of Islam, Jewish influence had been exercised primarily through example, and secondarily through the power of the written word. The example of the nation of Judah, a nation of some millions of people, was the main source of Jewish influence in the ancient world. After this nation was devastated by the Romans, there still remained millions of Jews throughout the Middle East to inspire others with their example. And throughout the period of close to 2000 years from the time of Moses to the time of Mohammed, the power of the Jewish example was further amplified by the power of the written word. Starting with the Jewish Scriptures, followed by the "apocryphal" and "pseudepigraphal" literature, a large number of Hebrew and Aramaic language Jewish writings were gradually translated into other languages and distributed over a wide area. Numerous Jewish writings were also composed in other languages, particularly Greek. The popularity of Jewish writings during this period was due in part to their inherent interest but also to the fascination with all things Jewish which was stimulated by the radical policies and heroic struggle of the nation of Judah.

With the emergence, first of Christianity, then of Islam, this phase of Jewish history came to an end. In the eyes of the world, including many former Jews, these two religions rendered Judaism unnecessary. And since the mass movement to restore Judah had been decisively defeated and the Jewish population of the land of Israel reduced to a small remnant, the Jewish example no longer inspired the same interest as before. The Jewish communities of the Middle East slowly declined in size until the total number of Jews in the entire world was reduced to a few million. These small communities were increasingly isolated from one another, and after the imposition of the ghetto system, from their non-Jewish neighbors as well. Jews continued writings books much as before, but these books were rarely translated or distributed to a non-Jewish audience. What the Jews thought and felt ceased to be of much interest to anyone except other Jews. For a period of at least 1000 years, from the time of Mohammed to the birth of the modern era, the Jewish people was relegated to the position of a small and insignificant minority scattered throughout Europe, Africa and Asia in tiny, isolated communities. When one of these communities did grow to a significant size, as happened in Spain during the early Middle Ages, it was soon reduced by persecution to a shadow of its former self. Under these circumstances, the power of the Jewish people to influence anyone, whether by example or by means of the written word, was severely limited.

And yet Jewish influence did persist. The clearest proof of this assertion is the imposition of the ghetto system on the Jews by Christians and Muslims alike during the Middle Ages. A complex set of regulations was gradually put in place which required Jews to live apart from their neighbors, to dress differently and to stay out of many professions. The avowed purpose of these regulations was to prevent the Jews from influencing non-Jews in any way. There would have been no need for the ghetto system if the Jews had not in fact continued to influence their neighbors in both the Christian and Muslim worlds. The Christian and Muslim authorities also testified to the persistence of Jewish influence by the frequency with which they denounced this or that "heresy" for "Judaizing" tendencies. Isolated, ghettoized and subjected to periodic persecutions of every kind, the Jewish people was still viewed by Christians and Muslims alike as a major source of "heretical" ideas within Christianity and Islam. Exaggerated and distorted as these accusations may have been, they must have rested on a certain foundation of fact, for why else would the Christians and Muslims make such a fuss about the Jews? Yet given the weak position of the Jews throughout this period, there is no obvious reason why they should have exercised the influence attributed to them.

A good example of the mysterious power of Jewish ideas in the era immediately following the rise of Islam is the conversion of the Khazars to Judaism. The Khazars were a nomadic people of Turkish origin who were one of the first Turkish peoples to move west from Central Asia into the Middle East and Europe. They arrived in the area of southern Russia in the 6th or 7th century CE and established a kingdom ruling over the indigenous peoples of the region. Around 740 CE, according to D.M. Dunlop in *The History of the Jewish Khazars,* their king and nobility converted to Judaism. There is a legend that this conversion was preceded by a debate between representatives of Judaism, Christianity and Islam which the Khazars felt was won by the Jews. No one really knows why they converted, for there were few Jews in their kingdom, nor did they have a long history of association with Jews prior to arriving in southern Russia. In fact, even after their conversion they had little contact with Jews elsewhere. Just what Judaism meant to them is largely unknown, but they remained Jews, at least in name, throughout their subsequent history. They ruled over a large area until the 10th century and fought numerous wars with both the Byzantine Christians and Muslim Arabs.

According to the legend, what impressed the Khazars during the debate that led to their conversion was that both the Christians and Muslims preferred Judaism to each other's religion. It would seem that somewhere at the heart of the persistence of Jewish influence in the medieval world was the simple fact that both Christianity and Islam were derived from Judaism. The two imperial religions came to completely overshadow the religion from which they were derived, but their very dominance also imbued Judaism with a certain prestige. Not many people dared to actually convert to Judaism as the Khazars did, but there did exist a strong tendency to gravitate towards Jewish ideas within a Christian or Muslim framework. Jewish ideas were ideas which were either associated with the Jews or which clearly served Jewish interests. Over time, these ideas made headway in both the Christian and Muslim worlds, gradually helping to create the conditions under which the Jewish Zionist movement was able to reemerge as an active force in world history during the modern era. Three ideas in particular may be said to have paved the way for the rebirth of the Jewish Zionist movement. These were: religious toleration, national self-determination and social equality.

RELIGIOUS TOLERATION

The concept of religious toleration is not normally viewed as a
Jewish idea, yet a moment's reflection will make it obvious that this
concept was the essential precondition for Jewish survival during the
medieval period. Jews, after all, were the prototypical religious minority. Outside of the remote Khazar kingdom, they were everywhere
confronted with Christian or Muslim majorities who might be incited
to attack the Jews at a moment's notice. Jews could only benefit from
a policy of religious toleration on the part of the Christian or Muslim
authorities. However, many writers see Christian or Muslim intolerance as derived from Jewish tradition. They point to the many passages
in the Jewish Scriptures where a policy of implacable hostility towards
various pagan religious beliefs and practices is enjoined. They maintain that the Christians and Muslims were influenced by these passages
to treat other religions with contempt. They were only doing, it is said,
what the Jews would have done had they been in a position to do so.

The important distinction here is that Jewish intolerance only
applied to the land of Israel. There is nothing either in the Jewish
Scriptures or in other Jewish writings which calls for the forcible
imposition of Judaism anywhere outside of the land of Israel. And
in practice, the Jews usually did tolerate rival religions in the land of
Israel as well. Pagan practices were frequently denounced but rarely
suppressed by force. The very frequency with which pagan practices
are denounced in the Jewish Scriptures testifies to their persistence.
Outside of the land of Israel, Jews normally lived in harmony with
their non-Jewish neighbors, whether pagan or Zoroastrian. Their con-
flicts with the Christians or Muslims were rarely initiated by the Jews
but rather by the Christians or Muslims, who both aspired to dominate
the entire world. Jews wished to influence the world, but only through
the power of example. Their hope was that the nation of Judah would
become a "light unto the nations", inspiring others to live according to
Jewish law. The Christian and Muslim ambition to dominate the entire
world did not derive from the Jews but rather from the fact that both
these religions were associated from the start with large empires.

Indicative of the difference between the Christian and Muslim attitude and that of the Jews was the religious policy of the Khazar kingdom. Dunlop brings out in *The History of the Jewish Khazars* that the bulk of the population under Khazar rule remained "pagan" despite the conversion of the king and nobility to Judaism. Zoroastrians, Christians and Muslims were also tolerated by the Khazars, whose capital Itil – located on the Volga river near the Caspian Sea – was noted for the many different faiths represented there. By way of contrast, most Christian kingdoms sought to completely eradicate both paganism and Islam and barely tolerated the Jews. The Muslims outside of Arabia were initially somewhat tolerant of both Judaism and Christianity but treated all pagan religions with extreme ferocity. Starting around the time of the Crusades, the Muslims also began to persecute Jewish and Christian minorities. The Christians too became much more repressive at this time, completely expelling the Jews from France and England and severely persecuting the Jews in Spain and Germany. Eventually the Jews were completely expelled from Spain as well. Religious persecution by Christians and Muslims was responsible for the death of literally hundreds of thousands of Jews during the Middle Ages, providing the Jewish people with a strong motive to advocate a policy of religious toleration everywhere.

The main promoters of religious toleration in the Middle East during the medieval period were the Seljuk Turks. During the course of the 10th and 11th centuries, the Seljuk dynasty led a coalition of Turkish tribes in the conquest of the greater part of Iran, Turkey, Syria and Iraq. Although nominal Muslims, the Seljuks believed in the separation of church and state. Ibrahim Kafesoglu stresses this point on page 89 of *A History of the Seljuks*:

> The Turks were known as state founders, that is, for their habit of establishing public laws, from the moment they appeared on the scene of history. In their early periods, especially at the time of the Gok-Turks, Uighurs, and Khazars, they followed the principle of separating religious from worldly affairs. This was a new kind of legal doctrine of state that appeared in the Islamic world with the Seljuks and must be considered one of the primary factors that assured the rise of the empire.

Kafesoglu goes so far as to call the Seljuks "secularists" and notes
on page 90 the connection between their "secularism" and their attitude towards religious minorities:

> On the one hand, secularism prepared the ground for the free
> development of science, thought, and literature, which made it
> possible for the Seljuk period, especially at the time of the empire,
> to enjoy a brilliant age; and, on the other, it lightened the obliga-
> tions to which the non-Muslim elements (*dhimmis*) in the state
> were subjected by Islamic legal prescriptions, and this assured
> winning their confidence.

Kafesoglu adds on page 115 that outside of a few Muslim centers
"the people in the empire were generally free thinkers in the Seljuk
period".

Kafesoglu saw the "secularism" of the Seljuks as characteristic of
Turkish culture, but another factor might be their link to the Khazars.
According to Tamara Talbot Rice in *The Seljuks In Asia Minor*,
Seljuk – the founder of the dynasty – was the son of a commander
in the Khazar army. Rice thinks Seljuk was probably Jewish, for he
named one of his sons Israel, a name hardly ever used by Muslims. At
some point the Seljuks converted to Islam, but they retained a favorable
attitude towards the Jews, who were permitted to occupy prominent
positions in their administration. Nizam Al-Mulk, the Grand Vizier
of the Seljuk ruler Malik Shah, complained bitterly about the tolerant
policies of the Seljuks in his tract, *The Book Of Government Or Rules
For Kings*. He states on page 164 that at one time public posts were
given only to those who were "pure alike in religion and in origin". He
continues as follows:

> But nowadays all distinction has vanished; and if a Jew admin-
> isters the affairs of Turks or does any other work for Turks, it
> is permitted; and it is the same for Christians, Zoroastrians and
> Qarmatis. Everywhere indifference is predominant; there is no zeal
> for religion, no concern for the revenue, no pity for the peasants.

Nizam Al-Mulk was a real bigot who finally prevailed on Malik Shah to at least let him persecute the Shi'ites; unfortunately for him, the Shi'ites responded by having him assassinated. Like their successors, the Ottoman Turks, the Seljuks were Sunni Muslims, but they clearly did not take their religion too seriously.

The Ottoman Turks, who gained control of the Middle East in the 15th and 16th centuries, also followed a policy of religious toleration relative to the Jews and other non-Muslim minorities. It was they who provided a refuge for the Jews expelled from Spain at the time of the Spanish Inquisition. Yet oddly enough, the Turks, like the Jews, are generally portrayed as religious fanatics in European Christian literature. The main pretext for the Crusades was that the Seljuk Turks, who were regarded as completely intolerant of Christianity, had seized control of the "Holy Land". It may well be that the real motive behind the First Crusade was the fear that the Seljuk Turks might prove amenable to increased Jewish settlement in the land of Israel. In any case, when the Ottoman Turks gained control of the land of Israel in the early 16th century, they did in fact permit large numbers of Jews to settle there. Many Jews now living in Israel are the descendants of the Jewish refugees from Spain who were permitted to settle in the "four holy cities" of Jerusalem, Hebron, Tiberias and Safed by the Ottoman Turks in the 16th century. It is also worth noting that at the present time Turkey is the only secular state in the entire Middle East and also the only one which enjoys relatively cordial relations with the state of Israel.

It is hard to say to what extent Jewish influence, beginning with the Khazars, was responsible for the traditional Turkish policy of secularism and religious toleration. What is clear is that the Jews throughout the Middle Ages tried to encourage such a policy as best they could. This is shown by the Jewish texts dating from this period which seek to compare Judaism, Christianity and Islam in such a way as to place all three religions on an equal footing. Judaism is naturally favored by the authors of these works but Christianity and Islam are treated with respect and understanding. One such work is *The Kuzari* by Judah Halevi, who lived in Spain during the 12th century at a time when both Muslim and Christian Crusaders were contending for control of

Toledo, his home town. It is a fictional account of the legendary debate between Judaism, Christianity and Islam which supposedly induced the Khazars to convert to Judaism. Another such work was published by Moshe Perlmann under the title, *Ibn Kammuna's Examination of the Three Faiths*. Ibn Kammuna lived in 13th century Baghdad; in 1284, he inspired a riot against him by writing a book comparing Judaism, Christianity and Islam. Ibn Kammuna did not actually say that he thought Judaism superior to Islam, but the mere fact that he suggested that Islam was open to criticism was enough to condemn him. He escaped the rioters but died soon thereafter.

In one way or another, the idea that all "monotheistic" religions basically teach the same truth gradually became an important part of the "mystical" religious culture of the Muslim world. This idea was expressed as follows by Jalalu'l-Din Rumi, a 13th century Sufi mystic:

> The lamps are different, but the Light is the same:
>   it comes from Beyond.
> If thou keep looking at the lamp, thou art lost; for thence arises
>   the appearance of number and plurality.
> Fix thy gaze upon the Light, and thou art delivered from the
>   dualism inherent in the finite body.
> O thou who art the kernel of Existence, the disagreement between
>   Moslem, Zoroastrian and Jew depends on the standpoint.

These lines appear in the poem, "The One True Light", on page 166 of *Rumi: Poet And Mystic* edited and translated by Reynold Nicholson. By way of contrast, it was not until the 17th century that similar views made their first tentative appearance in the Christian world. Throughout the Middle Ages, toleration of Jews by Christians was always granted within the framework of an ideology which explicitly stated that Judaism was a diabolic phenomenon which really ought to be suppressed. Needless to say, such toleration was generally brief and sporadic, to be followed by persecution or expulsion.

Religious toleration finally made its appearance in the Christian world mainly as a result of two historical developments: first the Protestant Reformation, and secondly the American and French

Revolutions. The Protestants were initially not all that tolerant of religious differences, but as a result of their numerous wars with the Catholics, the idea gradually became established in Christian Europe that religious conflict was a bad thing. The American and French Revolutions carried this idea a step further by introducing the principle of the separation of church and state. These historical developments were accompanied by a significant shift in attitudes towards Jews and Judaism. Like earlier "heretics", the Protestants were often accused of "Judaizing" tendencies by the Catholics due to their reverence for the so-called "Old Testament", which they carried to the point of learning Hebrew and studying with rabbis. And both the American and French Revolutions were associated with the position that Jews could be citizens of the new secular state with the same rights and obligations as Christian citizens. In Europe as in the Middle East, pro-Jewish attitudes and advocacy of religious toleration tended to go together. This connection was inevitable in view of the status of the Jews as the prototypical religious minority in both the Muslim and Christian worlds.

What is difficult to determine is the extent to which the Jewish people not only benefited from religious toleration but helped to bring it about. There were relatively few Jews in Western Europe and North America when the idea of religious toleration first became established in these areas in the 17th and 18th centuries. Most historians therefore view the acceptance of Jews in "the West" as a gift that fell from the skies and not something that the Jews themselves achieved. Of course, it could be argued that had the Jewish people not persevered in the face of persecution and discrimination throughout the Middle Ages, "heretical" and secular thinking would not have been so likely to emerge subsequently. But the validity of this argument hinges on the question of whether the early Protestants and secularists actually looked to the Jews as a model. Given the status of the Jews as a despised and persecuted minority, why would anyone wish to imitate them? However, it cannot be denied that the Protestants were fascinated with the "Old Testament" and the way of life which it portrayed. What was there in the Jewish Scriptures that was so important to them? The answer hinges on another Jewish idea: national self-determination.

NATIONAL SELF-DETERMINATION

Like religious toleration, national self-determination is not generally viewed as a Jewish idea, and yet its relationship to Judaism is obvious. From the start the Jews defined themselves as a nation, different
from other nations perhaps, but a nation all the same. When other
nations came and tried to force the Jews to conform to their ways, the
Jews resisted. To be sure, they did not resist in the name of the general
principle of national self-determination but rather in the name of their
own traditional laws and religion. All the same they did resist, and the
fact of their resistance marked them in the eyes of their neighbors as a
stubborn people who did not submit easily to foreign conquerors. This
impression was confirmed in the eyes of a large part of the entire world
by the lengthy and bloody struggle which the Jewish people waged
against the Roman empire. As a result of this history, the Jews even
in exile were perceived as an independent nation who had lost their
homeland but still maintained their ancient traditions and language.

Did the Jewish insistence on national self-determination also influence other nations to strive to remain independent? The desire for
national independence was certainly a major component in the history
of the Protestant Reformation. Throughout northern Europe – among
the Czechs, the Dutch, the Swiss, the Germans, the English and the
Scandinavians – the Protestant rebellion against the rule of Rome was
associated with an upsurge of national feeling. One manifestation of
this trend was the insistence of the Protestants on translating the Bible
into the vernacular language of their country rather than continuing
to study it in Latin. Another manifestation was the opposition of the
Protestants to the imperial ambitions of the Holy Roman Empire, whose
Habsburg rulers were closely aligned with the Papacy. Everywhere the
Protestants sought to bring into being national churches which spoke
the language of the country and defended its political independence.
As a result, the Protestants played a major role in the emergence of the
many independent European nation-states out of the undifferentiated
"Christendom" of medieval Europe.

One of the first peoples among whom Protestantism took root on
a mass scale were the Czechs. During the early 15th century they came

under the influence of the teachings of John Hus, a religious reformer who was burnt at the stake by the Roman Catholic church in 1415. Hus was burnt as a "heretic" because he believed that Christians did not necessarily have to obey the orders of the Pope. On page 161 of *John Hus' Concept of the Church*, Matthew Spinka offers the following revealing summary of the arguments which Hus directed against the "doctors" of the Roman Catholic church in opposition to the doctrine of Papal supremacy:

> Hus further argues that since the doctors deny such a right to the critical examination of the papal commands and profess to obey the papal or royal orders without a demur or scrutiny, they would have to obey even if they were ordered to kill all the Jews in Prague, as they accepted the command to exterminate the Christian Neapolitans...Thus there could ensure a terrible persecution of Christians.

As it so happened, Prague was one of the few cities in Europe where there still remained a good sized Jewish community at the end of the Middle Ages. Both Hus and his more radical followers, who were called Taborites, sought to maintain good relations with the Jewish community of Prague. R.W. Seton-Watson states on page 73 of *A History of the Czechs and Slovaks*: "It may be noted in passing that the Taborites were often reproached for the relative tolerance which they showed towards the Jews." Seton-Watson also brings out on page 78 that the early Czech Protestants were strongly influenced by Jewish tradition in their efforts to achieve national independence. He cites a follower of Hus, John of Rokycan, who stated in 1458 that "it would be better to follow the example of the judges of Israel and transform Bohemia into a Republic, if there were no native worthy to bear the royal crown."

It was at this time that George of Podebrad, whom Seton-Watson characterizes as "the first heretic and elected king in the Europe of his day", was chosen as king of the Czechs by a national assembly. The response of the Roman Catholic church was to send John of Capistrano, a noted preacher and member of the Papal Inquisition, to

Breslau to launch an attack on the local Jewish community. Frederick
Heymann, on page 80 of *George of Bohemia: King of Heretics*, states:

> But the act that was perhaps most instrumental in making
> Capistrano's stay in Breslau noteworthy and memorable through
> the ages was the way in which he helped to bring about and to
> direct the great persecution of the local Jewish community. Fierce
> attacks against the Jews were a standard element of his sermons.
> It was in this atmosphere of a boundless religious antisemitism
> largely created or at least whipped up by Capistrano that accu-
> sations of repeated debasements of hosts (which began to bleed
> when wounded, or jumped out of the fire into which they had
> been thrown) as well as charges of ritual murder were laid to sev-
> eral members of the old well-established Jewish community of the
> city. The ensuing trial was largely master-minded by Capistrano,
> who even instructed the hangman how most effectively to torture
> the "criminals". As a result of confessions thus obtained, forty-
> one Jews were burned at the stake, while the rest of the members
> of the Jewish community had to leave Breslau.

Just as Hus had feared, the Pope tried to demonstrate his supremacy
by inducing the Czechs to kill the Jews. George of Bohemia responded,
somewhat belatedly, by ordering John of Capistrano to leave Breslau
in 1454. For the Czech Protestants, defense of the Jews against Roman
Catholic persecution was closely bound up with their own claim to
national independence.

A similar pattern can be shown in all those areas where the emerg-
ing Protestant movement was able to come into contact with local
Jewish communities. In *The Radical Reformation*, George Huntston
Williams brings out numerous examples of direct Jewish influence on
the early Protestant movement in the Rhineland and Bavaria. On page
189, he describes the teachings of Augustin Bader, a radical Protestant
leader in Augsburg in the 1520s. Bader called for the elimination of
all Christian sacraments offensive to Jews and Muslims; and together
with his followers, he "sought out Jewish communities, tried to learn
Hebrew, and interpreted the Old Testament and the Apocrypha with

the help of rabbis." He was tortured and killed by Habsburg troops in 1530. On page 252, Williams offers the following description of a group of Protestant "Judaizers" in Strasbourg in the 1520s led by a weaver named Saltzmann:

> The Judaizers would accept only the Pentateuch as divinely bind-
> ing, denied the Trinity, insisted that there was but one God, and
> considered Jesus a false prophet who was rightly put to death. For
> this Saltzmann was decapitated shortly before Christmas 1527.

Radical Judaizers were also active in the town of Muenster, which proclaimed itself the "new Jerusalem" or "new Zion" in 1534. This movement too was drowned in blood by the forces of the Roman Catholic church. Generally speaking, the closer the ties of a given Protestant sect to Jews and Judaism, the more savagely it was perse-cuted and suppressed.

The pro-Jewish thrust of the early Protestant Reformation was most clearly manifested in the Protestant assault on the Catholic cult of "the Host". In the 13th century, the Roman Catholic church had officially adopted the doctrine of the "Real Presence", according to which the wafers and wine which the Christians consumed in church actually turned into the real flesh and blood of Jesus Christ during the ceremony. Not satisfied with thus emphasizing the cannibalistic nature of their religion, the Romans Catholics then used this emphasis as a pretext on which to persecute Jews for allegedly desecrating "the Host" – the wafers – in some manner. It was on charges of "desecra-tion of the Host" that the Jews of Breslau were persecuted by John of Capistrano. The response of the Protestants was to denounce the doc-trine of the "Real Presence" and call into question the entire Christian tradition of pretending to eat a Jew for brunch. In Germany, opposi-tion to the cult of "the Host" was most intense among the radical Protestants called Anabaptists. Claus-Peter Clasen notes on page 113 of *Anabaptism*:

> In general the Anabaptists refused to partake of the Lord's Supper
> in the churches. From time to time Anabaptists were discovered who

had not attended the Lord's Supper for years, sometimes even ten or twenty years. Those who under pressure finally agreed to attend church services still vehemently refused to take the Sacrament; the few who did simply regarded it as bread and wine only.

Clasen adds on page 114: "In the 1530s, some Anabaptists in Hesse and Thuringia seem to have discarded the traditional Lord's Supper entirely." And even the more conservative Protestants such as the Calvinists still rejected the doctrine of the "Real Presence". Only Luther among the Protestant leaders continued to uphold this doctrine in a modified form, substituting his own theory of "consubstantiation" of the wafers and wine for the Catholic doctrine of "transubstantiation".

Like Mohammed, Luther had begun his career as a religious leader by adopting a pro-Jewish stance and calling for greater toleration of the Jews by Christians. But as the conflict between Catholics and Protestants intensified, Luther changed his views and began to denounce the Jews. The tragedy of German Protestantism was that German nationalism could not be separated from German imperialism. The Holy Roman Empire was a German empire; its Kaisers had come from various dynasties, but they had all been German. At the time of the Protestant Reformation, the Holy Roman Empire was ruled by the Habsburg dynasty, which came from Austria. The German Protestants, including the Lutherans, were hostile to Habsburg rule, which they associated with Roman Catholic domination; but in the back of their minds was already the aspiration to found a new empire under Protestant auspices. This aspiration, which came to fruition in the 19th century with the establishment of Bismarck's Second Reich, caused Luther and the Lutherans to eventually adopt a much more hostile attitude towards the Jews than the other Protestants. They too associated Judaism with national independence, but the only national independence which the Lutherans respected was their own.

The Protestant sense of identification with the Jews was strongest among those nations, such as the Czechs or the Dutch, who had no great imperial ambitions. Protestants of this type naturally gravitated towards a conception of Europe as a federation of nations, a concept which was actually articulated by George of Bohemia. It was therefore no accident that the formation of the League of Nations in 1919 coincided with the formation of the newly independent state of Czechoslovakia, nor was it an accident that the dismemberment of Czechoslovakia in 1938 at Munich coincided with the start of the Nazi Holocaust directed against the Jews. It is also worth noting that the main supplier of heavy weapons to the state of Israel in its War of Independence in 1948 was the Communist government of Czechoslovakia. In general, the more Europe resembled a federation of nations, the better its treatment of the Jews; and the more Europe was dominated by some empire, be it Holy Roman or Nazi, the worse its treatment of the Jews. The struggle for national independence and pro-Jewish sentiment were linked in Europe, first by the "Old Testament" model of Hebrew independence, and second by the example of the European Jews, whose perseverance in the face of persecution could not help but impress the Europeans. How they reacted to the Jewish example, however, depended not only on their national outlook but also on their social background. Of all the Jewish ideas, the most deeply rooted and the most explosive was the concept of social equality.

SOCIAL EQUALITY

In Germany, for example, most of the Anabaptist "Judaizers" came from the artisan class. Conversely, the anti-Semitic Lutherans came mainly from middle class backgrounds and even from the nobility, which in northern Germany was hostile to the imperial pretensions of the Habsburgs. Among the Anabaptists, pro-Jewish sentiments went hand in hand with a radical social program. Karl Kautsky, the early 20th century German socialist leader, wrote an entire book, *Communism in Central Europe in the Time of the Reformation*, describing the radical social ideas of the German Anabaptists. However, like most Marxist writers, Kautsky paid no attention whatsoever to the role of the Jews in stimulating radical social thought among non-Jews. Although himself a disciple of a Jewish radical, Karl Marx, and although closely associated with such Jewish radicals as Rosa Luxemburg, Kautsky ignored the pro-Jewish tendencies of the Anabaptists and referred to the Jews only a few times in his book, always in connection with money. Like Marx himself, Kautsky thought of the Jews primarily as money-lenders, bankers and merchants. This stereotype of the Jewish people was taken over by the Marxists from the Christians, who had traditionally used it as one means among many of justifying their anti-Jewish outbursts.

In reality, most European Jews were artisans in the medieval period or workers in the modern period. Money-lenders, bankers and merchants formed only a small minority of the Jewish people, but anti-Semites everywhere focused on this minority, exaggerating its power and accusing it of all kinds of diabolic practices. Rich Jews did consti-tute the dominant social class among the European Jews, but rule by the rich was hardly unique to Jewish society. What did distinguish the social structure of the European Jews from that of their neighbors was the almost complete absence of Jewish farmers or landowners. By law, Jews were barred from owning land under the ghetto system. Usually confined to a small ghetto whose gates were locked at night, European Jews constituted an overwhelmingly urban people. They were excluded from the countryside, except as peddlers, and they were also excluded from the feudal social structure of lord and vassal. This meant that there were no Jewish nobles, no Jewish aristocratic class, no Jewish lords and ladies. Respect for inherited rank and status was therefore much weaker among the Jews than it was among their non-Jewish neighbors. This simple fact, taken together with the long history of Jewish involvement in movements for social equality stretching back to the days of the Habiru, inevitably imbued European Jewish society with a radical tone relative to the surrounding non-Jewish society.

In *Byzantine Jewry*, Andrew Sharf describes the complex interac-tion between Jewish and Christian radicalism in the Byzantine empire after the rise of Islam. Jews living under Muslim rule in nearby Iraq were slow to accept the defeat of their Messianic hope. In 645 a Jew named Pallughtha led a rebellion of Jewish "weavers, barbers and full-ers"; and around 700, another Jewish revolt broke out led by a Persian Jew named Abu Isa al-Isfahani. Al-Isfahani accepted both Jesus and Mohammed as legitimate prophets but called for the return of the Jewish people to the land of Israel. The rebellion, which was suppressed by the Muslims, led to the formation of a Jewish Messianic sect in Syria which "preached a militant, Palestinian-centered nationalism" until the 10th century. These teachings were in turn taken up by Byzantine Jews, leading to a decree by the Byzantine Caesar Leo 3 around 721 commanding all Jews to be baptized. Sharf thinks the main motive for this decree was fear that Jewish radicalism would promote Christian "heresy". Leo 3 saw Jewish influence at work in the spread of a radical "heresy" called Montanism, and in the 9th century, a Byzantine Christian sect called "Athinganians" openly preached adherence to Jewish law, excepting only the substitution of baptism for circumcision. Sharf thinks the doctrine of these sects may have been modeled on the teachings of a Christian convert to Judaism named Severus or Serenus who led a Messianic uprising of Syrian Jews around 720. Ironically, Leo 3, who came from Syria, was himself viewed as something of a radical by his contemporaries because of his "iconoclasm" or hostility to graven images. Sharf thinks his persecution of Jews and Christian "heretics" was intended, at least in part, to counter the suspicion that his destruction of Christian icons was caused by his own covert Jewish sympathies.

In Iraq, Syria and the Byzantine empire, the main support for both Jewish Messianism and Christian "heresy" came from the artisan class and in particular weavers and other workers in the garment trades. A similar pattern developed in medieval Europe, where Jews were noted for their skill in the manufacture of clothing. The cultivation of silk worms and manufacture of silk cloth was unknown in Europe until it was introduced by Jewish weavers from the Byzantine empire into Italy. However, once the ghetto system was instituted, Jews were gradually driven from the more lucrative garment trades and forced to concentrate on refurbishing old clothing. In *A History of Jewish Crafts and Guilds* on page 147, Mark Wischnitzer cites the following contemporary description by an Italian doctor of Jewish life in Italy around 1700:

> Nearly all Jews, especially the lower classes, to which most of them belong, are employed in work at which they must sit or stand. They are mostly giving to sewing and furbishing up old clothes:

the women, above all, whether married or single, make their living by needlework...Besides, in most cities the Jews live miserably, shut up in narrow alleys, and their women at all seasons stand during their work by open windows to get what light there is: this causes them to incur various afflictions of the head, such as headache, earache, toothache, cold, sore throats, and sore eyes. Many of them, especially of the poorer class, are hard of hearing and blear-eyed.

So well established was the association between Jews and refurbishing old clothes in medieval Europe that – as Leon Poliakov notes on page 196 of Volume 1 of *The History of Anti-Semitism* – rag pickers in France continued to be called "Jews" for many centuries after the expulsion of all Jews from France in the early 14th century. The ragpickers guild of Paris eventually lodged a formal protest against this usage.

It was mainly through contacts between Jewish and Christian artisans in the garment trades that radical ideas spread from one community to the other. In *The Pursuit of the Millennium*, Norman Cohn brings out that the growth of the cloth industry in the Rhineland was the main cause of the emergence of radical millenarian movements there during the Middle Ages. Cohn notes on page 53 that among weavers in the Rhineland "one can detect an apparently unbroken tradition of revolutionary millenarianism continuing down to the sixteenth century". The Rhineland was also the main center of Jewish settlement in Germany. Cohn feels that the most influential "prophetic system" in Europe prior to the rise of Marxism was based on the teachings of Joachim of Fiore, a 12th century monk who believed in a synthesis of Jewish and Christian doctrine. He taught that humanity would pass through three stages: the Age of the Law, based on Judaism; the Age of the Son, based on Christianity; and the Age of the Spirit, in which distinctions between the different monotheistic religions would disappear and all people would commune in a spirit of freedom, joy and love. These teachings became immensely popular in Germany, culminating in the emergence of overtly pro-Jewish radical sects in the Rhineland during the Reformation.

Underlying the various Messianic and millenarian beliefs which flourished among Jewish and Christians artisans during the Middle Ages was the egalitarian spirit of the Jewish community. A good description of this spirit appears on page 120 of *Life Is With People* by Mark Zborowski and Elizabeth Herzog. Describing a traditional Jewish "shtetl" in Eastern Europe, they state:

> The spirit of the talmudic training is the spirit of the shtetl itself. The same elements are present in the attitudes towards scholastic authority and in the attitudes towards social status. In any area, recognition of a clearly defined and minutely graded hierarchy is combined with an equally clear assumption that potentially all men are equal. The man at the top of the social or economic scale is subject to question and disapproval on the part of the poor and humble. The deeds and words of any leader are subject to criticism and discussion, if not openly then secretly, at home or in the besmedresh [shul or house of study]. For every individual the final appeal must be to his own judgment; if the subject matter itself is beyond him, then he must debate with himself the reliability of conflicting authorities.

In other words, Jewish society did recognize social distinctions based primarily on wealth or scholarship, but these distinctions did not have a hereditary, fixed character. There were no hereditary aristocrats and also no hereditary serfs. Power and prestige were based on actual accomplishment and therefore anyone could aspire to a leading position in the community. The transient nature of all social distinctions was further emphasized by the constant threat of persecution, which could easily strike at the rich and powerful as well as the poor and humble.

Indeed, one of the main goals of the ghetto system and the frequent anti-Semitic outbursts which accompanied it was to reduce all Jews to a state of poverty and degradation. The following description of the ghetto of Palermo in Italy, written by a 15th century Jewish observer, appears on page 567 of *A History of the Jewish People*, edited by Haim Ben-Sasson:

> Palermo...has about eight hundred and fifty Jewish householders all gathered in one street, very well situated. And they...are poor craftsmen of different kinds, copper and iron smiths and porters and men engaged in all kinds of heavy work. They are despised by the gentiles, being all ragged and filthy. And they must wear a red cloth as broad as a gold piece on their hearts as a sign.

Of course, in many Jewish communities there were also wealthy Jews, including some who lent money and charged high rates of interest. But it was close to impossible for a Jewish family to remain wealthy over several generations, since the Christian authorities were always seeking ways to seize the assets of Jews whom they knew to be rich. Before the last remaining Jews were expelled from England at the end of the 13th century, they were tortured in prison to make them reveal where their money was hidden. The method the English chose was to extract one tooth from their mouth each day that they refused to talk. Yet in Shakespeare's fictional play, "The Merchant of Venice", it is the Jew who demands a pound of flesh from his poor Christian victim. At the time this play was written, there were no Jews in England, nor had there been for hundreds of years.

When the English finally did decide to readmit Jews to England, it was as a result of the emergence of a radical Protestant movement in the 17th century. The English radical Protestants, who were called Levelers, were strong advocates of social equality. They played a major role in the English Revolution of 1640, which resulted in the execution of the king and a general attack on aristocratic and feudal rule. Under the leadership of Oliver Cromwell, the English Parliament then agreed to take up the issue of the readmission of Jews to England. A Jewish leader from Holland, Manasseh ben-Israel, was invited to England to address the Parliament on behalf of the Jews. Nahum Sokolow, in Volume 1 of his *History of Zionism*, brings out that the writings of Manasseh ben-Israel were translated into English and circulated in England during the 1650s, while Cromwell was still in power. Sokolow also shows that many of the radical Protestants favored not only the readmission of Jews to England but the return of the Jews to the land of Israel. On page 43 he cites the radical Protestant leader Thomas

Brightman, who wrote in 1641: "What! Shall they return to Jerusalem again? There is nothing more certain: the prophets do everywhere confirm it." Although the formal readmission of Jews to England was delayed by the restoration of the English monarchy in 1660, it is clear that in England as elsewhere, pro-Jewish sentiment and belief in social equality tended to go together.

The clearest proof of this connection is provided by the French Revolution of 1789. At the very same time as they adopted the slogan, "Liberty, Equality, Fraternity", the French also decided to grant the rights of citizenship to French Jews. Like the English Revolution of 1640, the French Revolution of 1789 was directed primarily against the aristocracy, which was also the main bulwark of anti-Jewish sentiment in Europe. The Roman Catholic church, which was primarily responsible for articulating this sentiment, was dominated by cardinals and bishops from the aristocratic class. It was for this reason that the French revolutionary assault on the aristocracy also took the form of an assault on the Roman Catholic church, many of whose leaders were sent to the guillotine along with their aristocratic patrons. For the next 100 years, whoever sided with the French Revolution tended also to side with the Jews, while those who opposed the French Revolution also tended to oppose the Jews. And throughout the period from the Protestant Reformation to the 20th century, the slow improvement in the status of the Jews and the gradual spread of a belief in social equality went hand in hand. This connection was also noted by the enemies of the Jews, including Adolf Hitler, who explicitly described social equality as a Jewish idea in his writings. It was therefore no coincidence that the attempt of the Nazis to reestablish a hierarchical and authoritarian social order in Europe was accompanied by a genocidal assault on the Jewish people.

KABBALAH

Just as the Nazi assault helped to precipitate the birth of Israel, so too did earlier Christian assaults help to precipitate the revival of the Jewish Messianic movement. Raphael Patai notes on page 155 of *The Messiah Texts* that there were at least nine separate Messianic movements in various parts of the Jewish world between 1087 and 1172 CE as a result of the First and Second Crusades. These Crusades were directed not only against the Muslims but also the Jews, who were slaughtered in the thousands by the Crusaders both in Europe and in Jerusalem. But like the earlier Jewish Messianic uprisings in Iraq and Syria in the wake of the Muslim conquest, the uprisings touched off by the Crusades were easily suppressed. By the 12th century the Jewish population was too small and scattered to represent much of a military threat to anyone. Jewish Messianism continued, but more as an intellectual tendency than an active movement. The name of this tendency was Kabbalah.

Kabbalah eventually developed a radical reputation among Christian Europeans, but it was not generally perceived by them as a Messianic tradition. In European eyes, it came to be seen as a form of "the occult", a compendium of magical lore which could be learned and utilized quite apart from Judaism, to say nothing of Messianism. Even Jewish authors such as Gershom Scholem, whose numerous scholarly studies of Kabbalah have dominated the field for the past 75 years, have tended to play down the Messianic side of Kabbalah and stress instead its affinity with classical philosophy, particularly Gnosticism. Kabbalah certainly contained both magical and philosophical components, but at its heart was a form of Jewish Messianism no less radical than earlier forms. It was the Jewish Messianism of the Middle Ages, a Messianism that could not proclaim itself openly because the restoration of Judah was not at that time a realistic goal. Instead Kabbalah aimed at a kind of intellectual restoration, a Judah of the mind which preceded and stimulated the emergence of the mass Zionist movement led by Shabtai Zvi in the 17th century. Kabbalah was the one original Jewish idea of the Middle Ages, and it remained the main expression of Jewish Zionist thought until well into the 19th century.

Kabbalah was first and foremost a literary tradition, and the great book of this tradition was *The Zohar*. Originally written in Aramaic, it was eventually translated into Hebrew and Yiddish but only excerpts were available in other languages prior to modern times. The first English translation did not appear until 1984 in a five volume edition translated by Harry Sperling and Maurice Simon. *The Zohar* purports to be a verbatim record of a discussion of the Torah conducted by the rabbi Shimon bar Yochai and his pupils during the 2nd century CE. Since Shimon bar Yochai was an actual historical figure and *The Zohar* was written in his language, Aramaic, it was generally accepted as an authentic text until modern times. However, modern Jewish scholars have shown that *The Zohar* was actually composed during the late 13th century by a Jewish Kabbalist in Spain named Moses de Leon. He seized on Shimon bar Yochai as the hero of *The Zohar* because the actual Shimon bar Yochai was best remembered for the fact that he had refused to accept Roman rule after the defeat of the Jewish forces in the "Second Jewish War". Instead he had hidden in a cave for 13 years, and *The Zohar* was a kind of literary reconstruction by Moses de Leon of what Shimon bar Yochai and his pupils might have thought and said during those years. He was able to write it in Aramaic because Jewish rabbis and scholars were traditionally expected to learn Aramaic due to the fact that a large part of the Talmud is written in that language.

The thoughts which Moses de Leon ascribed to Shimon bar Yochai and his pupils were Kabbalist, Zionist and Messianic. Philosophic discussions of the nature of the universe are interspersed with references to the coming of the Messiah and the restoration of the nation of Judah. For example, on page 249 of Volume 4 it is stated: "At the time when the dead will be awakened and be in readiness for the resurrection in the Holy Land, legions upon legions will arise on the soil of Galilee, as it is there that the Messiah is destined to reveal himself." This passage could be interpreted as mere wishful thinking, but in practice the actual effect of *The Zohar* was to motivate legions upon legions of rabbis to actually move to the Holy Land in order to await the Messiah. During the 1500s, literally thousands of Kabbalists, most of them from Spain or Portugal, emigrated to the "four holy cities" of Jerusalem, Hebron, Tiberias and Safed in the land of Israel, which had come under Turkish rule at the beginning of the 16th century. They were fleeing from the Spanish Inquisition, but the reason why they fled to the land of Israel was because Shimon bar Yochai in *The Zohar* had stated over and over again that only there could the Torah really be understood and implemented. It was the uncompromising Zionist spirit of *The Zohar*, more than any other single factor, which inspired the revival of the Jewish Messianic movement on a large scale at the end of the Middle Ages and the beginning of the modern era.

The Middle Ages was not a good time for the Jewish people. Penned into walled ghettos or squalid slums, the miniscule Jewish communities of this period were periodically ravaged by Christian or Muslim mobs bent on avenging some imaginary insult. Particularly galling were the numerous Christian persecutions inspired by charges of "ritual murder" or "desecration of the host". Precisely because the Christians themselves met each week to pretend to eat the flesh and drink the blood of Jesus Christ, they felt an overwhelming need to accuse the Jews of putting Christian blood in their Passover matzohs or stabbing the Christian wafers and making them bleed. Kabbalah was essentially the Jewish response to this situation. It abandoned any thought of a normal Jewish life in the Diaspora and instead glorified and idealized Jewish life in the land of Israel. On a philosophic plane, it denigrated material reality in general as a mere "garment" or "shell" for the invisible world of the spirit. This radical rejection of the material world was inspired by the harsh conditions under which the Jews of that time were forced to live. Kabbalah originated in southern France and Spain during the persecutions of the 13th and 14th centuries, and by the 16th century it had become the orthodox form of Judaism for most Jews. Joseph Caro, the 16th century author of what became the standard handbook of orthodox Judaism, the *Shulchan Aruch*, was a Spanish Kabbalist who emigrated to Safed in the land of Israel and claimed the right to ordain all Jewish rabbis everywhere from there.

Although Gershom Scholem viewed Kabbalah mainly as a philosophy, his biography of Shabtai Zvi, entitled *Sabbatai Sevi: The Mystical Messiah*. contains ample evidence of its Zionist and Messianic side. Shabtai Zvi was an obscure Kabbalist who became convinced that he was the Messiah destined to bring about the ingathering of the exiles and the restoration of the nation of Judah. During the decade of the 1660s he led a mass movement of Jews throughout the Mediterranean region who believed in his claims and expected him to compel the Turkish Sultan to permit the Jews to return to the land of Israel. Unfortunately, threatened with death by the Sultan, Shabtai Zvi broke down and agreed to convert to Islam. On page 392, Scholem offers the following description of Shabtai Zvi's supporters:

> "The frenzied rabble", "the miserable beggars", "the poorest of the land", and like expressions recur frequently in contemporary reports. Perhaps the most withering social definition was given by the emissary from Casale who wrote that "everyone who was in distress and trouble, and all vain and light persons followed him".

Like Kabbalah in general, the movement led by Shabtai Zvi was an expression of desperation. It was not realistic to expect that an unarmed Kabbalist, surrounded by unarmed followers, could somehow compel the Turkish government to set aside the claims of Islam and meekly accept not only Jewish emigration to the land of Israel but the establishment of a Messianic Jewish state there. All the same, the movement led by Shabtai Zvi did have the effect of popularizing the Zionist ideology of Kabbalah among the Jewish masses. It helped to set the stage for the emergence of the modern Zionist movement, which was a direct outgrowth of the Messianic movements of the pre-modern period.

All the Jewish ideas of the pre-modern period tended in this same direction. It was the tolerant attitude of the Turkish government towards the Jews which led Shabtai Zvi to believe that he actually had a chance to transform the Sultan into a Zionist. It was belief in the concept of national self-determination which led the radical English Protestants to begin advocating the return of the Jews to the land of Israel only a few years before the emergence of Shabtai Zvi as a Messianic leader. It was faith in social equality which led "the poorest of the land" among the Jews to believe that they had the right and the ability to make history. And after percolating slowly into the consciousness of the Christian and Muslim worlds during the pre-modern period, the Jewish ideas of this era went on to become the dominant ideas of modern times. Today they have become so widely accepted that it is hard to remember how radical they once appeared. What is also hard to remember is that these ideas were sustained and propagated by "miserable beggars" who endured centuries of torture and persecution to keep alive the flame of Jewish egalitarianism.

THE JUDEO-MASONIC TRADITION

Anyone familiar with the European anti-Semitic literature of the 19th and early 20th centuries will be struck by the extent to which this literature is directed not only against the Jews but also against the Freemasons. In the so-called "Protocols of the Elder of Zion" and similar expositions of a mythical Jewish conspiracy to rule the world, the Freemasons are assigned a major role in the alleged conspiracy.

There are two obvious reasons for this attitude. In the first place, Freemasonry was generally perceived as tolerant of Jews. Jews could become Freemasons – although not many did – because members were not required to believe in Christianity, only in the existence of a "Supreme Being". Freemasons were in favor of freedom of religion and took the lead in 18th and 19th century England, France and the United States in efforts to remove restrictions on the right of Jews to practice their religion in peace. And in the second place, Freemasonry originated as a secret society, whose very existence was concealed from the public prior to 1717. Known both for secrecy and pro-Jewish sentiments, the Freemasons were perfect candidates for inclusion in fantasies of a secret Jewish plot to rule the world.

There is also a third, slightly less obvious reason for the condemnation of the Freemasons in anti-Semitic literature. The 19th century Roman Catholic church viewed Jews and Freemasons as its principal foes. A large proportion of the anti-Semitic tracts of this period were written either by practicing Catholics or by people from a Catholic background. The Roman Catholic church also sponsored numerous attacks on the Freemasons during this same period, including an anti-Masonic Papal encyclical entitled "Humanum Genus", issued by Pope Leo the Thirteenth in 1884. It was the Roman Catholic church which first linked the Jews and Freemasons together and developed many of the accusations against both groups which were later to be taken up by other anti-Semites. Jews and Freemasons were perceived by the

Roman Catholics as the vanguard of modernism, the secret sponsors of atheism, secularism and hedonism in the modern world.

Although I come from a Jewish background, the knowledge that Jews and Masons were said to be involved in a conspiracy together never aroused much interest in the Freemasons in me. I thought the whole idea of a secret society rather silly, and what I knew of Masonic doctrine did not impress me. Some claimed the Masons were derived from the workmen who built the First Temple in Jerusalem in the days of Solomon. Others asserted the Masons grew out of the guilds of stonemasons who built the great cathedrals in Europe during the Middle Ages. The first claim is clearly absurd and the second only led me to associate the Masons with the persecutions of Jews which took place in the shadow of those same cathedrals. Since the Masons were condemned by my enemies, I assumed that there must be something good about them, but I was not strongly impelled to find out what it was.

What started me thinking along different lines was a book published in 1989 by John J. Robinson entitled *Born In Blood: The Lost Secrets Of Freemasonry*. Robinson was an American amateur historian with an interest in the Middle Ages and the Crusades. His study of the Knights Templar, a medieval crusading order, led him to the view that the Freemasons were formed as a result of the suppression of the Knights Templar by the Roman Catholic church in the early 14th century. In England the Templar order had several months advance warning of impending arrest, and most members were able to go into hiding. Robinson thinks they formed a secret society which then played a major role in the English uprising of 1381 known as Wat Tyler's rebellion. Robinson brings out that Tyler is also a Masonic title for the sentry who guards the door to Masonic meetings. Robinson argues that the Masons developed an ambivalent attitude towards Christianity as a result of the fact that many of the members of the Knights Templar were tortured and executed by agents of the Roman Catholic church at the time of the suppression of the order in 1307. *Born In Blood* is written in a reasonable, factual style and it convinced me that the Masons were in fact derived from the Knights Templar just as Robinson said. Particularly convincing is Robinson's derivation of a whole series of obscure Masonic terms from medieval French, the language of the Knights Templar in England as well as France. Tyler he derives from "tailleur", which now means "tailor" but whose literal meaning is "one who cuts", an appropriate term for a sentry who was supposed to stand with a drawn sword in his hand.

Seeing the Masons as derived from the Knights Templar made them appear both better and worse than I had previously thought. On the one hand, their status as a secret society no longer seemed so silly. The Masons did not originate as medieval guild members indulging a love of ritual but as hunted fugitives who had every reason to conceal their very existence from the authorities. Robinson theorizes very plausibly that also in later generations the Masons attracted genuine rebels against Church and State for whom secrecy was a necessity and not a game. On the other hand, the Knights Templar were associated with many more crimes against the Jewish people than any stone masons could possibly have been. The Knights Templar grew out of the First Crusade of 1096, whose members murdered whole communities of Jews in the Rhineland before departing for the Middle East. When they arrived in Jerusalem these same Crusaders murdered every single Jew in the entire city. The Knights Templar were clearly fanatic anti-Semites prior to their suppression in the 14th century. How did it happen that such people should have evolved into the tolerant, free thinking Masons of the modern era?

Or did they? The Masons, after all, remained just as focused on Jerusalem as the Knights Templar had been. Robinson reveals that when Masons are initiated into full fledged membership, they are taught the legend of Hiram Abiff. He was supposedly the real architect of the Temple of Solomon, who was murdered by traitors. Robinson sees him as an allegorical symbol for Jacques de Molay, the last Grand Master of the Templar order who was burnt at the stake in 1314 on orders of the Pope. The Masons are enjoined to continue his work, which amounts to a call to continue the European quest to conquer Jerusalem. Freemasonry originated in England, which as it turned out was the European country which did in fact follow in the footsteps of the Crusaders and conquer Jerusalem at the end of World War One. And Robinson himself, who was not a Mason, ends his book with a disquisition on how the Temple Mount is sacred to three religions, all three of which should have some place of worship on the site of the Mount.

Reading Robinson's book hardened a conviction in me that there is something called the Judeo-Masonic tradition which has played a major role in the history of the past 500 years or so. At the core of this tradition is the memory of the Temple. The Knights Templar were called that because their original headquarters was located on the Temple Mount, in the mosque of al-Aksa, which they had seized from the Muslims. And before the Christians and Muslims there were Jews, who died in the millions defending Jerusalem and the Temple against the Assyrians, the Babylonians, the Greeks and the Romans. It was we Jews who built the Temple; if its ground is holy, it is because we made it holy. Its secret is our secret. We started the Judeo-Masonic tradition, but it was the Masons who turned it into a vehicle of world rule. England, France and the United States, the three main centers of Freemasonry, have between them come close to ruling the world over the course of the past several hundred years. They did so by espousing "the modern". Did Leo the Thirteenth get it right: is "the modern" a Judeo-Masonic plot?

DEISM

What I am calling Judeo-Masonic thought might also be called Deism. Many of the leading Deists of the 18th and 19th centuries were in fact Masons. The Deists maintained that there must be a God because how else could the universe have come into being? They maintained that this God had so arranged the universe that good deeds would be rewarded and bad deeds punished. However, they did not believe in the divinity of Christ or in the need for God to directly intervene in the day-to-day workings of the universe. God's will was incorporated in the very structure of the universe in the form of laws of nature. The task of science was to discover these laws and apply them to the betterment of the human condition. Most of the leaders of the American Revolution of 1776 and the French Revolution of 1789 held views of this kind.

Deism is what Jews and Masons had in common. However, Judaism is not the same as Deism. YHVH does intervene quite frequently in daily life in the Torah. Deism as a historical movement was a radical form of Protestantism, one which denied the divinity of Christ while still regarding him as a great teacher. Deism grew up in scientific circles in England, France and the United States and placed great emphasis on the concept of natural law. Deism was gradually accepted by many Jews, including Einstein, but it was not originally a Jewish doctrine. YHVH does not govern by natural law but by sheer willpower. However, Deism is compatible with Judaism in a way that Christianity is not. Christianity is suffused with a spirit of blame relative to the Jewish people, while this spirit is absent from Deism. And even if the concept of natural law is not originally Jewish, it can be incorporated into Judaism without any great disturbance. Natural law is really just another word for the will of God, for there can be no law without a legislator.

The thing is, in reality there are no natural "laws", only tendencies, regularities and patterns. As many historians of science have pointed out in recent decades, the foundations of the modern scientific outlook are religious. To me it seems obvious that the universe always was and always will be. To speak of it being "governed" by "laws" appears to me an archaic mode of speech reflecting a need to prove the existence of God. I am therefore looking at Deism from the outside, for I do not accept its basic precept, faith in the existence of God. People are always telling me that this is also the basic precept of Judaism, but I still have trouble believing them. To me Judaism means attachment to the Jewish people. The words "Judaism" and "Jewish" are both derived from the Hebrew word "Yehudah", the name of the ancient kingdom called "Judah" in English. Judaism thus means literally loyalty to Judah. Jerusalem was the capital of Judah, and the Temple was the heart of Jerusalem.

Judaism can thus be interpreted to mean loyalty to the Temple, and it was thus that the Masons interpreted it. The Judeo-Masonic tradition is therefore something deeper and more extensive than Deism. Deism is probably best understood as the public form of this tradition. It claimed to be a religion but it was really a critique of Christianity. Its fundamental precept was denial of the divinity of

Christ, and it was this precept which linked it to Judaism. Deism was not a religion because it lacked a ritual and ceremonies of its own. Robespierre and his followers attempted to create Deist rituals at the height of the French Revolution but their attempt was still born. Deism remained essentially an intellectual stance and for this reason it gradually declined in popularity over the course of the 19th and 20th centuries. It was supplanted on the one hand by Marxism, whose critique of Christianity was even more radical than that of the Deists, and on the other hand by a wide variety of "post-modern" relativist doctrines. But both Judaism and Freemasonry were older than Deism, and they have survived it as well.

The difference between Freemasonry and Deism is brought out very clearly in *The Temple And The Lodge* by Michael Baigent and Richard Leigh. This book was published in the same year as Robinson's *Born In Blood* and also argues that Freemasonry originated with the Knights Templar. But for some reason, Baigent and Leigh made no reference to Robinson, nor Robinson to them. And although they develop the same thesis, the two books differ sharply in their view of Freemasonry. While Robinson sees it as a revolutionary force, Baigent and Leigh stress its conservative character. They see the Templar tradition as perpetuated by the pro-Catholic Stuart dynasty in England, whose Jacobite supporters they view as the true founders of modern Freemasonry. They pay no attention at all to the anti-Christian, Deist side of Masonic thought and instead stress its roots in Christian mysticism and the Rosicrucians. Whereas Robinson devoted a number of chapters to possible Templar-Masonic involvement in Wat Tyler's rebellion of 1381, Baigent and Leigh do not even mention it.

On the other hand, Baigent and Leigh do go into great detail on the role of Freemasonry in the American Revolution of 1776. But even here, they manage to depict the Masons in a conservative light. They see the main vehicle of the spread of Masonry from England to the American colonies in the "field lodges" active within the British army during the French and Indian War. American officers such as George Washington were drawn into Masonry through their contacts with British officers at this time. Baigent and Leigh see the British and American military Masons as striving to remain united but being pulled apart by non-Masonic radicals on the American side such as Paine and Jefferson. However, they also point out that most of the initiators of the Boston Tea Party were Masons, as were at least 9 of the 56 signers of the Declaration of Independence. And on page 181, they summarize the radical impact of 18th century Freemasonry as follows

> Insisting on a universal brotherhood which transcended national frontiers, English Freemasonry was to exert a profound influence on the great reformers of the eighteenth century – on David Hume, for example, on Voltaire, Diderot, Montesquieu and Rousseau in France, on their disciples in what was to become the United States.

But given their view of Masonry as a crypto-Catholic, neo-Platonic mystical cult, it is hard to understand why it was so intimately associated with all the major European and American revolutionary movements of the 18th and 19th centuries.

In any case, it is evident that Freemasonry, like Judaism, overlapped with but was not identical to Deism. Moreover, Freemasonry contained the rituals and ceremonies which Deism lacked. It was a religion in all but name, while Deism was a religion in name only. Viewed as a religion, Freemasonry differed from Deism in its focus on the Temple. Baigent and Leigh not only trace this focus to the Templars but also see them as the source of many of the radical ideas later upheld by the Masons. Thus they assert (page 54) that the Templars were "almost certainly "tainted" with religious heterodoxy, if not full fledged heresy" and (page 58) that "certainly, during years of activity in the Holy Land, the Temple had absorbed a good deal of both Judaic and Islamic thought". They cite little or no evidence for these assertions, which appear to be derived from the accusations directed against the Templars by the French monarchy and the Roman Catholic church at the time of the suppression of the Templar order in the early 14th century. Once the Templars were suppressed, however, they very definitely developed anti-Christian attitudes. Authenticated Templar grave sites from the 14th century onwards are distinguished by their complete lack of Christian symbolism of any kind.

If the Templars were heretics prior to their suppression, the only clear indication of their heresy was their focus on the Temple. Although neither Robinson nor Baigent and Leigh seem to be aware of it, pre-Templar Christian tradition was thoroughly hostile to any thought of rebuilding the Temple. When the Christians gained control of the Roman empire, including Jerusalem, in the 4th century CE, they used the former site of the Temple as a garbage dump. At no point during the next 300 years of Christian control of the Temple Mount did the Christians show the slightest interest in treating the site as a holy place. The respect shown by the Templars both to the site of the Temple and to its memory was a major novelty in Christian circles. It was no doubt prompted by the fact that the Muslims had built a number of religious structures on the site of the Temple Mount. By selecting the mosque of al-Aksa on the Temple Mount as their headquarters, the Templars testified to their desire to not only rival but also imitate the Muslims. This impulse might well have been viewed as heretical by the Roman Catholic church, but so long as the Templars played a leading role in the Crusades, their novel attitude was tolerated by the Catholic hierarchy. Only after the Crusaders were entirely expelled from the "Holy Land" at the end of the 13th century did the Templars become expendable. At this point their focus on the Temple could easily have become a major factor in the decision to suppress them. Certainly the Roman Catholic church never showed any subsequent interest in the site of the Temple, whose destruction by the Romans has always been pictured in Catholic circles as a divine punishment visited on the Jews for their failure to recognize Christ.

JEWS AND MASONS

In line with their tendency to trace the radical ideas of Freemasonry to conservative, Catholic sources, Baigent and Leigh even go so far as to assert that the Templars were friendly to Jews. They state on page 136 "Although nominally "knights of Christ", the Templars, in practice, maintained cordial relations with both Islam and Judaism, and are even said to have harboured ambitious plans for reconciling

Christianity with its two rival faiths." They advance no evidence for
this statement, nor do they make any reference to the role of the founders of the Templar order in the massacres of Jews carried out during
the First Crusade. On the other hand, it may be significant that Philip
4, the French king who was responsible for the suppression of the
Templar order, was also responsible for the attempted expulsion of all
Jews from France in 1306. Robinson sees Philip's attack on the Jews as
a kind of model and precedent for his attack on the Templars in 1307,
one year later. Be that as it may, there is no doubt that the Freemasons
in later centuries became associated with a tolerant attitude towards
Jews. But even here the picture is more complex than is usually admitted by Christian historians.

Jacob Katz brings out the complexities in *Jews and Freemasons
in Europe, 1723-1939*. In England, where Freemasonry originated,
all Jews had been expelled in 1290, only a short time before the suppression of the Templars. Jews did not return to England until the
17th century, and even then only a trickle. So far as is known, the first
English Jew to become a Mason was Edward Rose, who was admitted
to a lodge in London in 1732. By the 1750s a number of English Jews
had become Masons, but most of them were segregated in a "Jewish
lodge". In France, Jews were initially eligible for membership when the
first lodges were formed in the 1730s, but the French "Grand Lodge"
banned Jews in 1755 in reaction to Catholic attacks on the Masons as
Jewish-inspired. Jews were generally barred from the French lodges
until 1791 when the French Revolution extended French citizenship to
the few Jews who lived in France at that time. Jews had been completely
expelled from France in 1394 and only a small number had returned
over the course of the 17th and 18th centuries.

The situation was at its most complex in Germany, whose 18th
century Jewish population was considerably larger than in England
or France. Jews were completely barred from the German Masonic
lodges until 1780, when a certain Hans Heinrich von Ecker und
Eckhofen founded a new lodge in Vienna known as the "Order of the
Asiatic Brethren". Jews were not only eligible for membership but,
as Katz notes on page 26, the lodge was founded with "the avowed
purpose of accepting both Jews and Christians in its ranks". However,

members were required to eat a meal of pork with milk as part of their initiation. Even so the lodge was attacked as Jewish-dominated and went into decline after 1790. A "Tolerance Lodge" open to Jews was founded in both Berlin and Hamburg around this same time, but neither lodge was recognized by the other German lodges as official. Finally, in 1807 a lodge open to Jews was founded in Frankfurt, home of the largest and most influential Jewish community in Germany. This lodge became known as the "Jewish lodge", but most German lodges continued to bar Jews throughout the 19th century. In fact, from the 1880s onwards, Jews were even excluded from the few German lodges which theoretically admitted them.

Katz's study makes it clear that attitudes towards Jews among European Freemasons did not greatly differ from the dominant attitudes among their non-Masonic compatriots. In the 18th century, only the English Masonic lodges generally admitted Jews, and as Baigent and Leigh note on page 181 with reference to 18th century England "Anti-Semitism became more discredited in England than anywhere else in Europe, with Jews not only becoming Freemasons, but also gaining an acess hitherto denied them to social, political and public life." The same was true in the American colonies, but there too there were very few Jews. All the same, it cannot be denied that the Freemasons everywhere were in the vanguard of the movement to extend citizenship to Jews in the 18th and 19th centuries. Among the early leaders of the French Revolution, whose decision to grant citizenship to Jews in 1791 was the decisive step in what came to be known as "Jewish Emancipation", most were Masons, including Lafayette, Danton, the abbé Sieyès and Camille Desmoulins.

If there was a Judeo-Masonic conspiracy at work in these events, it was embodied in the person of Moses Dobrushka. Dobrushka was in fact a Jew, a Mason and a conspirator all rolled into one. He was born in 1753 in Austria into a wealthy Jewish family. In 1775, under the influence of the "false Messiah" Jacob Frank, Moses Dobrushka converted to Christianity and took the name of Franz Schoenfeld. He became a prominent figure in Viennese high society and in 1778 was elevated to the Austrian nobility as Franz von Schoenfeld. He went on to become one of the founders and leading members of the Masonic lodge known as the "Asiatic Brethren". Arthur Mandel recounts the story in great detail in his biography of Jacob Frank, *The Militant Messiah*. According to Mandel, the founders of the lodge sought to attract members with the promise of revealing the secrets of Kabbalah. Mandel continues as follows, on page 90

> But here they needed a "Cabbalist", and they found him in the person of Schoenfeld-Dobrushka. He managed to sell them a bill of goods, a hodgepodge of Jewish-Christian symbols which turned the Cabbala into a secret science for the forecasting of eclipses of the sun or moon and other natural phenomena. Some gullible persons, fascinated by the mysterious spell of the Cabbala, actually fell for it and joined the order, among them the future king of Prussia, Frederick Wilhelm II.

Von Schoenfeld also developed ties with the Austrian royal house and accompanied Leopold 2, the king of Austria, to Pillnitz in 1791 where the Austrians and Prussians decided to declare war on revolutionary France.

However, Leopold 2 died soon thereafter and the new ruler of Austria, Franz 2, did not like von Schoenfeld. The latter therefore fled to Strasbourg in France where he assumed the name of Sigismund Gottlob Junius Brutus Frey. Generally known as Junius Frey, he became active in Jacobin circles, and in 1792 he moved to Paris, where he established ties with the leading Jacobins of the day. His sister, now named Leopoldine Frey, married the head of Robespierre's secret police, Francois Chabot, "noted for his debauchery" according to Mandel on page 136. However, Frey was accused of being an Austrian or Prussian spy, and in 1793 he was arrested. He was sent to the guillotine on April 5, 1794 together with Danton, whom Robespierre accused of being in league with Frey in a "Foreign Conspiracy". To this day no one has succeeded in figuring out just what Dobrushka really stood for and what was the logic of his successive transformations into von Schoenfeld and Frey. A more perfect embodiment of the anti-Semitic stereotype of a Judeo-Masonic conspirator is difficult to imagine, yet Dobrushka has been forgotten by Jews, Masons and anti-Semites alike. He was indeed a prophet of the modern age, whose literary works include a Book of Entertainment (in Hebrew), David's War Songs (in German) and Social Philosophy (in French).

Dobrushka seems to be the exception that proves the rule. In general Jews and Masons continued to occupy separate worlds even after the Masonic lodges began to admit Jews. Having already converted to Christianity, Dobrushka obviously had no problem eating pork with milk, but most Jews were repelled by the numerous Christian elements in Masonic symbolism and lore. Radicals and free-thinkers in Christian eyes, the Masons look much like Christians from a Jewish point of view. Their famous members, men like George Washington, the Marquis de Lafayette, Simon Bolivar, Giuseppe Garibaldi, Winston Churchill and Franklin Roosevelt, are never viewed as non-Christians. The "Asiatic Brethren", it is true, featured numerous Jewish themes in their ritual and doctrine, but they did not survive much longer than Moses Dobrushka. On the whole the Jewish contribution to the Judeo-Masonic tradition remained miniscule. Yet miniscule as it may have been, it was nonetheless significant, for it was difficult to think of the Temple without thinking of the Jews. Lurking somewhere at the heart of the Judeo-Masonic tradition is, of course, Zionism.

ZIONISM

Numerous historians have already drawn attention to the Zionist strand in English Protestant tradition which formed an important part of the background to the Balfour Declaration of 1917. This theme was emphasized by Nahum Sokolow in his path-breaking *History of Zionism 1600-1918*, and it provided the main focus for Barbara Tuchman's later work, *Bible And Sword*. Both Sokolow and Tuchman show in great detail how many English Protestants, beginning in the 1600s, became convinced that the return of the Jews to the "Holy Land" would signal the start of the Messianic Era, which they associated with the "Second Coming" of Christ. Sokolow saw these views as intimately bound up with the decision to readmit Jews to England and grant them civil rights. Tuchman was more sceptical of British motives, stressing the extent to which Protestant Zionism was merely a pretext for Christian and English conquest of the "Holy Land". Yet despite the close ties between Freemasonry and Protestantism in England, neither Sokolow nor Tuchman saw fit to delve into the Masonic component in English Protestant Zionism.

Tuchman did argue, however, that Protestant Zionism was actually rooted in the Crusades. On page 39 she described the "self-identification with the ancient though not the contemporary Jews" on the part of the Crusaders, which enabled them to see themselves "as the rightful inheritors of the Holy Land". Nowhere was this self-identification stronger than among the Templars. Baigent and Leigh, on page 92 of *The Temple And The Lodge*, describe the Templars as follows

> Among biblical texts, they constantly invoked Joshua and Maccabees, promoting themselves as latterday avatars of the army that toppled the walls of Jericho, the army that nearly defeated Rome in the years just prior to the Christian era.

We may safely assume that this self-identification with Joshua and the Maccabees did not incline the Templars to a favorable view of the Jews of their own day, but it did put them somewhat at odds with Catholic tradition. And once the Templars had been repudiated by the Roman Catholic church, it is easy to see how this self-identification might have evolved in a pro-Protestant and even pro-Jewish direction.

The great merit of Robinson's book is that he develops a plausible theory of how this transformation might have taken place. He sees the fugitive Templars in England and Scotland forming underground networks closely aligned with other foes of Church and State. These networks then provided the organizational leadership for Wat Tyler's rebellion. Templar involvement in this rebellion is strongly suggested by the fact that the rebels made a big point of attacking everywhere the property and persons of the Order of the Hospitallers. The Hospitallers were the big rivals of the Templars, and it was they who had received the bulk of the confiscated Templar properties in England. Wat Tyler's rebellion was suppressed but according to Robinson the Templar underground found a refuge in Scotland, which had become independent of England with the aid of Templar fugitives. From Scotland in turn emerged Freemasonry at the end of the Middle Ages.

That Freemasonry did in fact emerge from Scotland is clear. This much was shown by David Stevenson in *The Origins Of Freemasonry*, which was published in 1988, one year before the appearance of *Born In Blood* and *The Temple And The Lodge*. Stevenson, who was a professor of Scottish history at the University of St. Andrews, had no interest whatsoever in the Templars. He completely accepted the conventional view that Freemasonry had grown out of medieval guilds of stonemasons; his goal was simply to prove that these were Scottish and not English stonemasons. Stevenson believed that Freemasonry was the creation of "one man", a certain William Schaw, who became "master of works" for the Scottish stonemasons at the end of the 16th century. Schaw issued "statutes" for the Scottish stonemasons in which Stevenson detected an occult influence. Stevenson's view of Freemasonry as Schaw's original creation is extremely dubious, but Stevenson does present extensive evidence tending to show that Freemasonry first surfaced as a distinct tendency at the court of James 6 of Scotland, who went on to become James 1 of England in 1603. James himself is thought to have been a Freemason, and the Masonic movement took firm root in England under his descendant, the Stuart king Charles 2.

Because the Stuart dynasty, which originated in Scotland, was hostile to the Puritans, both Stevenson and also Baigent and Leigh tend to associate Freemasonry with a kind of crypto-Catholicism. James 1 was a Protestant, however; the "King James Version" of the Bible is named after him. Scotland, moreover, was a Protestant stronghold throughout the 16th century. After stressing the fact that William Schaw was a Catholic, Stevenson adds, on page 123 "William Schaw may have been a Catholic, but his lodges were protestant, loyal to the established church." Many of the participants in Wat Tyler's rebellion had also held views similar to those of the later Protestants. They were called Lollards, followers of the teachings of John Wyclif, who is generally viewed as a precursor of Protestantism. And throughout its history, Freemasonry was always viewed with extreme hostility on the part of the Roman Catholic church. No sooner were the first Masonic lodges formed in France in the 1730s than a Papal bull was issued in 1738 banning them. Whatever crypto-Catholic tendencies it may have displayed, Freemasonry was therefore generally identified with rejection of Papal authority. More often than not this rejection assumed a specifically Protestant form, as shown by the popularity of Freemasonry among the Protestant English and Americans.

Tuchman, in *Bible And Sword*, saw a connection between Protestantism, rejection of Papal authority and Christian Zionism. As she put it on page 80

> Wherever the Reformation took hold the Bible replaced the Pope as the final spiritual authority. The Palestinian origins of Christianity were stressed more and more in order to reduce the pretensions of Rome.

The Masons too claimed "Palestinian origins", and pre-Christian ones at that. Their focus on the rebuilding of the Temple could and did align them even more closely with the Jews than non-Masonic Protestants. But it would prove little to put together a list of all the Masons who associated themselves with the Zionist concept in some way. Such a list would be difficult to compile in any case due to the extreme reluctance of historians of Zionism to look into the Masonic connection. This reluctance is a natural reaction to the anti-Semitic charges of a Judeo-Masonic conspiracy. Zionism certainly did not grow out of a conspiracy, whether Judeo-Masonic or any other. It was a broadly based movement rooted in 3000 years of Jewish history. The question is rather whether Judeo-Masonic thought tended to create a favorable context for the success of the Zionist movement. This question clearly has to be answered in the affirmative.

That Freemasonry was inherently favorable to Zionism is suggested by the fact that the three main supporters of the Zionist movement in modern times, England, France and the United States, were also the three main centers of Freemasonry. In the United States, today Israel's strongest supporter, at least 13 Presidents have been Freemasons, including Harry Truman, who was responsible for United States recognition of Israel in 1948. Freemasonry helped to create a receptive climate for Zionism by its legitimation of Judaism, by its association with movements for national independence and above all by its focus on the Temple. Although this focus could be interpreted in many different ways, it was difficult to resist the implication that the Jews would have to participate in some manner in the rebuilding of the Temple. This view in turn conditioned Freemasons to accept the Zionist movement when it arose among Jews in the 19th and 20th centuries. Zionism was in no sense their creation, but without their aid its success would have been considerably less likely.

THE TEMPLE

That the Temple was central to Freemasonry from the start is shown by Stevenson in *The Origins Of Freemasonry*. After a thorough examination of the few references to Freemasonry in 17th century Scottish texts, Stevenson concluded that the early Scottish lodges were consecrated to the memory of the Temple. He put it this way, on page 149

The lodge of the early Scottish masons was clearly intended to be Solomon's Temple. It does not seem to have been mentally furnished with the pillars of the temple, but they were present through the use of their names as secret words, and the references to the lodge being orientated like the temple and to the first lodge having been held in the temple porch help stress this identification – as does the grave of Hiram, the temple's architect. This being the case, the "work" to which the master puts the masons in the lodge was presumably regarded as symbolising the building of the temple. In the religious literature of the day "building the Temple" was frequently used as a synonym for building the new Jerusalem, the creation of a true godly community.

Stevenson's testimony is all the more suggestive in that it never occurred to him that this focus on the Temple might have derived from the Templars. Stevenson also had no interest in a Jewish connection, but noted on page 133 that a 1689 Scottish text referred to the "Mason Word" as a "Rabbinical mystery". Stevenson theorized that "as the words of the Mason Word were connected with Solomon's Temple it was natural to connect their use with Jewish tradition".

The point about the Temple is that it symbolized not only "the creation of a true godly community" but also physical force. It was built at the height of the power and prestige of the kingdom of Judah and it survived only so long as the Jewish people was able to defend it. Physical force was also the main concern of the Templars, who were a military order who engaged in constant military training. Physical force was also a prominent element in Masonic culture, as shown by the long list of generals and other military men who were Masons. It is just this point which makes Robinson's theory of the origins of the Freemasons so plausible. Wat Tyler's rebellion was also an expression of physical force, and one which was remarkably well organized and destructive. It is hard to understand how a group of neo-Platonic mystics could have given rise to most of the great revolutionary movements of the 18th and 19th centuries, but it is easy to see how a radical underground formed by ex-Templars might have done so.

The moral of the story is that the Temple matters. The modern Zionist movement paid little attention to the issue of the Temple, and yet it has continually surfaced all the same. The seizure of the Temple Mount by the Israeli armed forces during the Six Day War in 1967 was viewed by many as a dream come true. Since 1967 Israel has marked time, retaining physical control of the Temple Mount but leaving its administration entirely in the hands of Muslim authorities. Some forty years have elapsed in this manner, but forty years are but a moment in the 3000 year history of the Temple and its legend. Sooner or later the issue of the Temple will have to be addressed. Who will decide its future – Jews, Muslims, Christians, the United Nations? To me it appears equally inconceivable that the Temple Mount will remain entirely Muslim or that an entirely Jewish "Third Temple" will replace the existing Islamic structures. Some compromise will have to be devised, but what this compromise might be no one really knows. One thing is for sure the Judeo-Masonic concept of the rebuilding of the Temple remains very much alive, and much depends on how this concept will be translated into practice in the years to come.

JEWISH HISTORY AND WORLD HISTORY

Despite the proliferation of departments of Jewish Studies in colleges and universities in the United States in recent decades, Jewish history is still almost totally excluded from standard academic treatments of world history. The main reasons for this state of affairs are as follows:

(1) In most colleges and universities, the first thousand years of Jewish history are generally treated as a subset of "Biblical" studies. Characteristic of all forms of "Biblical" scholarship is a tendency to either credit the various religious versions of early Jewish history (whether Jewish, Christian or Muslim) or else avoid any analysis of that history which might conflict too sharply with a religious version. Since most historians approach the subject of world history in a strictly secular spirit, they are understandably reluctant to rely too heavily on a "Biblical" narrative which they rightly suspect to be tinged with a religious point of view.

(2) Academic historians in the West have inherited from Christian tradition a belief that once the "Biblical" period was over, Jewish history was no longer of any significance or importance. The Christian view that the Jews were doomed to suffer forever for their rejection of Jesus Christ was transmuted into the academic view that the only thing worth mentioning about the Jewish history of the past 2000 years was one or another persecution or massacre. And since the persecution and massacre of Jews has come to be considered a questionable practice in the wake of the Holocaust, historians who wish to speak well of some culture that traditionally engaged in torturing Jews tend to omit even this aspect of Jewish history from their narrative.

(3) Early academic treatments of world history were dominated by a concept of "the West and the rest", but as time goes on, representatives of "the rest" have become increasingly prominent in the field. Their attitude towards Jewish history is shaped in large part by the negative attitude of most Third World countries towards the state of

Israel. This attitude leads them either to ignore Jewish history altogether or to focus only on those aspects of Jewish tradition which can be linked to Western imperialism and colonialism. This tendency is further reinforced by the existence of a considerable body of Marxist literature asserting a close connection between Jewish tradition and capitalism.

The position of Jewish history within the academic concept of world history is mirrored in the position of Jewish Studies within the academic multi-cultural establishment. Superficially Jewish Studies might appear to resemble all the other multi-cultural fiefdoms, such as Black Studies, Women's Studies, Middle Eastern Studies and so forth, but appearances are deceiving. Most of the other departments of this type were created in response to political movements which demanded greater attention and respect for their particular constituency. This pressure naturally spilled over into the study of world history, leading to the emergence of a standard multi-cultural narrative in which the history and achievements of these various constituencies were given much greater prominence than had previously been the case.

Jewish Studies, however, was not created in response to political pressure from any part of the Jewish community. Most departments of Jewish Studies in the United States owe their existence to two factors: first, the presence of significant numbers of Jewish students on campus, and second, the readiness of Jewish philanthropists and organizations to fund Jewish Studies programs in whole or in part. Indeed, in many cases the facilities where Jewish Studies are taught are not even part of the college campus but are made available by local Jewish groups at their own expense. And since Jewish Studies did not arise in response to angry demonstrations, there was also little or no pressure to include Jewish history in the multi-cultural narrative of world history. To the contrary, the multi-cultural establishment has become permeated with hostility to the state of Israel, leading to the effective ghettoization of Jewish Studies within the academic world.

Because of these various reasons, the following bizarre situation exists. On the one hand, even the most casual student of world history has to be aware of a whole series of major developments which are linked to the Jewish people in some way. Two powerful religions

commanding billions of followers on a world scale, namely Christianity
and Islam, are clearly rooted in Judaism to one degree or another.
Moreover, there is a long history of Christian "heresies", culminating
in the Protestant Reformation, which resembled Judaism even more
than "Orthodox" or "Catholic" Christianity. Furthermore, the intellectual and cultural history of the past 150 years or so is filled with the
names of Jewish individuals, such as Marx, Einstein and Freud, who
played a leading role in the emergence of what is called "modern" society. Yet on the other hand, despite all this evidence of Jewish influence,
the Jewish people is nowhere to be found in most academic accounts
of world history. This or that Jewish individual or text might receive a
certain amount of attention, but as to the social, intellectual, cultural
and political history of the Jewish people itself, scarcely one word do
we hear.

It should nonetheless be obvious that all the famous literary vehi-
cles of Jewish influence which have appeared in the past 3000 years
are rooted first and foremost in the actual social practice of the Jewish
people. If Jewish thought has traditionally been somewhat more egalitarian, rational and humane than that of the surrounding peoples, it
was first and foremost because the Jews themselves embodied these
qualities in their social relations to a greater degree than was typical
elsewhere. The reason for this is not far to seek: it is because the Jewish
people originated as a nation of runaway slaves.

The memory of Hebrew enslavement in Egypt has been preserved
in a mythical form in the Torah, but behind the myth stands a well
documented historical reality. Over the course of the past 100 years,
innumerable inscriptions in Accadian cuneiform hieroglyphics have
been unearthed in various parts of the Middle East making reference to
a class of people called Habiru or Apiru. They were described as living
on the outskirts of the more settled areas, as subsisting as day laborers or mercenaries or bandits, and as being composed in large part of
runaway slaves. In particular, there are numerous references to Habiru
taking part in a major rebellion against Egyptian rule in Canaan in the
14th century BCE, to Habiru being taken prisoner by the Egyptians
and carried by them back to Egypt, and to Habiru working as slaves
on construction projects in Egypt for the Egyptians. Were it not for the

prejudices which surround the subject of Jewish history, the identity of the Habiru slaves in Egypt with the Hebrew slaves in the Torah would long ago have been recognized as a historical fact.

Two main factors have prevented this recognition. In the first place, most "Biblical scholars" have done everything in their power to avoid noticing the identity of the Habiru and the Hebrews because it means that the whole story of Hebrew descent from Abraham and Isaac and Israel and the twelve sons of Israel has to be treated as a myth. The Habiru could not possibly have all belonged to the same family, or even to the same ethnic group. And in the second place, both the "Biblical scholars" and the academic scholars of world history are not at all happy with the idea that the Hebrews really were runaway slaves. Insofar as they are prepared to discount the story that the Hebrews were all descended from one man, the "Biblical scholars" would much prefer that they be idealistic "peasants" and "villagers" rather than bandits and outlaws. And despite the existence of a considerable body of historical literature describing Messianic movements among just such bandits and outlaws in a number of different parts of the world, the last thing the scholars of world history want to see is the inclusion of the Hebrews in this category.

Unlike most such rebels elsewhere in the world, the Hebrews succeeded in creating a lasting political tradition embodying their conception of egalitarian social relations in written form. This tradition was preserved by the Jewish people, both in words and in deeds, for 3000 years. And just for this reason, the Jewish people has been subjected to unremitting persecution by the advocates of autocracy, empire and class rule continuing unto the present day. Yet despite this persecution, Jewish conceptions of social relations have gradually made their way, both in a religious and in a secular form, into the consciousness of a large part of the world. Were academic scholars to take note of these facts, they would have to place the Jewish people at the very center of world history. And last but not least, they would have to adopt a positive attitude towards the state of Israel.

In truth, the prejudice against the inclusion of the Jewish people in world history and the prejudice against the state of Israel are one and the same prejudice. It is the prejudice against the Jews as a nation. The world is full of people who have no problem espousing ideas which are derived from Jewish sources, but as soon as the subject of the Jews as a nation comes up, immediately some idiotic accusation comes into their head. Yet it is the Jews as a nation, and not God or a few Jewish individuals, who created the basis for all the famous Jewish ideas. You cannot have one without the other. And since the very idea of an objective, realistic account of world history owes more than a little to Jewish influence, those who uphold this idea owe it both to themselves and to others to show some respect for the source from which so much of their own thinking is derived.

THE FUTURE OF JEWISH SECULARISM

Ever since the early 1970s I have been searching for a Jewish secular organization in which I could feel comfortable. I have yet to find one, and not for want of trying. I was active in the Society for Humanistic Judaism (SHJ) for about ten years, much of that time as a member of the SHJ chapter in Queens, New York. I have also had some contact with a number of other Jewish secular organizations both in the New York area and also in Israel, where I now live. I have no doubt that Jewish secularism ought to be the wave of the future for the Jewish people, but at the present time I have to face the fact that it is mostly a weak and ineffective echo of the past.

Jewish secularism has always had two souls. One is an assimilationist soul, a desire to cast off the identifying marks of the Jewish religion and blend into the larger non-Jewish society. The other is a nationalist soul, a sense of solidarity with the Jewish people and a positive attitude towards Jewish culture, history and tradition. But if we examine the history of Jewish secularism over the course of the past 100 years or so, what we mainly see is a gradual weakening of its nationalist component and a gradual strengthening of its assimilationist component.

For obvious reasons, this is less true in Israel than it is in the Diaspora, but even in Israel it is true to some extent. However, without a nationalist component, Jewish secularism becomes just plain assimilationism, and that is what is happening to the younger generation in the Diaspora. They don't want to be identified as Jews, and therefore they don't join Jewish secular organizations. The result is that in the United States the membership of both the SHJ and its rival, the Congress of Secular Jewish Organizations (CSJO), is largely composed of people like myself, older adults who retain a sense of Jewish identity that is rooted in the period prior to the 1960s when Jews were still excluded from many sectors of American society. The total membership of both groups is quite small, no more than a few thousand people, and a majority of American Jews are probably unaware that they even exist.

The situation in Israel is different because Israelis, even non-Jewish Israelis, tend to be perceived as Jews regardless of what they themselves may actually believe. Yet even in Israel, secularism has come to be increasingly associated with assimilationism and a desire to see Israel become "a state of all its citizens" rather than a Jewish state. To be sure, someone who speaks Hebrew, serves in the Israeli army and pays taxes to the state of Israel can never be such a complete assimilationist as a secular Jew in the Diaspora. But even if others perceive them as Jews, more and more secular Israelis see themselves as advocates of supposedly "universal" values which are based more on "politically correct" thinking around the world than they are on Jewish tradition.

So far as I am concerned, Jewish secularism ought to base itself first and foremost on the recognition that the God of the Jewish religion, and Christianity and Islam as well, simply does not exist. This recognition does not stem from either assimilationism or nationalism but rather an awareness of the close correlation between theist and monarchical ideology in the history of the world's religions. God is an invention of the servants of kings and emperors, a king in the sky to justify and rationalize monarchy on earth. Of course, just because its basic premise is false does not mean that the Jewish religion is entirely without value. To the contrary, Jewish religious tradition is filled with ethical, cultural and practical elements well worthy of preservation, God or no God. But anyone who wishes to understand the world as it is, without illusions, cannot accept the fundamentally silly idea that the universe is ruled by a king in the sky.

Unfortunately, atheism is not a "universal" value. The pressure to believe in a king in the sky has become so strong, particularly in recent decades, that many or most Jewish secularists tend to fudge their beliefs on this score and identify themselves as something other than just plain atheists. For example, in the SHJ members were encouraged to identify themselves as "ignostics", a term coined by Sherwin Wine, which was supposed to imply that God might or might not exist but in any case was not relevant to solving the problems of life on earth. And in general, there is a tendency among the advocates of "universal" values to soft pedal or conceal their doubts about God so as to facilitate their efforts to make common cause with the religious believers in "God given" human rights. But a Jewish secularism that dares not avow the real basis of its secularism will always find itself at a disadvantage relative to the religious, who do not hesitate to proclaim their faith in God on every conceivable occasion.

However, even though there are no overtly atheist Jewish organizations, there are quite a few organizations in the United States which do call themselves "atheist" and include a significant proportion of Jews among their members. I agree with much of what these groups have to say on the subject of "the God delusion", but I could never belong to any of them. Their tendency is to downplay or ignore the role of the God idea as a prop for monarchy and instead treat it as a form of pre-scientific thinking on the part of people who were too "primitive" to understand the universe otherwise. And since they see the Jews as primarily responsible for the introduction of the God idea into the world, they tend to adopt a patronizing and often hostile attitude towards Jewish religious culture, about which they generally know very little. Their critique of Christianity and Islam is usually better informed, but I have yet to see one atheist writer make an issue of the anti-Semitic elements in Christian and Muslim tradition.

Concealed behind the myth of God is the fact that the Jewish people has played a progressive role in world history. What is unique and unusual about Jewish religious tradition is not that it contains yet another version of the God idea – an idea that is found throughout the world wherever monarchy appears – but that it enjoins a day of rest for laborers, hospitality for runaway slaves (see Chapter 23 of Deuteronomy), charity for the poor and the return to its rightful owner (in the year of the Jubilee) of all land lost through debt. It was for espousing such beliefs that the Jewish people has been subjected to intense persecution throughout our history, and it was because of the popularity of such beliefs that some aspects of Jewish tradition were taken over, in an anti-Semitic form, by Christianity and Islam.

And why did the Jewish people hold such unusual beliefs? Modern "Biblical scholarship" has unearthed a large mass of evidence indicating that the Jewish people are indeed descended from runaway slaves, just as the Torah states. But the runaway slaves in questions did not consistute one big family descended from Abraham, Isaac and Israel, but rather fugitives from many different families and ethnic groups who were known as Habiru and who formed armed bands on the outskirts of the more settled areas not only in Canaan but throughout the Middle East. The Torah is the mythical record of a process through which a small group of Habiru held as slaves by the Egyptians escaped from Egypt and organized a confederation of the Habiru bands in the area of Canaan which succeeded in gaining control of the entire area around 1200 BCE. It was because they themselves had been runaway slaves that the Jews enjoined hospitality for runaway slaves and the other progressive features of Jewish religious tradition.

In modern times, as monarchy has begun to be replaced by democracy throughout the world, it has become possible for Jews to cast off the religious coating of Jewish tradition and espouse the progressive ideals at its core in an overtly secular form. Thus it was that Jews came to play a prominent role in a wide variety of secular movements aimed at the creation of more just, compassionate and rational society for all. Unfortunately, as the force of such movements has weakened in recent decades, Jewish secularism has been gradually stripped of its progressive content and reduced to the "politically correct" advocacy of "human rights", an advocacy which does little or nothing to alter the basic facts of life for the great majority of people in the world. At the same time, Jewish secularism has also made its peace with the God idea, which has enjoyed an astonishing revival thanks to the "clash of civilizations" between Christianity and Islam. This is the situation in which we now find ourselves, and which makes the prospects of Jewish secularism appear so dismal at the present moment.

So does Jewish secularism have a future? I think that it does, and that the name of this future is secular Zionism.

Over time I see an inevitable tendency for all forms of Jewish identity to transmute themselves into forms of Israeli identity. The reason for this is simple: it is that Zionism is the logical outgrowth of Judaism. Jewish religious tradition did not merely preserve the progressive ideals embodied in the Torah; it also preserved the desire to see these ideals implemented through the reestablishment of a Jewish state in the land of Israel. This is what was meant by the belief in the coming of the Messiah, a belief which was an integral part of traditional Jewish religious culture. But now that the Messiah has come and gone, the Jewish religion has lost its most basic functions. It is no longer necessary to dream of the "ingathering of the exiles" but rather to engage in the prosaic tasks of building and defending the Jewish state. And it is no longer necessary to encapsulate the progressive ideals of Jewish tradition in a religious form when it is so much easier and more convenient to express those ideals in strictly secular terms.

It follows that anyone who wants to remain true to Jewish tradition must strive to see that tradition expressed in a Zionist form. But although Zionism is clearly derived from Judaism, an Israeli identity is not and cannot be identical with a Jewish identity. Israeli Hebrew is derived from ancient Hebrew but has a much larger vocabulary and a somewhat simpler grammar. Israeli holidays are derived from Jewish holidays but are celebrated by most Israelis in a much more secular way. Most Israelis are Jews but Israeli citizenship is open to non-Jews as well and there are many hundreds of thousands of Israeli Arabs who hold Israeli citizenship, speak Hebrew and form an integral part of Israeli society. Moreover, as time goes on, the differences between Israeli culture and traditional Jewish culture will tend to increase, not decrease. Some may welcome this trend while others bewail it, but the trend will continue regardless of how anyone might react to it.

In the Diaspora, this trend is reflected in the obsession with Israel on the part of all shades of Diaspora political and religious opinion. Assimilationism is rapidly eroding the Jewish identity of most younger Jews in the Diaspora, but no matter how assimilated they may become, most Jews still recognize that the fate of the Jewish people will be determined by the fate of the nation of Israel. If they are indifferent to what happens to Israel, it is because they have become indifferent to the survival of the Jewish people as well. However, the longer that Israel survives, the greater the tendency for Jewish identity in the Diaspora to become more like Israeli identity and less like the Jewish identity of the past. It is for this reason that there is an inherent tendency for the Jewish secularism of today to transmute itself into the secular Zionism of tomorrow.

I see the main function of secular Zionism to be the promotion of a positive attitude towards the nation of Israel on a strictly secular basis. This means understanding Jewish history, and also understanding the relationship between Jewish history and world history. Because the ancient kingdom of Judah was founded by the descendants of runaway slaves, its culture and institutions were significantly more egalitarian, both in theory and in practice, than those of the neighboring kingdoms and empires. For a period of roughly 1000 years, from the time of king David to that of the Maccabees, the Jewish nation maintained its independence of the surrounding kingdoms and empires either as a kingdom in its own right or as a priestly temple state. For 200 years, from 63 BCE to 135 CE, the Jewish nation then struggled to resist the domination of the Roman empire, the largest and most militaristic of the various kingdoms and empires which had yet appeared. After several million Jews had been killed by the Romans and their Greek allies, this struggle ended with the formal abolition of Jewish rule in the land of Israel and the creation of a Roman province called Palestine.

These facts, which are well attested, explain why first the Greco-Romans and then their Arab rivals subsequently sought to give their respective empires a pseudo-Jewish appearance in the form of Christianity and Islam. They explain why the Jewish people, although scattered, decimated and subjected to constant persecution, refused to disappear and continued to believe that one day justice would demand the reestablishment of a Jewish state in the land of Israel. They explain why the emergence of democratic and egalitarian institutions in the West in modern times was accompanied by the emergence of a more positive attitude towards the Jewish people than had previously characterized Christian and Muslim culture. And in particular they explain why the establishment of the state of Israel took place as the result of the military victory of democratic and egalitarian forces over the most Satanic empire the world had ever seen.

It is the responsibility of secular Zionism to develop a comprehensive historical narrative along the lines which I have briefly sketched out and to make this narrative available to the widest possible circle of people. The establishment of the state of Israel was not the result of a divine plan, nor was it an act of charity meted out to the Jewish people to make up for the Holocaust, nor was it (as our enemies affirm) the result of a colonialist plot. It was the outcome of 3000 years of struggle on the part of the Jewish people to popularize a more progressive concept of social relations than that favored by the dominant kingdoms and empires of world history. The modern state of Israel has continued this struggle, instituting a far more democratic, liberal and egalitarian social system than that found in any other part of the Middle East. Israel is indeed a "light unto the nations", but in order for this light to be seen, we secular Zionists must play our part in disseminating the truth about Jewish history and its relationship to world history.

A comprehensive understanding of Jewish history carries with it not only a positive attitude towards the state of Israel but also a number of other implications for Jewish secularism. The following are some of the areas in which a secular Zionist movement will necessarily differ from existing Jewish secular organizations.

(1) The fight against anti-Semitism. It cannot be said that existing Jewish secular organizations have made the fight against anti-Semitism a high priority. In all the years that I was active in the Jewish secular movement in New York, I never once saw either the SHJ or the CSJO lend their name to a demonstration or petition directed against some manifestation of anti-Semitism in the United States. I also noticed an extreme reluctance on the part of both groups, and also such Israeli secular organizations as Meretz, to characterize expressions of anti-Zionism as anti-Semitism. Starting from an attachment to the "universal" values of "human rights", the general tendency of existing Jewish secular organizations is to adopt a hypercritical attitude towards most forms of Jewish nationalism, whether religious or secular, while bending over backwards to find some element of validity in the anti-Jewish accusations of all but the most violent and bigoted anti-Semites.

Once you understand the progressive role which the Jewish people has played in world history, then the real basis of anti-Semitism immediately becomes apparent. Although it has a complex history, anti-Semitism is first and foremost an expression of political opposition to the egalitarian strand in Jewish tradition. Throughout its history, anti-Semitism has been typically associated with authoritarian regimes seeking to impose their rule on captive peoples and nations.

Anti-Semitism was founded by the Hellenistic empires of the Greeks, perpetuated by the Roman empire of the Caesars and then continued right down to modern times by a long succession of autocratic rulers culminating in the empire of the Nazis. Anti-Semitism in the form of anti-Zionism is today promoted by a global coalition of autocratic states whose control of most of the world's oil enables them to disseminate their anti-Semitic poison on a world scale.

The thing which we rational and reasonable secular Jews need to understand is that you cannot reason with anti-Semites and you cannot appease them. That is because their stated grievances are not their real grievances. They say they are angry because we don't believe in their religion, or because we are trying to rule the world, or because we have returned to our original homeland, but actually what bothers them about us is that we don't like autocracy. Our religion forbids the worship of autocratic rulers, our laws apply equally to rich and poor, our culture encourages diversity of opinion. Opposition to autocracy is too deeply rooted in Jewish tradition to conceal or eliminate even if we wanted to, and so autocrats the world over, whether big or small, are constantly racking their brains trying to dream up some new absurd accusation to direct against us in order to prevent our egalitarian point of view from interfering with their program of domination. There is only one rational and reasonable response to the autocratic offensive, and that is to intensify our opposition to autocracy even further, until the day comes when there are no more petty tyrants anywhere on earth.

However, it must also be recognized that autocracy is not the only source of anti-Semitism. Autocrats were primarily responsible for stigmatizing the Jews in the first place, but once they did this, all kinds of people climbed on the anti-Semitic bandwagon. Some were commercial rivals, others coveted Jewish property, still others wanted to supplant the Jews as preachers of morality. In today's world a major source of what might be called secondary anti-Semitism is the fear of a reduction in the supply or an increase in the price of oil. First the autocrats who control the supply of most of the world's oil declare that the Jews are no good, and then all kinds of otherwise reasonable people leap on the bandwagon and declare that Zionism is a threat to world peace. The problem is, you can't reason with these people any more than you can with the hard core anti-Semites. Their stated reasons are also not their real reasons, which boil down to anxiety over the future of their suburban way of life. Rather than trying to counter the endless accusations of the anti-Semites, we secular Jews ought to focus on our own positive message, that the defense of the Jewish people and the promotion of liberty and equality in the world are one and the same cause.

(2) The affirmation of Jewish nationalism. Zionism is the most important and the most powerful manifestation of Jewish nationalism in the modern world, but it is not the only manifestation. Prior to the Holocaust, Jewish nationalism manifested itself on a large scale in the form of devotion to the Yiddish language and Yiddish culture. In the United States the CSJO and also the largely secular Workmen's Circle grew out of this tradition. Today there are no more cohesive Yiddish speaking communities, apart from a few Hasidic enclaves, to sustain a Yiddish language Jewish nationalism, but nostalgia for the vanished Yiddish speaking world remains a significant force in Jewish life. And of course Jewish nationalism continues to manifest itself, as it has always done, in a religious form, whether Orthodox or Conservative or Reform or whatever. Can secular Zionism project a conception of Jewish nationalism that speaks to all of these disparate tendencies and includes but also transcends its core Zionist message?

Jewish nationalism is about strength. It was Jabotinsky, a Jewish nationalist if ever there was one, who said: "Strength is the only consolation". Strength to weather the storms of an anti-Semitic world, strength to remain faithful to our ideals and beliefs, strength to tell the truth. "Schver tsu sein a yid", "It's hard to be a Jew" runs the old Yiddish saying, meaning: it takes strength. The starting point of all forms of Jewish nationalism is a positive valuation of the strength necessary to remain a part of the Jewish people come what may.

From strength come achievements. All forms of Jewish nationalism celebrate the achievements of the Jewish people, but opinions differ as to what those achievements might be. Some say that the greatest achivement of the Jewish people was to introduce the idea of monotheism to the world, but I have never understood just why it is so much more wonderful to worship only one imaginary entity as opposed

to a number of imaginary entitles. In my opinion the great achievement of the Jewish people was to popularize the Messianic vision of
a more peaceful, prosperous and enlightened society on a world scale.
Whatever achievements you might wish to emphasize, no one familiar
with the facts can deny that the Jewish people has exterted and continues to exert a powerful influence on world history. Knowledge of the
influence we have exerted in the past is the surest basis for persevering
in our efforts to exert a progressive influence in the present as well.

Jewish nationalism is probably best defined as a sense of identity
with the Jewish people – past, present and future. More than any other
form of Jewish nationalism, secular Zionism has the potential to promote a sense of identity with the entire Jewish people. That is because
it is grounded in the historic ambition of the Jewish people to establish
an independent Jewish state in the land of Israel, while at the same
time it affirms the progressive social ideals which Jews everywhere have
played such a large part in disseminating. A true understanding of
Jewish history reveals a complex dialectic in which the struggle for a
Jewish state and the struggle for social progress mutually reinforced
one another and advanced in tandem as well as separately. All forms
of Jewish endeavor, whether religious or secular, Zionist or Diaspora
oriented, can be encompassed in this narrative which is nothing other
than the real history of the entire Jewish people.

(3) The vision of a better world. In the past, Jewish secularism
was typically associated with one or another form of the socialist
ideal, and in particular with the concept of democratic socialism.
Democratic socialism was at one time a mass movement within the
Jewish community, whether in Eastern Europe, in the United States or
in the land of Israel. However, times have changed, and little is heard
about democratic socialism in the Jewish world today. To the extent
that the notion of social progress is still upheld, it is usually associated
with the term "social justice". Most people do not realize that the term
"social justice" was first popularized in the 1930s in the United States
by Father Coughlin, a rabid anti-Semite, who used it as the title of
a magazine he published. Coughlin was opposed to socialism but in
favor of justice in the sense of punishment, and he left little doubt as
to precisely whom he wanted to see punished. Those who use the term

today usually mean by it the advancement of the interests of some group or groups whom they consider disadvantaged relative to the Jewish people. But in its origins, democratic socialism aimed neither at punishment nor preferment but simply a more humane, rational and equitable organization of society.

Today the great need of the entire human race is for a system of planet management that is capable of meeting the material needs of the world's peoples, of providing them with a basic education and of reversing the current trend towards global warming and the degradation of the world's environment. Bits and pieces of such a system already exist on a capitalist basis, but any objective observer would have to conclude that the capitalists are not doing a very good job of planet management. How could they, when they themselves say that their primary goal is their own personal profit rather than the welfare of the entire world? It seems obvious to me that what is needed is a system of planet management that is both more democratic and more socialist than the existing system. More democratic, in that there has to be an established mechanism whereby the world's peoples can vote for the kind of world they want to see. And more socialist, in that public has to replace private decision making and control in the key sectors of the world's economy.

Secular Zionists have every reason to adopt such a program as their own. It is in the interest of the entire Jewish people, and most especially the nation of Israel, for the world to become a more peaceful, prosperous and humane place. Rational planet management is the only way in which this is going to happen. Both in Israel and in the Diaspora, secular Zionists ought to be in the forefront of the movement for solving the world's problem on a global rather than piecemeal basis and transferring authority over the world's economy from a small group of wealthy capitalists to a representative public body. The idea is not to penalize or punish anyone, simply to make crucial decisions affecting the welfare of the entire planet in a more sensible way than is currently being done. Anyone familiar with Jewish history will recognized that this is an ideal with deep roots in Jewish culture and tradition. It is also an ideal with a future, and that future is the future of Jewish secularism.

Why I Am a Zionist

In the year 2001 of the Christian era my wife and I became Israeli citizens and moved from New York City to Netanya in Israel. We are living there still. I guess that makes me a Zionist. But when people in Israel ask me why I gave up our comfortable life in the United States to live in a nation under siege, I have trouble coming up with a good answer. I usually say, "Because I want to live in a Jewish neighborhood."

That answer is not false, but it's not entirely true either. Before making aliyah we lived in Forest Hills in Queens, which is or was as close to a Jewish neighborhood as it gets in the United States outside of a few Hasidic enclaves. But even then Forest Hills was becoming less Jewish, and I don't doubt that the trend has continued. The normal pattern in the United States is for Jewish neighborhoods to gradually change character as Jews move out to the suburbs and new immigrants move in. Only in Israel do Jewish neighborhoods stay Jewish.

On the other hand, most of the people in the Jewish neighborhood where we now live speak Hebrew, a language which I only began to study late in life and still do not speak or understand all that well. As a result many facets of the culture of our neighborhood are closed to me because of the language barrier. If choosing a Jewish neighborhood were my only motive, I am not sure which I would prefer, Forest Hills or Netanya. And for that matter, I am not even sure that I would insist on a Jewish neighborhood, assuming that I could find a non-Jewish one where I could feel at home. Of course I never have, but I might still be looking for one in the United States if there weren't something more to my Zionism than wanting to live in a Jewish neighborhood.

I was born in 1937 and grew up in Washington Heights in New York City, a neighborhood that was about half Jewish when I was a boy. My family was Jewish, most of my friends were Jewish, but because my parents were not at all religious, I had very little in the way of a Jewish education. I was eleven when the state of Israel was founded but I have no memory of any celebration at the time or even someone mentioning that this had happened. The goal of my parents was to be Americans, and that was my goal too. Due to my grandfather's influence we did celebrate Hanukah and Passover, but that was about it. Being Jewish in my eyes was a kind of minor or incidental aspect of being American, which was the main thing. Little did I know that having grown up among Jews and absorbed a good deal of secular Jewish culture I was a typical Jew in the eyes of most non-Jews.

My first inkling that my being Jewish was more than an incidental detail came when I went away to college at Wesleyan University in Connecticut. There were no public dining facilities at Wesleyan at that time; to eat you had to belong to the eating club of a fraternity, or else to the John Wesley Club. I applied to three fraternities but was rejected by all three. Only then did I discover that almost all the fraternities on campus had a clause barring membership to "Jews, Negroes and Orientals". Not feeling the need for Christian fellowship, I ended up as a waiter for the John Wesley Club, which solved my eating problem but left me feeling like an outsider in relation to the non-Jewish world.

Fortunately I was not the only one, and I gravitated to a circle of proto-beatniks, would-be poets and writers, mostly non-Jewish, but nonetheless in rebellion against the cultural norms of the America of the late Fifties, Yet even in this circle I was a little bit different; my cultural rebellion had more of a political tinge. In the Jewish world where I grew up, people took politics very seriously. Republicans were unknown; the political spectrum ranged from Communists on the left to liberal Democrats on the right. Spurred on by a few left wing professors at Wesleyan, I decided to become a Marxist and devote my life to the theory and practice of revolution. After a year "on the road" in the beatnik mode, I entered graduate school in the fall of 1959, an aspiring history professor by day and cultural radical by night. Yet even then, the thought that all this was happening because I was Jewish never entered my head.

As you might imagine, I took to the Movement of the Sixties as a duck takes to water. It was just what I needed: revolutionary politics and cultural radicalism all rolled into one. I became a "Movement person" and by the early Seventies I was an ex-history professor living on welfare after serving a 3 month prison term for my political activities. The Movement was all I had left, but just around this time came the first stirrings of anti-Zionism on the American left. Only now did I feel compelled, for the first time in my life, to learn something about Jewish history in order to decide for myself whether Israel had a right to exist. I also joined a small group called the Jewish Socialist Community and began to think of myself as Jewish in a way that I had not previously done. I had never denied it, but neither had I affirmed it until now. Strangely enough, the more anti-Zionism came to permeate the Movement (or what remained of it), the stronger my need to identify as a Jew became.

My study of Jewish history played a key role here. At first I consulted Marxist writers, like Kautsky and Rodinson, who maintained that the Jews were a merchant people (Kautsky) who had established a "colonial settler state" (Rodinson) in "Palestine". I later learned that "Palestine" is a Roman term which was applied to the country which the Romans had previously called "Judea" in 135 CE following the "Second Jewish War" during the course of which the Romans killed 580,000 Jews according to their own account. Something like 1 million Jews were also killed by the Romans and their Greek allies during the "First Jewish War", from 66 to 73 CE, and many additional hundreds of thousands of Jews were also killed by the Greeks and Romans during the "Diaspora revolt" of 115-117 CE. This entire history of mass murder spanning a century is almost completely invisible in the standard academic accounts of Roman history, which focus instead on the growing popularity during this same period of a new mystery religion focused around pretending to eat the flesh and drink the blood of a Jewish man once a week.

Most of the Jews murdered by the Greeks and Romans were farmers, or landless laborers who had lost their farms, or urban artisans. Kautsky's view of the Jews as a merchant people turned out to be completely fraudulent, not only with reference to Greco-Roman antiquity, but also with reference to later Jewish history as well. Most Jews in Kautsky's own day were artisans, urban workers or impoverished peddlers. As for Rodinson's "colonial settler state", close to half of the current Jewish population of Israel is composed of Jews of Middle

Eastern descent whose ancestors lived in North Africa, Iraq, Iran and Yemen long before the Arab conquest of these areas. The other half is largely composed of Jews from Europe who were forced to flee murderous persecution there, culminating in the Holocaust, motivated on the grounds that they were Middle Eastern "Semites" and therefore unfit to live in Europe. And no one can deny that the Jews of Israel speak Hebrew, a Middle Eastern language, and are descended, whether physically or spiritually, from the population of the ancient Jewish kingdoms of Judah and Israel which were situated in the region which is universally known as the "land of Israel" in Jewish tradition.

Gradually it dawned on me that the values which I had derived from the Jewish community in which I grew up, values of sympathy for the underdog and the desire for a more peaceful, equitable and rational social order, were Jewish values, values which the Jewish people had upheld throughout our history and been persecuted for doing so by one autocratic ruler after another. And as it so happened, those countries and organizations which took the lead in attacking and denouncing Israel were also, without exception, founded on autocratic principles and therefore hostile to the democratic socialist principles on which Israel was founded. But although this realization led me to reject the growing anti-Zionism of the Movement and become a supporter of the state of Israel, it did not turn me into a Zionist. By the late Seventies I had begun to find work as an adjunct teaching history at various colleges in the New York area, and I had also begun the first of several drafts of a book on Jewish history, which I eventually self-published under the title of Dark Star in 1984. I became a Jewish nationalist, one with a secular bent, whose mission in life was to promote a greater understanding on the American left of the progressive role which the Jewish people has played in world history.

I was shocked to discover that the American left wasn't interested in what I had say. I should have got the message early on, when Monthly Review, a Marxist publishing house, rejected an early draft of Dark Star. Just to show that there were no hard feelings, they invited me to their Christmas party. Evidently Marxism and Christianity coexisted in their mind in a way that Marxism and Judaism never could. And in general it became increasingly clear to me that most leftists just didn't want to hear about the Jewish roots of their own beliefs. They were perfectly willing to ascribe a progressive content to Christianity and Islam, but Judaism was becoming more and more identified in their mind with the twin evils of "patriarchy" and "racism". Since I had impeccable Movement credentials they couldn't really denounce my critique of this stereotype, but they could and did ignore me.

I found this attitude on the part of the left particularly galling because in the course of my study of Jewish history I had become convinced of something which I thought would fascinate my leftist friends. Unknown to the general public, the small world of "Biblical scholarship" had been debating for years whether the ancient Hebrews were in fact "Habiru", runaway slaves who had organized themselves into armed detachments and eked out a living as bandits or mercenaries in many parts of the Middle East during the 2nd millenium BCE. I found that the evidence of the identity of the Hebrews and Habiru was overwhelming, but most Biblical scholars had resisted this conclusion because it conflicted with the Biblical image of the Hebrews as all descended from the twelve sons of one father. Never mind, I thought, my leftist friends will have no diffculty understanding that it was precisely because the Hebrews had formed a revolutionary social class rather than an enormous extended family that Jewish tradition had such an egalitarian tone and was so hostile to the idols of ruling class culture. But to my amazement I found far more interest among religious Jews in what I had to say on this subject than among leftists, who just didn't want to know anything which would make the Jews look good from a leftist perspective.

What created this need on their part was above all the anti-Zionism of the international left. In order for anti-Zionism to be justified, Israel had to be a bastion of reaction, and in order for Israel to be a bastion of reaction, Jewish tradition had to be a reactionary force. This conclusion was all the more necessary in that the American left was composed in large part of Jews who were trying to get away from being Jewish. It was so much easier to do this if you thought that you were getting away from a reactionary ideology. Nor were non-Jews on the left at all averse to a situation in which Jewish leftists had to continually prove their right to be considered leftists by denouncing the one and only Jewish state. To be sure, the growing anti-Zionism and anti-Semitism of the American left did not make it all that popular among most Americans, but by this point organizing the masses was no longer the aim of the left. Its goal was rather to advance the personal and professional career of its members in the "politically correct", "multi-cultural" world which it had created for itself in academia and the professions, and here it was a resounding success.

My answer to this trend was to start visiting Israel. My wife and I visited for the first time in 1981 after winning a monetary settlement from a landlord who wanted to evict us so he could raise the rent. That initial visit had a big effect on me. I remember sitting on the balcony of a cheap hotel with a view of Zion Square in Jerusalem and thinking, "I could live here". I felt differently in Israel than I did in the United States, more relaxed, more at peace with myself. Of course this was before the first intifada and Israel did not seem so dangerous as it later appeared. But making aliyah was not a realistic option for us then. Instead my wife and I fell into a pattern of visiting Israel every three years or so, usually for a month in the summer but once for an entire year at the time of the first Gulf War. We seriously considered making aliyah at that time, but eventually decided not to. By this time I had pretty much given up hope of having an impact on the American left, but there was one alternative to aliyah that I had not yet explored. This was trying to make a life for myself as part of a community of secular Jews.

I had taken a step in this direction back in the Seventies by joining the Jewish Socialist Community, but this group didn't last very long. It was not until after we returned from our year in Israel that I began to actively involve myself in a number of Jewish secular organizations. After my wife and I moved to Forest Hills in the early Nineties, we joined the Queens chapter of the Society for Humanistic Judaism. I also became a member of The Generation After, an organization founded by Holocaust survivors with a left wing outlook dedicated to understanding and teaching the lessons of the Holocaust. And at the same time I started an organization of my own, the Jewish Radical Education Project (J-REP), with a small office and classroom in a building just off Union Square in Manhattan. During the Sixties the

Students for a Democratic Society had formed an organization called
the Radical Education Project, and my goal was to do something similar but with a Jewish outlook. The idea was to teach secular Jews to
identify with the egalitarian values embedded in Jewish history as an
alternative to either religious belief or loss of Jewish identity.

All of these groups had some success, but as time went on certain
problems became evident. For one thing, most of the secular Jews I
came to know were, like myself, aging veterans of involvement with
one or another left wing cause. Few young people flocked to our ban-
ner, preferring either the path of religious Judaism or that of complete
assimilation. For another thing, I didn't feel entirely comfortable with
the attitude towards Israel which I found in the secular Jewish community. Although many had visited Israel at least once and were basically
supportive of Israel's existence, there was a definite tendency to emphasize the negative side of things, to criticize and complain, echoing in a
milder form the standard litany of anti-Israel accusations so prevalent
elsewhere on the left. And when it came to opposing manifestations of
anti-Semitism in the New York area, especially those associated with
the Afro-American community, I found that most secular Jews had
little or nothing to say.

Gradually it became apparent to me that if I really wanted to feel a
part of a secular Jewish community, I had to move to Israel. Israel was
founded by secular Jews and even today, after all the changes that have
taken place, a clear majority of the members of the Knesset, Israel's
Parliament, is composed of secular Jews. And whereas many secular
Jews in the United States have a somewhat defensive, critical attitude
toward the rest of the Jewish community, secular Jews in Israel have
necessarily to cooperate with religious Jews to deal with the many
threats which we all face. The emphasis is less on what divides us and
more on what unites us, which I feel is the right approach. Both secular and religious Jews in Israel, each in our own way, are striving to
affirm the traditional Jewish vision of a more equitable social order,
and although I much prefer the secular to the religious way, I see us
both as part of one Jewish nation, something which no longer exists
in the Diaspora.

In short, I am a Zionist because I believe in the Jewish people. My study of history has convinced me that the Jewish people was the force behind the crypto-Jewish, semi-progressive ideologies of Christianity, Islam and Marxism, the three dominant ideologies of the modern world, but unfortunately all three assumed an anti-Semitic veneer in order to make their way in a world dominated by kings and tyrants. Moreover, my experience of Jewish life, which is extensive, has left me with a feeling of profound admiration and respect for my fellow Jews. Like they say, "Jews are like everyone else, only more so". We have to be "more so", because that is the only way that we can cope with the destiny which the Habiru bequeathed to us, the destiny to act as a "light unto the nations". Israel is that light, and that is why I am a Zionist.

CPSIA information can be obtained
at www.ICGtesting.com
Printed in the USA
LVOW10s1603200317
527823LV00039B/1798/P

9 781936 780587